ASSESSING THE PORTFOLIO

PRINCIPLES FOR PRACTICE, THEORY, AND RESEARCH

WRITTEN LANGUAGE
Marcia Farr, senior editor

ASSESSING THE PORTFOLIO

PRINCIPLES FOR PRACTICE, THEORY, AND RESEARCH

Liz Hamp-Lyons
Hong Kong Polytechnic University

William Condon
Washington State University

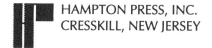
HAMPTON PRESS, INC.
CRESSKILL, NEW JERSEY

Printed in the United States of America

Library of Congress Cataloging-in-Publication Data

Hamp-Lyons, Liz
      Assessing the portfolio : principles for practice, theory, and research / Liz Hamp-Lyons, William Condon
            p. cm.-- (Written language series)
      Includes bibliographic references and indexes.
      ISBN 1-58283-230-X -- ISBN 1-57273-231-8 (pbk.)
      1. English language--Rhetoric--Study and teaching. 2. Report writing --Study and teaching. 3. Portfolios in education. I. Condon, William 1950- II. Title. III. Series.

PE1404.H357 1999
808'.042'07--dc21

                                                                                                99-051366

Hampton Press, Inc.
23 Broadway
Cresskill, NJ 07626

CONTENTS

SERIES PREFACE

This series examines the characteristics of *writing* in the human world. Volumes in the series present scholarly work on written language in its various contexts. Across time and space, human beings use various forms of written language—or writing systems—to fulfill a range of social, cultural, and personal functions, and this diversity can be studied from a variety of perspectives within both the social sciences and the humanities, including those of linguistics, anthropology, psychology, education, rhetoric, literacy criticism, philosophy, and history. Although writing is not often used apart from oral language, or without aspects of reading, and thus many volumes in this series include other facets of language and communication, writing itself receives primary emphasis.

This particular volume of the series focuses on writing in formal educational settings, and, specifically, on ways to assess that writing. Research on writing in school has burgeoned in the last few decades to the point that there are now several identifiable subfields; one of these subfields is research on the assessment of writing. Work in this area too has burgeoned, taking off at a time when writing was assessed indirectly, with multiple choice tests, rather than directly, by evaluating actual pieces of student writing. Now the (sub)field has moved on from the direct assessment of writing through timed tests (in which students write an essay under testing conditions within a limited time frame) to the direct assessment of multiple pieces of student writing written as part of the regular curriculum. As Hamp-Lyons and Condon show, techniques have been developed that make this form of assessment quite reliable and certainly more valid. Such research is extremely important and timely, given the increased emphasis on standards and assessment in education, and, moreover, the centrality of writing to learning.

   While the study of writing is absorbing in its own right, it is an increasingly important social issue as well, as demographic movements occur around the world and as language and ethnicity accrue more intensely political meanings. Writing, and literacy more generally, is central to education, and education in turn is central to occupational and social mobility. Manuscripts that present either the results of empirical research, both qualitative and quantitative, or theoretical treatments of relevant issues are encouraged for submission.

ACKNOWLEDGEMENTS

We both with to acknowledge our ECB colleagues over the years, whose willingness to experiment and stimulating critiques kept us always moving forward. Liz thanks the TAs at the University of Colorado-Denver who (mostly enthusiastically!) participated in the early years of a portfolio program there. Bill thanks colleagues and TAs at Washington State University.

Liz acknowledges the following support to her work in portfolio assessment: University of Colorado-Denver for a Faculty Fellowship; University of Melbourne for a Visiting Scholarship; Hong Kong Polytechnic University and the Hong Kong Research Grant Committee for a Central Allocation Research Grant (#S434). However, none of these bodies and individuals are responsible for our opinions or our text!

And last but first, we recognize the support of our families: Mike Lyons, Chris and Nick; Pat Condon, Jenny, Maggie, Nick, and Mischa.

INTRODUCTION

This book has a long history—longer than either of us had expected when we began it, in 1991, and readers should keep this in mind as they puzzle over why two academics at Hong Kong Polytechnic University and Washington State University, respectively, should be writing so much about programs of which they are not part. It began its life soon after Liz Hamp-Lyons had left the University of Michigan and had begun to think about how a pretty good system of exit portfolio assessment might have to be adapted for a very different context, the University of Colorado in Denver. It arises from more E-mail exchanges than either of us can imagine let alone remember, and from four interstate visits: one by Liz back to Ann Arbor and three by Bill to Denver; and even one visit by Bill out to Hong Kong, where Liz moved in 1996, the same time as Bill moved from Michigan to Washington State University. The temptation with a book like this, in a field that is growing and changing faster than we can write about it, is never to stop, to try always to include everything, and to keep going for a higher level of excellence. In working on this final revision, we have been tempted to add two further layers and write in detail about developments at our new universities. But we have resisted, because we believe the book will fill a need that exists now and has existed for a while, and we hope there will be opportunities to add to it later as we receive feedback from its first edition.

Our involvement with portfolios has a still longer history: We might argue that it begins with two claims made in the late 1970s by senior faculty at the University of Michigan to argue for a university wide writing requirement, together with an entry-level direct test of writing (Fader, 1986) that judging writing ability by scoring writing samples was more valid than judging it with multiple-choice question tests; and that writing samples could now be scored with sufficient reliability for the resulting scores to be taken seriously. The acceptance of these arguments and the passing of these proposals by the University of Michigan Senate resulted in the establishment of the English Composition Board (ECB), where both of us worked, in the case of Liz, as associate director for assessment from 1986 to 1990, and in the case of Bill, as associate director for instruction from 1987 to 1994, and as director from 1994 to 1996. In 1986, the field of writing assessment was still concerned about developing better forms of timed writing test and better ways of scoring and reporting on these tests (and indeed, this is a concern that is still with us, for these forms of assessment have not gone and will not go away, and there is still a great deal to be learned about how to do them well: but that is another book . . .) and Liz's first year at Michigan was spent wholly on this endeavor, an endeavor that continued through to 1991. But in 1986, Pat Belanoff and Peter Elbow published their piece in *College Composition and Communication* about the portfolio assessment they had developed at the State University of New York, Stony Brook. In 1987, some of us in the ECB were talking about the (possibly crazy) idea of trying out some such system ourselves. That summer, along came Bill, and a professional relationship began between the two of us that slowly grew to an exciting synergy. Out of our conversations, sometimes the two of us and sometimes others, notably Emily Decker and George Cooper, grew the first model of exit portfolio assessment, and then a more adventurous portfolio, and later, after Liz had left, a truly daring and exciting entry portfolio assessment spearheaded by Emily. Bill and I learned to write together and liked it; and when we went our separate ways, difficult although it was, we wanted to continue.

WHY PORTFOLIOS NOW?

In the years since Janet Emig (1971) began a reform movement in composition studies with her landmark work on the writing process, composition pedagogy has undergone several interesting shifts in focus, from formalism, through expressivism, cognitivism, process, collaborative learning, social construction—and perhaps next we'll see contributions from postmodern theory. Through all the changes, what has emerged is a "composition universe" that shares some key values.

　　　First, the focus in teaching writing has shifted. Pre-Emig, writing classes focused on rhetorical modes and literary analysis. Post-Emig, the variety of writing encountered in composition classes and countenanced by composition programs has grown exponentially. As alternatives to formalism have developed, the range and variety of writing has increased. In addition, throughout the 1970s and 1980s, the emphasis on teaching the writing process, from a variety of theoretical bases, also grew. Expressivists, cognitivists, social constructionists, and others may all have differing approaches to and differing views of the writing process, but all teach their versions of it. The emphasis on the writing process, at least in the form of drafting, has even crept into most formalists' teaching practice. Along with the increasing focus on the writing process have come ways of assessing the effectiveness of different processes and learner strategies (think-aloud protocols, keystroke capture utilities for word processors, double-entry journals, and so on). This shift toward process, and the emphasis on measuring effectiveness in the face of a much greater variety of writing, creates a natural opening for performance assessment, and for portfolios in particular. As the variety of writing increases, teachers have an increasingly difficult time dictating, controlling, keeping up with, responding to, or evaluating the forms and strategies students will use, and so an assessment tool that looks broadly at what students have written addresses the teacher's need to evaluate students' performances in an increasingly open and variable context.

Second, as the emphasis on the writing process and an acceptance of a greater variety of forms has proceeded, a natural desire to make the learning process more democratic, to allow all the participants more of an impact on learning, has also emerged. Although teachers are still in charge—if for no other reason than that institutional structures require them to be, whether they want to be or not—the greater thrust toward involving the learner in every phase of the learning experience acts as an encouragement for learners to accept more responsibility for their own learning and to take a more active role in that learning. The more active the learner, this line of reasoning goes, the more invested he or she will be in the writing, and the more he or she will learn. At this point in time, the emphasis on active learning and on motivating students to spend more time on-task has been validated experimentally to the extent that it is at the heart of the department of education's recommendations for "Instructional 'Good Practice' Indicators in Undergraduate Education" (1994). Practice in composition studies has moved to involve students more directly in their own learning processes, to open the curriculum to students' input, to involve students collaboratively in course and assignment design. This process enriches the learning environment for both teacher and learner because it involves both in the process of addressing the learner's needs. Along with involving learners more directly in their learning process, teachers, too, have been more actively involved in curriculum and program development. The top-down administrative model of the past has faded into an environment in which teachers become knowledgeable about and invested in curriculum through participating in its design and in implementing the courses that will carry out that curriculum. The final step along this pathway has come with the emergence of the portfolio. Portfolios involve teachers with assessment. That involvement takes testing out of the hands of the so-called experts and, by using actual classroom performances, puts it into the hands of teachers—where it belongs.

Involving teachers with assessment brings up the third shift in emphasis that we discuss here: the integration of assessment with curriculum. In the past, the classroom was completely divorced from assessment, completely self-contained. Teachers offered courses, students enrolled and did the work, professors calculated grades, and students moved on to their next course. At some point, an outside agency would administer a test—almost always a norm-referenced multiple-choice test—to validate what the student had learned. The CAT or some other, similar test, assigned a percentile ranking to the student, and the average of all the percentile rankings for students in a school became the number by which the school's effectiveness was judged. (Often, too, the average from a class became the means for judging the teacher's effectiveness as well.) Or, near the end of high school, college-bound students sat for the ACT or SAT, in order to receive a score and percentile that would in large part determine which college(s) they could attend—or whether they could attend college at all. Even college graduates bound for graduate or professional study take norm-referenced standardized tests that weigh heavily on their acceptance into the more desirable schools of law, medicine, business, nursing, or graduate study. None of these tests are in any way connected to the curriculum to which students are exposed in their schooling. All the tests are designed independent of any actual curriculum—in fact, they tend to drive curriculum, instead of being driven by it (M. Smith, 1991).

Integrating assessment with curriculum changes that whole situation. If assessment occurs as a natural outgrowth of learning, then each can affect the other; each can make the other more responsive to students' needs. Using actual classroom performance as the basis for diagnoses of needs, for placement into further courses of study, or for referral to different support services creates opportunities to examine what students in a class have produced in relation to where those products take them. Teachers can see what has and has not worked, what students can do as a result of the time spent studying the class's curriculum and performing the tasks the class required. Thus, the emphasis on student-centered teaching, discussed previously, is joined by a move toward student-centered assessment. Portfolios allow students to bring their work, their learning, into the testing context. The resulting assessment gives far more information than any percentile ranking can, and so is far more useful to the student. The fact that recent developments have demonstrated that performance assessment can also serve the public policy needs heretofore addressed by norm-referenced tests (LeMahieu, Gitomer, & Eresh, 1995; Mislevy, 1995) only makes the move toward portfolios more rapid and more robust.

Fourth, and finally, we sense that portfolio-based writing assessment stands more or less where direct tests of writing stood in the mid-1970s. By 1978, when Michigan's ECB instituted its v test, the groundwork had already been laid—at ETS by Cronbach and by Edward White in California (White, 1994). By 1974, we knew that direct tests could be administered cheaply and that they could be scored with acceptable reliability—not as high as on multiple-choice tests, but good enough, when we factored in the much greater validity of the direct test. Then, for 20 years, the research continued to refine and document the successes of direct tests of writing, holistic scoring, multiple-trait scoring, expert-rater scoring, and so forth. Perhaps the culmination of this kind of writing test is the volume edited by Williamson and Huot (1993), where the leaders in the field, from Ed White to Bill Smith to Williamson and Huot themselves, described the state of the art in direct testing--and discuss its unavoidable limitations. Today, portfolios stand at that earlier juncture. Before they could be taken seriously, the issue of reliability had to be solved. Even considering the far greater validities a portfolio exhibits over timed writings, early portfolio assessments suffered from extremely low reliability. Today, that hurdle has been overcome, as several large-scale portfolio assessments, including those at Michigan and Miami University, have achieved reliability levels consistent with those of holistically scored timed writings. With this book, then, we hope to contribute to the next stage, the process of theory-making and research that will establish portfolio-based writing assessment as firmly as, today, we see with timed writing tests.

Why portfolios now? Because portfolios answer today's need for a measurement system that can have a generative, rather than a reductive effect on education, because portfolios reinforce what we know about good teaching practice, because portfolios help teachers help learners assume more responsibility for their own learning, and because portfolios provide a rich source of information to teachers as they continually reconsider their theory and practice and to researchers and administrators as they continue to assess educational progress in our schools and colleges.

Chapter 1

PORTFOLIO-BASED WRITING ASSESSMENT: CURRENT TRENDS AND PRACTICES

"Would the passenger who left his portfolio behind Row 3 please contact a flight attendant?" This announcement over the Boeing 727's public address system started an emblematic chain of events. The culprit came forward and met the flight attendant in the doorway that divides first-class from coach. She addressed this middle-aged artist in an uncharacteristically strident tone: "That space is where the captain stows his bags. Luckily, the captain has no luggage on this trip, but you should know that in the future you cannot use that space."

"The clerk wouldn't allow me to check it as baggage, and it wouldn't fit in the overhead or in the compartment where you put the hanging bags," the artist replied, "so I put it there."

"Well, that's the *captain's* space, so you won't be able to use it on any other flights."

This exchange pointed out a flaw in the system, a point at which a passenger's legitimate need to store a not entirely unusual piece of baggage exceeded the parameters of the airline's storage systems. The company had assessed the need for storage, architects had designed systems for moving the baggage from check-in station to plane, and aircraft manufacturers had constructed baggage areas to accommodate suitcases, hanging bags, containers for golf clubs and skis, cardboard boxes, shopping bags, diaper bags, briefcases, carrying bags for computers—seemingly, an all-encompassing system. However, what if a passenger brings to the airport an item that exceeds the expected parameters? How was the artist, under normal circumstances, to get himself and his portfolio from St. Louis to Denver?

Artists have been carrying awkwardly shaped flat folders containing their finest drawings or paintings from door to door for a long time, transporting their work to galleries or hoping to impress potential employers sufficiently to be given a job or a commission. We cannot say why an airline might refuse to allow an artist to check a portfolio. Perhaps the question centers on liability for works that are unwieldy, or highly valuable. Perhaps the overall dimensions are too large to allow the portfolio to fit on the conveyor belts that take the bags from the check-in counter to the baggage area. Or perhaps the portfolio's thinness causes some other risk that it will be lost or damaged. In any event, the airline had not anticipated a piece of luggage like the portfolio, and neither its baggage moving systems nor its storage spaces could accommodate the artist's needs.

If a process as relatively straightforward as baggage handling demands complex systems and is limited by the breadth of the designers' assumptions about what sort of baggage passengers will bring with them, how much more difficult are the systems we devise for writing assessment! Basically, baggage exists in three dimensions. Those who design systems for handling and storing it need to think primarily in terms of weight and capacity. Not much else matters. We who plan systems for assessing writing, however, must contend with far more variables. Genre, subgenre, length, language, levels of usage, audience and purpose, assignments, curriculum, the writing process, collaboration, differences in tools and settings, variability of resources, all these considerations and more complicate the very nature of the task of assessing writing. This complexity rendered indirect measures of writing virtually useless, prompting their replacement with direct tests such as holistically scored essays. And now those direct tests are giving way to various kinds of performance assessment—in particular, in colleges and universities—to portfolio-based assessment.

The move toward portfolios is being driven by the need to measure more complex phenomena, for more complex reasons. Once, it was enough to set a measurement objective (e.g., a test score) as a mark that students who wished to pass a course or to acquire entrance to college had to achieve: Meet the mark, win the prize. Today, however, we want to know how the course of instruction is meeting its objectives in more ways than merely whether a certain proportion of students can meet the exit or entry requirements. In addition, we want more detailed assessments of students' strengths and needs, of teachers' performances, of the degree to which different portions of an institution's writing curriculum prepare students adequately for the challenges presented in other portions of the curriculum. In other words, we have increased the amount, kinds, and complexity of the information we want to gather in a given assessment. In today's atmosphere of continuing improvement and reform—and in an age of far greater institutional accountability than was required in the past—we simply need to know more and know it more fully than we could in the past, with the tools that were typically applied.

More than any other single improvement, we need to find ways to integrate instruction and assessment. Our tests have to test what we teach, not what someone in New Jersey thinks we teach. The move to performance assessments in general and to portfolio-based writing assessment in particular allows assessment to accommodate instruction; the writing portfolio provides an instrument that incorporates the products of instruction and that can, if the assessment is designed carefully, provide an evaluation that feeds back into the process of instruction. In other words, thoughtfully constructed performance assessments bring their contexts with them. We cannot reliably or validly (in any of the increasingly complex senses of those terms) evaluate a performance without knowing its context, without knowing the conditions under which the performance was accomplished. Thus, we can adequately judge a portfolio only if we know something, at least, about the instruction that led the writer to produce the portfolio; as a result, we cannot evaluate the performance without, in some respects, evaluating the instruction. The latter knowledge, then, becomes vital in continually improving instruction. This interrelation between assessment and instruction is one of the few features of portfolio assessment that is not negotiable. Almost every other feature of this form of assessment is extremely fluid. Portfolios accommodate a wide range of writing, of writing classes, of writing programs, of writing contexts. Portfolios can be designed to fit any writing curriculum and to yield a wide range of information the designers wish to extract about the performances of students in a wide range of learning experiences. But amid all this flexibility, the fact is that a credible portfolio assessment must incorporate the learning context within which it was produced. This is the fundamental element of the theory of portfolios as assessment instruments. We must not forget that portfolios of writing began as classroom instructional tools and as teacher development tools, and that their power as alternative assessment tools is tied to this inseparable teaching-assessment link. Although in K-12 education there have been attempts at portfolio assessment programs that were not linked to instruction—the National Assessment of Educational Progress (NAEP) program comes to mind—these programs have been very unwelcome to most teachers, and they exhibit few of the characteristics of portfolios described in chapter 2. Perhaps the greatest theoretical and practical strength of a portfolio, used as an assessment instrument, is the way it reveals and informs teaching and learning. Without this, the portfolio is not much more than another test, only of a particularly large and unwieldy kind. Therefore, in this book we assert and carry through a belief that a book about portfolio assessment also has to be about writing instruction. In chapter 2, we discuss not only writing theory in order to reach a position from which we can derive a theory of portfolio assessment, but we also show how theories of instruction and assessment interact. In chapter 3 we discuss the portfolio classroom, and describe some of the aspects of modern writing instruction that marry well with portfolio-based writing assessment.

THE DYNAMICS OF CONTEXT

It follows from what was just presented that portfolio-based assessment is context-rich. The goal is to collect several samples of a student's writing in a real class, a real context—some revised, some not; some produced under controlled conditions, some under more open conditions. From these samples the student, perhaps with the help of the teacher, will make a selection. The *collection* and selection of pieces is driven by the context. Context-appropriate choices work to provide as complete a picture as possible of the writer's level of competence (or, rather, levels of competence in a given set of skills, tasks, or modes) at a given moment—for example, at the end of a semester-long course. The writer's own sense of what the writing accomplishes can be seen because most portfolios include *reflective* writings that describe, explain, or otherwise account for the samples included. Validity of the construct behind the assessment, therefore, is the portfolio's strength: In a well-conceived portfolio program with teachers who fully understand not only what they are doing but also why they are doing it, the writing in a learner's portfolio will quite accurately reflect his or her abilities, and will do so far more extensively than could a sample of the same writer's performance on a one-shot essay test.

Although a portfolio-based writing assessment, like more traditional direct tests of writing, focuses on a product, this product can accommodate the writing process unlike any other timed assessment. Instead of examining a single, limited sample of writing, a portfolio-based assessment examines several samples, written over time and under different constraints, in order to produce an assessment of what the writer can do with the written form, rather than an assessment of a single text. In addition to working with a collection—a fact that demands that students produce a large enough corpus of work from which to make a reasoned selection—a portfolio-based writing assessment requires higher order decisions: Students (with or without the advice and collaboration of their teachers) have to select those pieces that present the best portrait of their abilities. Thus, *selection* adds a dimension to readers' experiences of the writer, as it exposes them to a much wider range of choices on the writer's part, allowing them to judge not merely the choices writers have made within a piece of writing, but also the choices they have made among pieces. Writers have to decide which are their best or most representative pieces (and to know what those pieces represent); thus, selection engages self-assessment, and it encourages writers to make conscious, deliberate choices regarding the quality of their writings, as well as the relative importance of the different features of good writing that their collection exhibits. Finally, the element of *reflection* exposes yet another facet of metacognition to the reader's view. What the writer says about the writing exposes more of what the writer knows, consciously, about the performance. This troika of collection, selection, and reflection help ensure that the portfolio yields not only information about the writer's performance, but also significant information about the instructional context—about what the writer learned about writing.

Traditional writing assessment, operating on a top-down model, does not provide such extensive information. Instead, the system's requirements dictate the topic, length, structure, and so forth, of the writing, and what the writers will do to produce the specified text and what the readers will do to judge it. Portfolio-based writing assessment has the potential for employing a bottom-up structure, in which writer, teachers, readers, and system are all involved, not only in producing portfolios, but in negotiating and renegotiating a local definition of the portfolio. Although not all portfolio-based writing assessments work this way, and a range of types of portfolio assessments are possible (see Fig. 4.3), at least in theory both the present needs of the writers producing portfolios and the concerns of teachers teaching the students and evaluating the portfolios can have a major influence on the components of the portfolio and the process of assessing the portfolios. Any carefully designed portfolio assessment must take into account the roles of all the major stakeholders. To the extent that the writer or the teacher are left out of full involvement in the portfolio development and evaluation process, some of the potential of portfolio-based writing assessment is not being fulfilled. The ethos of portfolio assessment, in many contexts but most especially in composition contexts—which lend themselves to collaboration in all dimensions—is such that it is quite difficult to remain unaffected by its potential for open, shared assessment.

Increasingly more programs at every level, from grade school to college, are responding to the shortcomings of traditional, holistic assessment by moving to portfolio-based assessment. The nature of the portfolio program as a living system, as a vital, reactive force, keeps it responsive to and reflective of local needs, especially as these needs change as a result of the influence of the portfolio assessment itself. We referred to this responsive process as *iterative* in an earlier study (Condon & Hamp-Lyons, 1991), but in fact, as local knowledge increases, the process becomes *recursive;* that is, each new reading is influenced and informed, to some extent, by every reading that preceded it. A careful, contextually sensitive process of introducing a portfolio-based writing assessment, with a carefully developed and tested scoring instrument, can be one that possesses the traditional psychometric quality of reliability, but is a far more valid instrument for assessing the students' academic writing skills than a timed impromptu, or even a take-home writing test. From the writer's perspective, a portfolio permits a better reflection of his or her effort and of the range of writing. For faculty, a portfolio offers more writing, longer individual essays, and (for those who choose it) a view of the "process history" that underlies completed texts.

Whatever the former method of exit assessment, whether an average of grades or performance on a single written assignment, once a writing instructor replaces other grading practices with a portfolio, or even simply makes a portfolio a part of the course grade, the method of determining a student's progress at the end of a course has changed radically. In our own early work designing and implementing a portfolio-based exit assessment for the English Composition Board's (ECB's) Writing Practicum, we found that our difficulties began before we had even started, as we decided on the precise makeup of a portfolio (Condon & Hamp-Lyons, 1991). Obviously (in retrospect—it was not so obvious to us at the time), nested within that question lay the need to formulate a new definition of writing competence, a definition that would in turn ensure that the specified contents of these portfolios would allow students to display their full potential for competent writing. Perhaps most obviously, this new context for judgment presented the need to define competence in such a way that it could include revision. But competence also had to be defined in a way that allowed students to present a variety of writing within their own portfolios, and that allowed instructors to teach with various approaches, methods, and materials. This meant that a variety of writing would appear from portfolio to portfolio within any single class. We had to serve apparently contradictory needs: To ensure uniformity, we had to dictate the contents of a portfolio, yet in order to acknowledge diversity among students and classes we had to leave open the essential form. We had to learn what we felt we needed to know about the students' writing while leaving room for them to reveal the full range of writing that they were capable of producing. Through the development of our exit portfolio program, we learned much more about our local definitions of competence in writing, and we reached a much closer consensus among our faculty about what it means to be competent in writing, within that context. We learned much more about our *instruction* through our focus on our *assessment*. Only those who have never paused for long to question their underlying assumptions and definitions for and about what they do will see this as a small thing; for us it was a major step, and a major benefit.

CHANGING THE ASSESSMENT PARADIGM

Traditionally—and oddly enough—writing assessment has not been directly related to instruction. The tools for assessment—indirect testing and, more recently, direct tests of writing—proceed out of a positivist scheme of assessment that focuses on limited information sets. That is, the assessment itself is viewed as a kind of scientific study of an objective, external, knowable reality that is independent of its context and infinitely replicable, under a given set of testing conditions. Positivist evaluations are generally conducted in order to rank or compare individuals with relation to the set of test-takers, and these rankings most typically take the form of percentiles (SAT, ACT) or placement into different levels of a course of study (writing placements, language testing, etc.). The positivist paradigm, as Murphy and Grant (1996) pointed out, insists on standardizing the testing instrument, as opposed to customizing the evaluation to fit a local context. As a result, decisions affecting the assessment are made by the designers of the test (top-down), rather than in conjunction with the various stakeholders in the evaluation (collaborative decision making). The positivist paradigm has obvious limitations: Murphy and Grant argued that "there is little ground for the all too common practice of generalizing from a single sample to a student's ability in other kinds of writing" (p. 287). In other words, when we collect one sample of writing performed under one set of conditions, we can measure a given writer's ability to produce that kind of writing under that set of conditions.

If we want to measure more than that, then we have to collect more than that.

In effect, if we wish to measure any construct as complicated as writing, we have to move beyond the limitations of the positivist model to some kind of constructivist paradigm. Writing, to adopt a term from chaos theory, is a *complex system*, involving a complex set of actors (student-teacher, writer-audience, curriculum designers—and, of course, assessors, etc.). Assessments that ignore most of that whole in order to make limited judgments about a small aspect of a part simply cannot prove, and have not proven, very useful. Because writing—and writing instruction—is complex, it cannot be assessed as if it were simple. We need a system of measurement that can accommodate many variables and that can exhibit flexibility, not rigidity, over time and across circumstances. A constructivist paradigm leads to a kind of hermeneutic approach to assessment (Guba & Lincoln, 1989) and thus views embedded concepts such as reliability and validity (Moss, 1994) as constructed forms of knowing that can be shaped to fit the circumstances or characteristics of a given situation. Whereas the positivist paradigm produces a test that exists outside and independent of the instructional setting, the constructivist paradigm demands that we build our assessment values and processes into the instructional setting so that the assessment itself can further the objectives of that instruction. Furthermore, the positivist paradigm's assumption that truth is simple and knowable results in top-down decision-making processes wholly outside the instructional setting, and the lack of connection that results disempowers learners. In such a system, evaluation serves as a disincentive for learners to assume responsibility for their own learning or to invest in the learning itself, as opposed to merely investing in the test. In the positivist belief system, learners need not care how they achieve a high score, only whether they achieve one. Any correspondence between learning and test performance is concealed by the test-makers' methods.

A constructivist paradigm, in contrast, leads to an assessment that incorporates evaluation into the learning experience, thus accepting and valuing the participants' (teachers and learners) perceptions of and judgments about the work they do in class from day to day and the levels of achievement on work that matters to the participants. Finally, a constructivist belief system tends to value progress, as opposed to the positivists' practice of ranking individuals against each other. In accepting that there is no simple "truth" or reality, a constructivist view of assessment helps learners understand where they are with regard to several continua, rather than where they stand in relation to other individuals. This emphasis, in turn, helps learners see the stakes they hold in their own learning, and it helps them see more clearly their current levels of ability and to set agendas that will result in progress over time. Because the evaluation is directly related to—indeed results from—the context in which learning takes place, the learner can more effectively perceive and engage in improvement. Finally, because the evaluations come from the instructional setting, rather than being separated from it, the outcomes actually provide useful[1] information for evaluating and improving instruction as well as learning—an area where traditional positivist assessments have been notoriously weak (Kilian, 1992; Mehrens, 1992; Popham, 1991; M. Smith, 1991; M. Smith & Rottenberg, 1991).

Portfolios do not, in and of themselves, enact a constructivist paradigm of evaluation. It is possible to design a portfolio that excludes the products of the learning environment (e.g., the State of Michigan's Employability Portfolio) or that is intended to provide a score by means of which test-takers can be ranked with relation to each other (e.g., ACT's pilot portfolio project) or that in other ways enacts a positivist paradigm. However, portfolios open the possibility of a constructivist evaluation; positivist measures do not, by definition, admit that possibility. Therefore, if we want to involve instruction with assessment, if we want the benefits that attend performance assessment, we need to move beyond the positivist model.

A SHORT HISTORY OF WRITING ASSESSMENT

The history of writing assessment in the United States, seen from the perspective of educational measurement theory, is a history of development from a traditional positivist approach and set of beliefs to an assertively, unapologetically, constructivist approach and set of beliefs. This change is less marked in other English-speaking countries, mainly because they never fell prey to mass, standardized testing to the extent that the United States did, but the pattern of development is generally the same.

In the United States, indirect tests, particularly multiple-choice, standardized, indirect tests were the usual method to reach judgments about people's command of written prose from World War II until the late 1970s. Indeed, these so-called "objective" tests are still in common use in the late 1990s: most college writing programs still allow students to "CLEP[2] out" or to receive credit for college writing courses based on standardized test scores of one kind or another. These objective, indirect,

---

[1]See Bachman and Palmer (1996) for a discussion of the concept of *usefulness in language testing*; they employ usefulness as a governing concept that helps set priorities for more traditional assessment concerns such as reliability and validity.

[2]CLEP stands for College Level English Proficiency test, a standardized test.

multiple-choice tests are highly reliable: that is, the same answer is scored as "right" or "wrong" every time, regardless of who (or what machine) is scoring it—saving only a technical error. Complete agreement on scoring is generally accepted as the working definition of reliability. However, the reality is not that simple. These tests are not really objective because, although scoring is done by an objective machine, the questions (items) are written by human beings and the "right" answers are decided and programmed into the computer or coded onto a scoring template by human beings. Either or both of those human beings may not be objective—indeed, as several successful appeals against standardized tests by minority groups have shown, test writers often unintentionally build their own subjective prejudices, experiences, and values into the test items they write. This problem is so endemic with standardized test item development that Educational Testing Service (ETS) have a formal sensitivity review process for their test items; even so, they have been criticized extensively by test-taker activist groups such as FairTest (Medina & Neill, 1990), and have admitted that there is a large gender gap in performance on the SAT, GRE, and other similar tests (College Board Report 92-7). All these tests are "reliable"—the problem is that they are not "fair" in either the lay person's sense or the technical sense.

Moreover, offsetting the supposed benefits of objectivity are several major problems with indirect tests. They provide a kind of contextless evaluation: All the score provides is a comparison of one person's answers to extremely limited kinds of questions with another person's answers to the same or very similar questions. Nothing can be known on that basis about how the person responds to different kinds of writing activities, what the person likes to write, what ideas excite him or her. Not only are these multiple-choice question (MCQ) tests contextless, they are constructless as well. They do not acknowledge what writing is, what we do when we write, what is revealed when others read our writing. They convey a view that writing is a collection of discrete elements that can be identified, and for each of which a multiple distractor probe can be created that will reveal whether the individual has control of that element: Add all these elements together, and the result is *writing*—which is defined by implication as the sum of these parts. The scores on such tests may be highly reliable, but writing teachers have never accepted that they can give valid information about how well a person writes because the tests themselves do not examine the person's writing. In short, writing is greater than the sum of those parts that indirect tests measure. Furthermore, the claim has often been made (Lunsford, 1986) that the use of indirect testing leads to a de-emphasis on actual writing skills in educational settings.

As the 1970s wound down, concerns about indirect testing of writing were growing for the reasons just sketched, and colleges increasingly began to introduce direct tests of writing. As White (1994) described in detail in the second edition of *Teaching and Assessing Writing,* the direct testing of writing in the United States had its roots in the essay test research and program development carried out at ETS in the 1960s, an endeavor that resulted in a careful approach to the holistic assessment of writing that is still used by ETS and many other large-scale testing agencies, as well as by many major universities. A similar method had been developed in Britain slightly earlier, and under its familiar name of the Devon method is equally common on that side of the Atlantic.

Direct tests of writing are far more credible to students, parents, teachers, and employers than indirect tests because they involve the writing and scoring of an actual writing sample. Where indirect tests provide no context within which judgments can be made about how well a person can write, direct tests do give human readers or judges a textual sample as a context within which to make a judgment. Where indirect tests provide a construct of writing that sees writing performance as merely the sum of a finite number of identifiable and controllable elements, direct tests do make human writers actually perform the skill on which they are being assessed, and do give human readers that performance to judge. A major criticism of direct assessments of writing has always been that these tests are of doubtful reliability, and it remains true that no assessment of a performance sample (such as a piece of written work) can be as reliable in the psychometric sense as a machine-scorable test. However, the ETS and Devon methods of holistic scoring, as well as more recent innovations in holistic scoring and newer, more complex and context-sensitive methods such as primary trait and multiple-trait scoring, have improved the reliability of scores to the point where in properly conducted and carefully monitored direct writing assessments the scores are fair, that different readers would assign a similar rating to a sample of writing, even if those readings were separated by a significant period of time. Writing teachers almost universally have argued that the somewhat lower reliability of direct writing assessments is more than counterbalanced by the greatly increased validity[3] such assessments have. Although assessing texts instead of counting crosses made in one of four possible boxes does not of itself make a direct writing assessment valid—that depends on how the assessment is done and what use is made of the scores produced—assessment of writing samples does have the validity of authenticity (Messick, 1989).

---

[3]The term *validity* is used fairly often, and not always in a strictly educational measurement, tightly defined, sense. In general, however, when referring to *validity,* we use the term in the way Messick (1989) did, to suggest an approach to educational assessment—including writing assessments—that does not abandon empirical validation, but defines it more broadly, to encompass the meaning and consequences of measurement, including the consequences of score interpretation and use (Messick ,1996).

At the end of the 1970s, and throughout the early 1980s, direct assessment of writing seemed to give the field of composition what it needed. However, just as the battle to establish the legitimacy of direct assessment of writing seemed to be ending in victory, teachers of writing were becoming increasingly dissatisfied with direct tests of writing and with holistic scoring. A period of intensive investigation into and development of modern writing theories, coupled with the resultant development of process approaches to writing instruction, led to the realization that in direct writing assessments, samples are typically collected under artificially constrained circumstances: limits of time and place, requirements that writers use set topics that may not be familiar or interesting to them, the necessity of writing under conditions that are not conducive to most people's writing processes—small desks, rooms packed with writers scribbling away in absolute silence, and so on—all these conditions affect the validity of the sample. So, although such a direct sample is a far superior instrument than the indirect test, teachers increasingly saw it as a context-poor assessment and began looking for an even better instrument. In short, although assessment by means of timed writing constitutes a huge advance over standardized test scores, in the field of composition, and specifically in writing assessment, a point has been reached where the limitations on the validity of the timed writing test are clear and the meaningfulness of the interpretations that can be made of scores from such contextually limited assessments can be questioned. It might seem ironic that as holistic scoring is finally well understood, and procedures for conducting excellent direct assessments are firmly established (see, e.g., the collection by Williamson & Huot, 1993), the field of composition and writing instruction has sought to abandon it. There are, however, sound reasons for this.

The traditional system of holistic assessment of writing provides a top-down kind of model. Its goals are *efficiency* (i.e., essays are mass produced and then mass evaluated in as little time as possible), and *reliability* (consistency across readers and time). The typical direct writing assessment is designed so that its components conform to the requirements of the system. Prompts are designed so they perform like other prompts; readers are trained to score essays as other readers do. These kinds of stability are bought at the cost of many of the values that are held, and taught, in most composition programs today. Prompts are highly structured, topic choices are typically not permitted, writers produce only one piece of writing, time is very restricted, writers are not given the personal space to show evidence of their facility with their own writing processes, and readers are required to respond within the agreed parameters of the program. Basically, writers can do only the most limited kinds of planning for the essay and only the most limited kinds of revision;

they must almost solely rely on their drafting skills in order to perform well on the test—the assessment mode eliminates most of the writing process from consideration. Using such a test as an exit assessment in particular raises the problem of teaching students a range of skills, but testing only one. In such a situation, students are free to ignore any part of the course or curriculum that is not a part of the test. Judgments about this kind of writing can have little relation to a student's actual writing abilities under normal writing conditions; this disparity leads to questioning whether a timed test can reveal the necessary information. Certainly it is not enough to know whether the test was "reliable," that is, how consistent the readers' judgments are across time and among readers. Although White (1994) viewed reliability as equating roughly with *fairness;* we see fairness as much more than whether a writer will get the same score for the same work every time. That may happen, and yet the test may not be fair: We cannot, for instance, see the fairness of teaching many genres of writing but testing only one; or of teaching writing as process but testing only the writer's ability to draft quickly; or of accommodating writers' needs for time, space, and flexibility in the instructional setting, but severely constraining all these—and more—in the testing setting. Readers' judgments of such limited samples may be consistent, but we can rely on those consistencies for only the most limited forms of judgments.

The implications of these limitations would be worrisome enough even if student populations were relatively homogeneous—even if, that is, the writers being compared were similar to each other in background, culture, training, and experience. Over time, however, college student populations have become increasingly diverse. In the United States, the student body of the late 1990s contains more African Americans, more Hispanic Americans, more of all minorities, more single mothers, and more economically disadvantaged students than the overall makeup of student bodies in the past. This increasing diversity of the college student population is occurring too in Britain, Canada, and Australia. Wherever it occurs, it brings a need to consider more factors in any assessment of writing ability: more cultural differences to account for, a wider range of instructional histories, often widely divergent life experiences, and so on. These increasing complications demonstrate a need for better instructional and assessment tools, as definitions of literacy shift and as the interconnection between literacy and political consciousness is clarified (Graff, 1988). As Collins (1993) showed, developments in assessment practices occur not only because of developments in the understanding of the field, as though the field itself existed outside the cultural and economic politics of the day; but in tune with, or in reaction against (depending on the political forces ascendant within the discipline) the political trends of the times. Thus, the history of writing assessment is a disciplinary history and a political history.

Although direct writing assessments have been asserted (e.g., by Brown, 1986) to be fairer for minority students, there is very little concrete evidence to support such a claim. Perhaps the best known study is one by White and Thomas (1981), which looked at the scores of more than 10,000 California State University students on the Test of Standard Written English (TSWE; part of the College Board's Scholastic Aptitude Test), a wholly multiple-choice test, and the English Placement Test (EPT; administered by the ETS for California State University), which includes an essay test. White and Thomas used self-reported ethnicity information correlated with score data to conclude that the TSWE is biased against Black, Mexican-American, and Asian-American students by comparison with the scores of the same students on the essay component of the EPT. White and Thomas argued for expanded essay testing of minority students and the reduction of multiple choice testing. However, Chaplin (1988) showed that merely switching from standardized testing to essay testing would not eliminate test bias against minority students. Chaplin's study used NAEP and New Jersey High Schools Proficiency Test (NJHSPT) writing assessment data, and focused specifically on the writing of Black students, because Black students have consistently scored below White students on the NAEP. Although Chaplin found occurrences of Black Vernacular English (BVE) in the essays, she found that only 5% of students were using BVE consistently; and not all these students proved to be Black. Chaplin asked essay readers whether they thought a particular essay was written by a Black or a White student; most readers usually thought they could tell, but were right less often than they were wrong. This raises questions about possible rater bias in essay scoring. Similar questions and concerns about bias have been raised for nonnative writers (Chiste & O'Shea, 1988; Hamp-Lyons, 1990; Sweedler-Brown, 1993a, 1993b; Tedick, 1993), and there are other technical issues that remain unsolved about essay tests.

Despite all the concerns and limitations reviewed here, we still believe wholeheartedly that the traditional one-shot, timed writing assessment is far better than the standardized, multiple-choice testing that it succeeded. Within their obvious limitations, timed writing tests meet their objectives for greater validity and similar reliability when compared with indirect tests. There are many contexts in which writing teachers and writing programs may have to be content with this kind of assessment, particularly in large-scale national testing, where efficiency is a major concern. We must also remember that, even in the late 1990s, there are still college writing programs that are struggling to make the conversion from standardized placement tests to an entry assessment based on a direct writing sample; or from an "objective" exit test to a direct test of writing. We support those who are still facing those battles in their efforts.

But within a single college, and within a single program, we are increasingly aware of the limits of essay tests and increasingly dissatisfied with such a context-poor assessment; we turn, then, to portfolio assessment as a key alternative mode for evaluating writing in college programs.

PORTFOLIO-BASED WRITING ASSESSMENT: AN OVERVIEW

The notion of a *writing folder* has been common in the British education system since at least the 1950s, and the writing folder became part of the British school examination system in the early 1970s, when it became part of the General Certificate in Education "Mode 3" examination. The term *portfolio* became current in the United States during the early 1970s as well, although for more than a decade it referred almost exclusively to a collection of writings prepared in a single writing class and graded by a single teacher. The current explosion in portfolio-based writing assessment began in the mid-1980s, once Belanoff and Elbow (1986) demonstrated, in their project at the State University of New York-Stony Brook, that using portfolios across a writing program was not only practical, but beneficial to the students, teachers, and the curriculum, not to mention to the people who run the program. Since that landmark event, portfolios have spread like wildfire. At the close of the 20th century, portfolios are being used as the grading mechanism for individual classes in many subject areas, and at many levels; as an exit assessment tool for multisectioned first-year writing courses; as an entry-level assessment, in order to determine where in a sequence of writing courses a student should begin; as a tool for assessing a student's progress through a school's curriculum or for assessing the curriculum itself; as a mechanism for promoting writing across the curriculum and for certifying that students have met the objectives of their school's Writing Across the Curriculum (WAC) requirement, and so on.

Looking at what people are doing with portfolios, in one place and in one way or another, an incredibly broad range is found, too broad a range certainly for just one book to describe, let alone for developing a theoretical account. However, before we proceed, in chapter 2, to lay out a theoretical basis for portfolio-based writing assessment in the context of college writing classes, programs, and curricula, we must place the particular values of and problems with portfolios, the theoretical and practical issues of portfolio-based writing assessment at the college level, within the context of work being done with, and attitudes toward, writing portfolios more generally. Portfolios are being used for everything from kindergarten-level tracking of whole-language skills (Batzle, 1992; DeFina, 1992) to college-level curriculum reform (Larson, 1991) with plenty of stops in between. In fact, the range of uses found by educators at every level and those they are finding for portfolios continually expands, inviting a comparison with the world of information technology: What is said today may well be out of date tomorrow. The principal users of portfolios fall into three groups, which, it seems, range from the group with the broadest set of concerns (i.e., the assessment community itself), to a group with a somewhat narrower but still quite broad range of concerns (i.e., the K-12 education community), and finally to the group that has more narrowly focused concerns (i.e., the college writing community).

These three constituencies—assessment, K-12, and college-level writing programs—have traditionally been alienated from each other, even though they share many interests and even though each depends, to some extent, on the other for information, justification, or support of many kinds. That the groups are so separate from each other is not a fact we celebrate, but it is one we can understand, because their interests and concerns have been so different. Even when it seems that an interest in the use of portfolios in instructions and assessment might bring them together, the fact is that each community uses portfolios for reasons that are both similar and divergent: Each bases its use of portfolios on a different set of theories; and each has a different stake in the success or failure of portfolio assessment or, more generally, performance assessment.

Portfolios and the Assessment Community

For many years, psychometricians and even many in the educational assessment community, were resistant to alternative assessments; the reasons for this lie in the genesis of the field of psychometrics itself. Psychometrics had its roots in the scientism of the turn of the 19th century and particularly the new "science" of statistics (Witte, Trachsel, & Walters, 1986) and was fed by the rationalist-empiricist 1930s and 1940s (the period of behaviorism in psychology) and funded by the need during World Wars I and II for fast, reliable decisions about the suitability of personnel for military and ancillary jobs. Psychometrics provided the tools for making large numbers of decisions rapidly and cheaply. As shown in the beginning of this chapter, the rationalist-positivist measurement experts believed that there was truth "out there" (or "in there") somewhere, and that their job was to capture and record it for the purpose of making decisions about people. Psychometricians played a vital role at that time in social engineering, developing and applying reliable tests for the selection of personnel for the armed forces, and for specific duties within the armed forces. The validity of those tests, and the decisions that came from them, were never questioned (except for interrogations of *internal validity*, a kind of validity that uses its own internal logic to validate itself).

It was a small step to introduce similar tests into public education, in order to discriminate effectively between more and less capable students, and to make decisions, such as who would receive admission to college, easier and cheaper. Such was the mood of the time that people believed in (or at least, did not question), the concept behind the Bell curve, that is, that human mental and moral qualities like intelligence, honesty, language aptitude, and writing ability were "normally distributed" in the same way as physical characteristics such as height or weight; people believed in the inherent truth of test scores. We must remember that during this period, an understanding of statistics was undeveloped even among highly educated people who were not themselves psychometricians, and it was years before questions began to be asked by significant numbers of people about whether these pure measures were really so pure, or whether they were too closely related to other measures such as quality of schooling received, per capita expenditure of the local school district, parents' educational or socioeconomic level, and so on. Because it had not been looked for, the evidence of the strong relations between test scores and variables such as social class, income, race, and gender had not yet been discovered. The key elements of test development were expediency and the design of time-, cost- and labor-saving assessments (Witte, Trachsel, & Walters, 1986). Construct validity[4] was neither mentioned nor discounted, whereas in the past decade its importance in psychometricians' hierarchy of validities has consistently risen until construct validity is now said, even by psychometricians themselves (Messick, 1989), to be "the overarching validity" (p. 101). Within this background, it was a significant move for members of the educational measurement community to accept that alternative forms of assessment were becoming common enough in educational use that measurement people needed to look at them seriously, and begin dealing with the difficult questions of how to ensure the adequacy and appropriateness of interpretations and actions based on judgments deriving from portfolios and other forms of alternative assessments.

In recent years, then, portfolios have attracted a considerable amount of attention from some members of the educational assessment community. This community presently looks at portfolios so broadly that portfolio almost becomes an abstract concept. This is mainly because they look at portfolios of all types—not only writing, but science, social science, art, music, and more—from all levels of student, from kindergarten through college level. One example of this eclecticism is a 1993 report of ETS portfolio projects in science (sponsored by National

---

[4]*Construct validity* refers to the ability of a test to capture and measure a hypothesized "construct" (such as "intelligence," "beauty," or "literacy").

Science Foundation), in the arts (Pittsburgh's Arts PROPEL project), in middle-school science classes (the SEPIA project, also in Pittsburgh), in college-level writing classes (the Composition Plus Portfolio project), and a K-2 project aimed at tracking the progress of these early learners across subject areas and grade levels ("Developing a Prognosis for Portfolio Assessment: ETS Staff Share What They've Learned"). Involvement across such a wide range of types and kinds of portfolio at such a span of grade levels means that the assessment community looks at the portfolio *qua* portfolio, rather than at a single instantiation of portfolio-based assessment within a coherent educational stratum and inside a particular skill area.

Another reason for the high level of abstraction in work on portfolios stemming from the assessment community is that, historically, psychometricians have been disengaged from education, and even educational measurement specialists have viewed curriculum and classrooms from a distance, not as part of what their work in test development and validation needed to be concerned with. Furthermore, conscious of the dangers of being cast in the role of villain as local school districts employed test scores in ways that the tests had not been designed to support, and seeking to retain the "pure" form of assessments as they had imagined them, the testers themselves reinforced the separation. The conflicted nature of educational assessment as an activity can be seen in recent work on test uses and the ethics of test preparation practices (Kilian, 1992; Mehrens & Kaminski, 1989; Popham, 1991).

As the educational assessment community takes more confident steps toward new methods of assessment, new kinds of measures to solve new kinds of questions, its work gets more difficult, but many educational assessment specialists find themselves less conflicted about what they do. These changing attitudes are a response to the social forces loose in the United States and other English-speaking countries at the end of the millennium. Today's context demands sensitivity to social conditions and the impact of racism, poverty, inequitable opportunities for schooling, and so on, and in response to these demands, newer assessment methods, generally referred to as "authentic" assessment or "alternative" assessment, are predominantly performance assessments and are most importantly represented by portfolio assessment. Responding to the same climate of change, teachers and schools are no longer willing to allow "the assessment people" to decide what is to be measured and how. Teachers and students expect to participate in those decisions, and they have views on what kinds of decisions will be acceptable to them.

This new democratic approach to assessment and accountability is afoot too across the nation, among parents and citizen groups. In President Bush's Education 2000 statement, Goal 5 read, "By the year 2000, every adult American will be literate and will possess the knowledge and skills necessary to compete in a global society and exercise the rights and responsibilities of citizenship." This goal had the potential to draw in large numbers of community members to considerations of educational excellence and assessment, and had the potential too to trigger a search for new ways of reaching literacy goals, and assessing whether and which literacy goals had been reached. And matters started hopefully. The U.S. Department of Education's Office of Educational Research and Information (OERI), in response to Goal 5 (which was later revised as Goal 6), carried out many fact-finding activities including public hearings across the country, sponsored workshops, and invited conferences.

But the urge toward increasing democratization of assessment and accountability issues by well-intentioned bureaucrats remains under siege from conservative forces in education, educational assessment, and bureaucracy itself. In pursuit of Goal 5 (6) of *Education 2000*, a "study design workshop" was held for the OERI by the National Center of Education Statistics, and the report of this workshop ("National Assessment of College Student Learning," 1993) is candid about the diverse voices and viewpoints that were heard in the prepared papers and discussions at that workshop. Among these diverse voices were several asserting the value of portfolio assessment methods, not only for the assessment of writing but for wider application to the assessment of the elements of thought; macroabilities such as analyzing or evaluating arguments and dialectic reasoning; and affective dimensions such as thinking independently and developing intellectual curiosity. Among these voices, White's (author of *Teaching and Assessing Writing*, 1994, and the "father" of first-language writing assessment) was loudly heard, and the report of the discussions make clear his influential role in the debate: A separate section toward the close of the report confronts head on his arguments for portfolio assessment. Following extensive extracts of White's text and citing of his points, opposing opinion was heard from Facione, who argued that "Many of the current tests effectively address higher order thinking skills" (p. 170; in a footnote, he cited LSAT, GRE, SAT, and AP) and concluded that adequate validity and reliability are a pipe dream for a national portfolio system. Larson, known to college compositionists for his work in writing across the curriculum, was also present and made specific suggestions for addressing problems in ratings, but despite these voices, "the general drift towards portfolios as a panacea to the many difficult issues involved . . . raised . . . a compulsion to warn" in those present (p. 172). These warnings, summarized by Pete Cappelli, were as follow:

- There is a need for assessment of portfolios by scoring guides that mirror the skills, knowledge, and abilities we want to measure.

- Portfolios might not capture a wide enough range of skills.
- There is a lack of studies of reliability or validity.
- Logistical problems exist.

The summary editorial comment (unattributed) is that the question will be whether insights from portfolio assessments can be defended and properly reported. A second "study design workshop" was held in 1992, to which a different set of participants was invited. In the report of this workshop ("National Assessment of College Student Learning," 1994), which includes the invited paper by Witte for the group on writing, there is no mention at all of portfolios: White was not invited. Attention had shifted, as the title of the report suggests, to inventories and taxonomies. As an outcome to this second workshop, the National Center for Education Statistics, under Sal Corrallo, contracted The National Center on Postsecondary Teaching, Learning and Assessment (NCPSTLA) at Penn State University to carry out consensus-finding activities to determine what was important in college education in the fields of writing, speech, listening, and critical thinking. The NCPSTLA recruited 600 volunteer judges drawn fairly randomly from colleges and businesses across the country to make judgments about an extensive list of specific skills in college ("National Assessment of College Student Learning," 1995). Six *hundred* judges! Among the many questions asked of the judges about practices in developing writing skills, not one was about portfolios.

As expectations shift in the educational community about what schools measure and how they measure it (Sheingold & Fredericksen, 1995), the people who make their livings from tests find themselves performing a difficult balancing act. On the one hand, they have to devise new tools that satisfy old demands. Thus, not only do these new tools have to meet established psychometric measures, but they also have to meet the demand for tools that can be used to ensure public accountability for schools, they have to come close to the former measures in terms of cost in time and money, and they have to fit existing ways of measuring a test's effectiveness: reliability, validity in its several forms, the ability to detect and adjust for test bias, and so on. Not surprising that it has so far been difficult for alternative assessments to measure up to the traditional expectations while setting and meeting new, expanded and more enlightened ones.

However, there are signs that the educational assessment community is responding to the potential for these new tools to act as an agent for change in education instead of as an inhibitor of change, as was the case with standardized tests (M. Smith, 1991; M. Smith & Rottenberg, 1991). These new methods inevitably implicate instruction with assessment, and those in educational measurement have had to rethink their ways of doing business and create new agendas and heuristics for themselves. Linn, Baker, and Dunbar (1991) described a set of criteria for evaluating the quality of new forms of assessment, and Moss et al. (1992) showed how portfolio-based conclusions about learning might be used to provide accountability information publicly.

Finally, the principal emphasis in assessment projects at agencies such as ETS, American College Test (ACT), and CRESST[5] is to establish ways portfolios in general can be useful, informative, valid, and reliable measures of performance. For a while, and to an extent even now, the assessment community seemed thwarted by the issue of reliability, as if there could be no value in portfolios without reliability: "Issues of validity, reliability, and so on," complained Calfee, speaking of teachers' enthusiasm for portfolios, "have simply fallen through the cracks" (cited in Flanagan, 1993, p. 1). Early—and as recently as 1991—the assessment community looked on performance assessment with suspicion (see, e.g., Frechtling, 1991), but more recently, the assessment community has begun to view performance assessment as a challenge to be met: "Performance assessment challenges methodologists to devise observational situations that evoke evidence about what we want to infer, to learn how to extract and summarize this evidence, and how to monitor and improve assessment systems" (Myford & Mislevy, 1995, p. 1). In fact, the growing acceptance of performance assessment within the assessment community itself has even led to questions about the old ways:

> Traditional methods alone will do no more than insist that the evidence be produced in traditional forms. The questions posed by the psychometric tradition persist and are compellingly important. However, the procedures for addressing them are mere technique. We must be willing to re-examine them in order to appropriately insist on quality even as we invite and accommodate new forms of practice. (LeMahieu et al., 1995, pp. 26-27)

As portfolios begin to measure up to psychometric standards—or as new ways for describing the effectiveness of these new tests arise—the assessment community has turned increasingly to activities that "push the envelope," that stretch ideas of what portfolios are and what, beyond the traditional ends of assessment, we might do with them.

---

[5]We have already cited several projects from ETS' Center for Performance Assessment; in 1998, ACT entered the second pilot year for a portfolio-based assessment of math, science, and verbal skills that augmented or replaced its standardized test; the spring 1994 newsletter of the National Center on Evaluation, Standards, and Student Testing (CRESST) contains several reports on activities in that organization.

These efforts involve portfolios for every conceivable purpose, always guided by a few basic principles, and always accompanied by a rigorous examination of what kinds of results one can obtain and how reliable those results are. Here we see the portfolio as a tool for performance assessment (Dietel, 1993), for example, as a potential tool for tracking literacy (Valencia & Calfee, 1991) or for evaluating writing teacher effectiveness (Hult, 1994). Basically, as the teaching community demands forms of assessment that are more responsive to students', teachers' and even parents' needs, the emphasis on performance assessment—as opposed to the more traditional test scores—has opened the door to portfolio-based assessment, with the portfolio as the site for gathering together a student's performances. Basically, as Stiggins (1991) argued,

> . . . we [the assessment community] are experiencing fundamental changes in the way we view and conduct assessment in American schools. Such in-depth reexamination of our assessment principles is not unprecedented in our educational history. But it has been 60 years since we have experienced such a deep-seated and thoughtful reevaluation of our assessment priorities. . . . We are asking searching questions about the student characteristics to be assessed in the 1990s, the kinds of assessment alternatives to be used to reflect those traits, and the very meaning of sound assessment. We are examining both the technical challenges posed by performance assessment and the practical issues we face in applying this methodology in the classroom and in large-scale assessment. (pp. 263-264)

Thus, for the assessment community, the portfolio exists as a tool for gathering performances of widely varying kinds, and the problems posed by this new kind of assessment are those of assuring, on the one hand, that the portfolios themselves are valid samples of students' manifold performances (Dietel, 1993) and, on the other, that the evaluations of those portfolios are sufficiently reliable—in assessment terms—to be called fair (Mehrens, 1992). In this realm, the portfolio exists, paradoxically, both as a complicated metaphor and as a simple tool. In either case, its existence and its efficacy depend not so much on what a particular instantiation of the portfolio (tool) collects—art, writing, math, science, videotapes, and so on—as on the concept (metaphor) of the portfolio itself, the aspects of portfolios that cross the boundaries of particular manifestations and affect portfolios no matter where they are used, no matter what they collect, and no matter how they are evaluated.

This emphasis is not only understandable, it is a necessary part of establishing portfolio-based assessment's credibility for audiences outside the teaching community. But the emphasis on testing the concept of performance assessment (the category into which portfolio assessment fits), on pushing these assessments to be valid and reliable in already established ways, and, more recently, on finding new and more extensive applications of performance assessment sets the assessment community apart from the teaching community in ways that sometimes seem to place the two communities at odds with each other. Calfee's remarks at a meeting sponsored by NCTE's New Standards Project indicate the distrust members of the traditional assessment community can feel for the teaching community, whom they often see as "outrageously enthusiastic" (Flanagan, 1993, p. 1). At the same time, teachers often seem impatient with the assessment community's insistence on what they see as unnecessary encumbrances (Elbow, 1994). This unfortunate schism tends to hide the assessment community's actual goals of establishing whether portfolio assessment yields useful results that both educators and the public at large can trust, and it also tends to obscure the very real benefits that will accrue to portfolio assessment as the assessment community itself moves away from more traditional measures and into "authentic" assessments, including performance assessment. Here, the interests of both communities come together, and both can be served by more contact and cooperation. In order to push its performance assessment agendas, the assessment community needs the cooperation of teachers; in order to gain access to conversations about accountability and school or curriculum reform, the teaching community needs the endorsement that assessors can lend to newer, more humane forms of assessment that also serve educational goals.

Portfolios in the K-12 Community

The uses to which primary and secondary schools put portfolios share much with the ways they are used by the assessment community— although largely for political reasons. Various state-mandated tests for students at certain grade levels, and even for teachers themselves, create a natural interest in how these assessments work, how they reinforce or undermine teaching, and how they might change in the future. The principal difference between the two communities, of course, is a matter of focus. The assessment community's interest, first and foremost, resides in the tests themselves, and although the interest in the effects of tests on curriculum, teaching, and learning is growing, those interests are and will probably remain secondary. The assessment community will continue to look at what happens in classes in order to determine whether decisions based on test results (and, increasingly, on the basis of other forms of assessment) are accurate and reliable, and whether the new instruments can meet traditional measures and enable traditional kinds of inferences, but there is no indication that assessors will become interested primarily in what happens in those classes to generate those results.

Teachers, of course, are most interested in what happens in their classrooms, with and for their students, and less interested in the details or precise machinery of assessments, whatever their kind. On the broadest level, K-12 teachers trust assessment tools that can incorporate the theoretical and practical bases of K-12 classrooms. Teachers know quite a lot about learning, especially about how learning occurs in children of school age as they grow into young adults. This knowledge comes from relevant studies in the fields of learning theory; cognitive, developmental, and educational psychology; and from studying the ways curricula incorporate both higher order skills (critical thinking, analysis, problem solving, etc.) and lower order skills (error detection in grammar and spelling, straightforward calculation in math, memorization of facts, etc.). Teachers see that standardized tests tend to focus on lower order skills, and that national or statewide norm-referenced tests must, of necessity, be irrelevant to local curricula, needs, and standards. In the past, students did their classwork and then at a specified time they took a national test—typically, the California Achievement Test (CAT), the Scholastic Aptitude Test (SAT), ACT,[6] and so on—that had no particular relation to the curriculum the teachers were using. Then, on the basis of these scores, schools and even teachers themselves were evaluated, ranked according to students' performances on essentially irrelevant tests. Thus, teachers see the extent to which the tests that supposedly measure their and their students' performances are in fact incomplete and unfair measures. These perceptions only increase the level of cynicism the teachers themselves feel about assessment, as well as add to the teachers' feelings of powerlessness (M. Smith, 1991). In turning toward performance assessment, teachers seek a test that is more fully integrated into their school's and classroom's curricula and that is grounded in the same theories about learning and human development as their teaching methods. Teachers want to focus on higher order skills because they realize that those skills are the basis on which their students will succeed in higher education, in a trade or career, and in life in general. Studies from the assessment community indicate that performance assessment can meet teachers' goals. Performance assessment provides richer information

---

[6]The CAT is commonly administered to students in order to measure their achievement in all subjects, and it is also (mis)used to rank school districts by the average scores their students attain; the SAT and ACT are both used to predict a potential student's success in college (although both tests correlate best to a family's socioeconomic status, rather than to eventual success in college), but the national averages on these tests are often used to measure whether education is improving or declining.

about what students can do, and it leaves room for students to show more than the test asks. Thus, performance assessment acts as an inspiration for meaningful conversations about students' work, and it helps students and teachers alike feel that what they are doing in the classroom is, first, worthwhile and, second, meaningful at assessment time (Sheingold & Fredericksen, 1995).

Teachers' interest in testing also springs from the ways tests influence their classrooms and their careers. Teachers want students to perform well, they are cognizant of state-mandated tests, and they are aware of increasing—and appropriate—demands for accountability, demands that come most frequently from legislators, school boards, and parents, but also from colleges and from students themselves. However, teachers are all too painfully aware that the old means of accountability— norm-referenced standardized tests—caused more problems than they solved in the classroom. Teachers, more than any other group, know how much time tests steal from learning activities, and how extensively the curriculum is geared to successful performance on standardized tests, rather than to helping students learn "how to think strategically, to understand concepts and ideas in curricular domains, to apply what they learn, to be able to pose questions, and to be able to devise and solve problems" (Sheingold & Fredericksen, 1995, p. 1). Teachers know that the curriculum focuses on what the tests ask, and that instructional methods come to resemble the tests, whether or not the tests present the most important material—studies indicate they don't—and whether test-dictated materials and methods promote learning—studies indicate they do not (M. Smith, 1991; M. Smith & Rottenberg, 1991). Everyone—most especially the teachers—wants to make schools work better, and to the extent that performance assessment can help drive change for the better, teachers are interested in participating.

The advent of performance assessment—and in the schools, performance assessment is heavily identified with portfolios—does mean that assessment and instruction are likely to become more fully integrated. Many studies emphasize the problems the disjuncture between test and curriculum raises (cf. Aschbacher, 1991; E. Baker, Freeman, & Clayton, 1990; Nickerson, 1989; M. Smith, 1991; Smith & Rottenberg, 1991) and the potential for solving the inherent problems by shifting to some form of performance assessment as a way of supporting the improvement of schools (Aschbacher, 1989). Because performance assessment involves producing or collecting samples of students' work in which the students go beyond simple recall of information to demonstrate problem-solving and critical thinking skills, such assessments are much more likely to draw on activities and products from a student's schoolwork; hence, such assessments are necessarily tied more closely to school curriculum and, by extension, actual classroom instruction. Teaching to these tests is less problematic because the activity involves students in the pursuit of knowledge, the creation of knowledge, and a spirit of inquiry—activity that goes considerably beyond fact-retrieval and test-taking strategies.

Performance assessment, then, promises to remove or at least de-emphasize the current barriers between assessment and teaching, primarily because the instruments used in performance assessment must come from or more closely resemble classroom products than standardized tests can or do. Integrating instruction and assessment is one of the most common effects of instituting portfolio-based assessment (Hamp-Lyons & Condon, 1993; Myford & Mislevy, 1995; Sheingold & Fredericksen, 1995), and one of the most significant because it brings together, in the case of primary and secondary education, the people responsible for both the teaching and the testing that will be needed for genuine educational reform. Portfolio assessment enables both groups to focus on the same student-generated products in order to assess student learning on specified tasks at particular points in a student's school career, as well as over time. In this regard, the portfolio(s) provide "footprints" that show students' achievements or competencies at a particular time, and portfolios act as a trace of a student's progress from one testing occasion to the next. Thus, the same instruments serve both local and state accountability purposes and basic classroom learning purposes. As these communities come more fully into contact and develop a more secure understanding of each other's needs, each community will be able to enrich the other, sharing information, contextualized knowledge, experience, and expertise.

Portfolios in the College Writing Community

The third major site for the development of portfolio-based writing assessment is the college-level writing program. Here, just at the place in a student's life when a thorough inventory of learning would be most useful, the scope narrows, so that in general only one aspect of students' accomplishments is assessed (writing), and, generally, at only one level—first-year composition. The potential for assessing students' writing as they enter college exists, but to date that potential has only begun to be explored (see Anson & Brown, 1991; Daiker, Sommers, Stygall, & Black, 1994; Decker, 1995). Currently, a few schools, most prominently Miami University, are asking a few students to submit portfolios in order to determine which of the most highly qualified students may exempt first-year composition. Only one school, the University of Michigan, has assessed the writing of all incoming students by requiring them to submit a writing portfolio (Decker, 1995). As of Fall 1999, that innovative attempt has been abolished. The literature on portfolio assessment indicates that portfolios are most often used by individual teachers (see, e.g., the section on classroom portfolios, in Belanoff & Dickson, 1991); next most frequently, portfolios are used as an instrument for assessing students passing out of a first-year composition course, in order to ascertain their readiness for the next step in the program or curriculum (cf. Belanoff & Elbow, 1986; Condon & Hamp-Lyons, 1991; Roemer, Schultz, & Durst, 1991). Much less frequently, portfolios are used to examine a college's curriculum (Larson, 1991), as a diagnostic assessment as students enter their junior year (Haswell & Wyche-Smith, 1994) or barrier test as they prepare to graduate from college (Holt & Baker, 1991), or as a means of certifying that a student has met the objectives for a college's writing across the curriculum requirement (Eckerd College). For the most part, however, portfolio-based writing assessment is less robust and less varied—although perhaps more widespread—in the college teaching community than it is in the assessment or K-12 communities.

The narrowness of focus (testing only one aspect, and generally at only one level) reinforces many other ways in which the college community is set apart from the other two. Although we note that the portfolio metaphor itself comes from a discipline other than writing (art), we also note that, outside art, architecture, and other visually oriented fields, portfolios are widely employed only for purposes of direct measurement of writing or, through an examination of the writing, measurement of performance in other disciplines—math, science, history, and so on. The specialization of college-level education has resulted in the separation of fields of study and even performance media (writing, music, oral interpretation, multimedia, and so forth), so that, for example, a psychologist may legitimately feel inadequate to deal with more than the content of an assigned paper—and may not even recognize student achievement if the form of the writing does not fall within a fairly narrow set of discipline-specific expectations (Harrington & Condon, 1998). This kind of isolation means that college-level assessments focus on single subject areas—biology, French, English/American literature, mathematics, writing, and the like. The fragmentation of learning into colleges and departments means that rarely does any individual or agency step back to look at learning on anything like the scope that is common in the primary and secondary schools. Or, when such an examination does happen, it is carried out by deans, who generally do not teach and may not have taught for some time.

Even when portfolios are used to evaluate or assess writing, approaches tend to be essentialized—that is, the focus is on what kind of portfolio this program or that program uses, how it is read and evaluated (in logistical terms) in a specific context, what local faculty's and students' reactions have been, and so forth. In the literature to date, little has been done in the way of theory-making for portfolio-based writing assessment, and what little is there generally has come not from the college writing faculty who work in those assessments, but from the educational assessment community (see, e.g., Camp, 1985; Valencia & Calfee, 1991).

This dearth of theory is perhaps a natural extension of the nature of teaching in higher education. First, "theory," as it applies to higher education classes, refers to more localized considerations of disciplinary content, rather than to the broader concerns of readiness, learning, and human development. College professors learn—and, in their classes, teach—the theories of their individual disciplines. Because students come to college, for the most part, as adults, and since they choose classes from a wide selection, the need to know about or consider issues such as readiness is not as great as it is in K-12. Second, and unfortunately, college teachers' preparation does not necessarily include exposure to the range of educational theory that the assessment community and K-12 community must acquire. College professors usually do not study how to accommodate different learning styles, for example, or how learning itself works. Instead, they study theories of quantum mechanics, evolutionary biology, cultural anthropology—or writing. For these two reasons, college-level classes focus on content and on discipline-centered theory, and college professors think less of assessment (i.e., grading) and they think about it in a less complicated way than the other two communities do. Finally, the undertheorization of portfolio assessment stems from the fact that portfolio-based writing assessment, as it occurs today, has only been in existence since the mid-1980s. Before that time, individual teachers used portfolios as a way to put off assigning grades until students had time to revise—and learn from—their essays. But in 1986, Elbow and Belanoff's article about the portfolio method employed at SUNY-Stony Brook began the current wave of expansion of portfolios beyond the individual classroom. Their portfolio project replaced a timed essay exit assessment from a first-year writing course, contributing in now familiar ways to faculty development and to maintaining an acceptable level of uniformity among different sections of the same course.

Portfolios are being used as tools for exit assessment from first-year composition classes at many institutions, in many differing institutional contexts (see, e.g., Camp, 1989; Condon & Hamp-Lyons, 1991; Roemer et al., 1991). In each context, programs have accounted for the differing curricular, institutional, and political demands of their local context, so that by now we are beginning to have enough practice from which to develop theory. Unless that theory is forthcoming, portfolios cannot evolve much further. Hence, this volume focuses on college-level portfolio-based writing assessment, rather than on the other areas. Where appropriate, of course, we intend to tie the interests of each of these constituencies together, but for the most part the demands of space dictate that we leave any detailed examination of portfolio-based assessment as it applies directly to the concerns of those other two communities for someone else's book.

Having said that, we nevertheless note that portfolio-based writing assessment at the college level shares much of the same theoretical base as in the other two communities. Inevitably—and knowingly or unknowingly—when we assess learning, we must confront issues about testing that are common in the assessment community, issues about learning that prevail in the K-12 community, and discipline-centered issues that are the direct concern of the college writing community. So, at the same time as we decry the divisions between the college community and the K-12 and assessment communities, we recognize that all three communities seek the far greater face validity of the portfolio (Elbow, 1991b) and that all three seek to solve the same problems, even though each faces the problems to a differing degree. Thus, each community must find fair and accurate tools for assessing students' achievements; each faces the challenges that stem from cries for accountability; each is genuinely interested in improving students' learning; each seeks assessment measures that reveal more about what happens in the course of a student's educational career. Performance assessments of one kind or another—including portfolios, of course—offer each community the hope of such measures.

Chapter 2

PORTFOLIO-BASED WRITING ASSESSMENT
IN COLLEGE WRITING PROGRAMS

CHARACTERISTICS OF PORTFOLIOS

What we see when we curl up with a portfolio are texts. What we don't see—but what is present nonetheless—are the contexts from which those texts arose. Although much of the discussion that follows, for the sake of (relative) simplicity, proceeds on the assumption that portfolios flow out of instructional contexts, we must keep in mind that this is merely a convenient assumption, one that can be made only for the moment, for the sake of the present discussion. In fact, portfolios come from a full context. Any student's worldview, which is largely the result of growing up in one culture, affects the texts seen in his or her portfolio. Any piece of writing grows out of the writer's frame of reference, the set of values that come from culture, home, school, church, workplace, and so on. The writing in most portfolios will come from school settings, so teachers have had an impact on the texts. The writer who assembles the portfolio is of necessity aware that an assessment will take place, and so the writer prepares the portfolio with the assessor in mind. In that way, and in the reader-response sense that the reader creates the text in the act of reading it, the assessor also affects the texts (see, e.g., Murphy & Ruth, 1993). In any optimal form of portfolio assessment, of course, the learner has the greatest role in initiating, revising, and preparing the texts and the portfolio as a whole, and the collection that results is as much an expression of the learner's various selves—the ones the learner has chosen to display, as well as the ones he or she has chosen to conceal—as it is evidence of the learner's competencies as a writer. So, as we enter this more focused discussion of what portfolios are and what they do, we should remember that portfolios always do more than we ask them to, always contain more than we expected, and that more is generally, but certainly not always better. We can choose what aspects of the portfolio we will focus on, but we can never fully control what the portfolio contains nor severely limit the uses to which it can be put.

This aspect of the portfolio—that the test, in effect, always tells us more than we have asked—results from different combinations of nine characteristics of portfolios themselves. To the extent that a given portfolio design includes more of these characteristics, then the portfolio assessment can yield richer, more useful information. To the extent that a portfolio design excludes some of these characteristics, then it will provide less information and be therefore less useful as an assessment tool. The nine characteristics that thoughtfully designed portfolios share are collection, range, context richness, delayed evaluation, selection, student-centered control, reflection and self-assessment, growth along specific parameters, and development over time.

Collection

Portfolios, by their nature, collect more than one performance. Because the principal object of using portfolios is to enable assessors to survey a broader range of performances, produced in the writer's normal way, under the writer's usual circumstances, portfolios by definition must include more than one product, and usually they include three or more, in addition to some kind of reflective statement or self-assessment. No matter the context for portfolio-based writing assessment in college writing programs, the current *raison d'être* seems to be the portfolio's greater "face" validity—if the portfolio contains samples of the writer's "normal" writing, then the portfolio closely resembles that which is being tested. As Elbow (1991a) pointed out, the portfolio simply gives a better picture of a student's writing ability—of what we, elsewhere, called multiple competencies (Condon & Hamp-Lyons, 1991). Portfolios typically invite students to display more than one text, in more than one genre, written for more than one audience on more than one occasion, for more than one purpose. Thus, portfolios allow readers to draw conclusions about writers, not only about the pieces of writing themselves. Collection, then, is the source of the portfolio's greater face validity, of its ability to represent the writer more fully than earlier forms of assessment allowed.

Range

Collection enables the writer to display and the assessors to judge a *range* of performances. That range stems from the fact that a course or course of study should present frequent opportunities to write, in a variety of forms or genres, for a variety of purposes and a variety of audiences. The nature of the curriculum in a writing course ensures that students will produce a range of writing from which the writer can select samples that, in turn, present the range of the writer's accomplishment, both in terms of the kinds of task the curriculum requires and the quality of performance the writer is able to achieve as a result of the opportunities presented by that curriculum. Thus, whether the portfolio encompasses writing from a single course, a specific sequence of courses, or the entire curriculum of a high school, college, or university, the ability of the writer to construct a portfolio of high face validity depends on the range of tasks and performances available to the writer at the time he or she assembles the portfolio.

Context Richness

Insofar as the contents of the portfolio represent the opportunities that a curriculum has presented to a learner, then the portfolio will be *context rich.* In the days of indirect tests of writing and of timed, holistically scored essays, the whole question of connecting assessment with instructional context was moot. The testing situation simply assumed that the writer came into it *tabula rasa*, and the test explicitly demanded that the writer prove what he or she could do, given the (usually severe) constraints—of time, subject matter, genre, place, test type, and so on—dictated by the test and the testing situation. Portfolio assessment, however, assumes that writers bring their experiences, in the form of their writings, with them into the assessment, that the portfolio comprises samples of the writing produced in those learning experiences. This characteristic means that instruction and assessment are intertwined, that the context within which the learning took place determines the contents of the portfolio. The greater the extent to which the portfolio is open to works the writer has produced in a given learning program, the more closely assessment and instruction will be connected; therefore, range allows access to one of portfolio-based writing instruction's greatest strengths.

Delayed Evaluation

Another strength, and a characteristic of portfolio evaluation that teachers and students find attractive and useful, is *delayed evaluation*. Even under the constraints presented in a traditional, graded course where the sole authority over evaluation and grading is centered in the teacher, the fact that reading for the purpose of grading occurs at the end of the term is significant. This timing promotes revision by providing both time for revision to occur and motivation to revise, invites students to assume responsibility for their own learning by placing some measure of control over success into the student's hands, and generates a "success now" atmosphere that helps students and teachers alike feel better about the learning experience. Moreover, at that point in the term, teachers will not read solely in order to assign grades. The timing prompts the teacher to re-evaluate course assignments, teaching methods, course and program curricula, sequencing of assignments and topics, and so on. So, even in situations where the constraints are heaviest, portfolio assessment moves teachers beyond judgments about students' competence, leading them to make judgments about the effectiveness of their course(s) as a whole.

Most portfolio programs use the characteristic of delayed evaluation to some extent. Most, probably, provide some sort of midterm evaluation, in the form of a mini-portfolio (Elbow & Belanoff, 1991; Roemer et al., 1991). These systems provide students with information about their progress, to the extent that progress is reflected by the student's grade, yet they still provide a period within which delayed evaluation can work. Only portfolios that consist of graded essays that students are not allowed to revise eliminate this characteristic and its attendant benefits.

Selection

The combination of several characteristics—range, context richness, and delayed evaluation—enables another significant characteristic, *selection.*

A portfolio generally contains selections of a writer's work, not the entire corpus, nor the entire output from a course. The selection will be guided, in most instances, by requirements laid down by the assessors, but often there is room within those requirements for the writer to present her best work, not just a cross section. *Selection* means that the assessor sees some evidence of a writer's ability to make extra-textual choices, to present a selection that represents the writer well across the specified requirements for contents and the announced criteria for judgment. *Selection* puts one kind of control over self-representation into the writer's hands, because he or she chooses which pieces to submit for judgment, in part, at least, according to the writer's criteria. The act of making the selection leads writers to implicit—and often explicit—decisions about quality. Thus, selection promotes self-assessment.

Student-Centered Control

Several other characteristics of portfolio assessment combine to create the potential for placing a large measure of control over success into the learner's hands. Some characteristics are primarily under the teachers' control: collection, range, and context are usually controlled by the teacher and the writing program; for the most part, these features are determined by the design of the course, the theory that informs it, and its role within the institution's curriculum. But when he or she can choose, even in limited ways, what to place into the portfolio, then the writer gains a measure of control over what kind of "snapshot" the portfolio will contain—the greater the freedom to select, the more control the student can exercise. To the extent that writers receive feedback early and have opportunities to revise before grading occurs, portfolios can foster a learning environment in which effort and time on task are explicitly rewarded. In such a system, learners can see a direct relation between how much effort they put into their early drafts, how extensively they revise, and so on, and how high a rating, score, or grade they receive on the portfolio.

Reflection and Self-Assessment

In the days before collaborative learning pedagogies and process approaches to writing became widespread, students typically wrote one essay, received a grade and some feedback from the teacher, and moved on to the next essay—most often, an essay of a different genre from the previous one. Feedback came after the grade was assigned—too late to do the writer much good—and the shift to a different *kind* of essay limited the extent to which the learning from the one experience could carry over to the next. Today, however, even without portfolio assessment, students usually have opportunities to gain feedback on a draft from their peers and from teachers before they "finish" the draft (i.e., hand it in for a grade). Often, too, even without portfolio assessment, most writing teachers provide opportunities to revise even after a (usually tentative) grade has been assigned. These changes have occurred for many reasons. Many writing teachers have realized that the most effective way for students to learn how to write better is *by making their writing better*—by revising pieces of writing to make them better (however we might define "better" in different contexts). Another prominent reason involves "teaching a person to fish"; writing teachers still want students to produce good writing, of course, but they also want students to develop the writing habits that good writers use. In this way, students can leave a course of instruction less dependent on a teacher to tell the writer whether the writing is effective. In order to accomplish these new goals, teachers must put more control into the students' hands, inviting students to reflect on their writing and on their progress as writers, and fostering self-assessment.

Portfolio designs usually call for some kind of reflective writing about the portfolio as a whole, or a self-assessment that often involves discussing the process that led to the written products and a plan for further revision. This kind of writing promotes a greater awareness of learning, both in the sense that learning is taking or has taken place and in the sense of how successful the learning process has been for the individual learner. Emphasizing *reflection and self-assessment* helps put control for learning into the learners' hands. When the learning environment promotes the learner's greater involvement in and investment in the learning, then it stands to reason that the learner will be more conscious of her or his progress. Asking students to write about their own development can promote further learning, as well as provide assessors with useful evidence that some learning has already occurred.

Growth Along Specific Parameters

Of course, the fact that portfolios provide a robust means of tracking the learning that occurs means that tracing *growth along specific parameters* is also possible. Has a writer developed a stronger ability to write unified essays? A portfolio that contains successive drafts or that requires inclusion of unrevised work from early in the term can yield an answer to that question. Has a writer become a better speller? Again, a portfolio can be designed to ascertain whether this kind of progress has occurred. The assessment criteria, of course, embody these parameters, and the extent to which students exhibit the strengths or needs specified in the criteria allows both learners and assessors to measure progress along those parameters for performance. If we clearly define, in the criteria, the characteristics that add up to a strong performance (not an easy task, certainly, but a necessary one), then we can design a portfolio that will allow students to show the extent of their progress toward exhibiting those characteristics of good writing and writers.

Development Over Time

Finally, depending on the timing of the assessment, portfolios can provide a means for measuring a learner's *development over time*. As long as the portfolio contains drafts of the finished products, for example, then readers can trace the development of each piece. If the portfolio contains both earlier and later work, then readers can perceive ways the writer improved (or declined) over time. Even if this measurement occurs only in the time that elapses between midterm and the end of the term, the degree of progress—the amount of learning and the kinds of learning—between those points is measurable, and that measurement is useful to the learner, who sees visible evidence of progress, and to the teacher, who can demonstrate the effects his or her course is having on the students. In addition, thinking about development over time as separate from growth along specified parameters opens the door for surprises, allowing learners to exhibit and even to emphasize their development in ways or areas that the teacher may not have specified or even anticipated.

All nine characteristics are available to the writing teacher or to the writing program administrator (WPA). Together, these characteristics form the basis for a theory of portfolio assessment because they at least begin to explain the phenomenon of the portfolio and to account for how it acts as it does. As we work our way through current practice toward a theory of portfolio-based writing assessment, we discuss this point further (see chap. 4). For the present, we look at ways these characteristics also begin to reveal how and why portfolios fit into writing programs.

In designing a course or a program's curriculum around a specific theory and the pedagogical practice that theory enables, teachers, administrators, or both, determine how many of these characteristics they will employ, decide which characteristics will be central and which peripheral, and decide just what role each characteristic will play within the confines of their courses or their program. Teachers and WPA's may make decisions that take full advantage of all the characteristics we have listed, or they may restrict the list, making more conservative uses of portfolios; either way, these decisions involve both knowledge of how portfolios work and a clear definition of the theoretical basis for the writing course or writing program involved. As we have argued more than once already, portfolio-based writing assessment inevitably involves assessment with instruction.

For this reason, the next step in exploring the relation between portfolio theory and writing theory, is to examine the several theories of writing in order to survey the intersection between them and portfolio assessment.

THEORIES OF WRITING

In classifying the theories that inform writing programs, we have expanded on catalogs provided in the work of, among others, Berlin (1982, 1984, 1987), Fulkerson (1979), and Kemp (1990) in order to arrive at a list that is both sufficiently comprehensive to encompass the field, yet sufficiently specific to enable useful explorations of portfolio theory as it relates to each category. Some of the items on our list (e.g., process and collaborative learning) are more often classified as pedagogies than as theories, but to the extent that each category names a different explanation of how writing happens, how writers write, and how learning occurs, we have designated them, *arguendo,* as theories. In chapter 3 we consider the "practice side" of what Berlin (1982) called "pedagogical theories"; here, we relate the theoretical side with portfolio theory in order to discover where the two kinds of theory are compatible and where they are at odds. For present purposes, then, our list of writing theories includes formalism, expressivism, cognitivism, collaborative learning, social constructionism, and process. We do not intend these categories to be mutually exclusive (e.g., one might combine aspects of formalism with aspects of collaborative learning theory or of process theory with cognitivism), nor do we assert that they are definitive. Each category of theory engenders such a range of practices that no brief summary can do the category justice. We simply use the summaries to indicate the range of theory available in composition studies, and to argue that portfolio assessments can be designed to accommodate the tenets of each theory.

Formalism

Characteristics Available   Most Prominent Characteristics

- Collection   - Collection
- Range   - Range
- Context Richness   - Selection
- Delayed Evaluation
- Selection

Perhaps the oldest and still the most widespread theory that informs writing courses and programs is formalism (AKA current-traditionalism), a school perhaps best described in the work of Corbett (1971), Hairston (1982), and Kinneavy (1971). Classes based in this theory focus on the study of rhetorical modes such as description, comparison and contrast, definition, classification, argumentation, and so on, and they often involve students in *imitatio*—that is, students model their essays after the writings of acknowledged "masters," in order to learn how to write like those model writers. Often, classes based on formalist theory involve students in the direct study of classical rhetoric and of the rules of grammar and mechanics. Formalism centers authority in the teacher, who defines the tasks, dictates the criteria, and judges the performances. The emphasis in such a class is on the written product: on its adherence to the rules of genre, grammar, and style. The underlying assumption of formalism is similar to that of the Old Testament Covenant: Outward conformation to a detailed set of rules and laws will eventually result in an inward transformation—in this case, the ability to employ the forms and practices of "good writing" and to do so in standard written English.

For differing reasons, the proponents of portfolio assessment and the proponents of formalism might doubt the efficacy of portfolio assessment in formalist writing classes. On the one hand, college-level use of portfolios grew out of the process theory and expressivist traditions, out of the work of people like Elbow (1973) and Murray (1980). So far, those who promote portfolio assessment have done so in terms that appeal to co-practitioners, not to those colleagues whose writing theory differs from the promoters' own. However, an assessment tool as flexible and variable as the portfolio should be able to support almost any theoretical approach. So how might a formalist portfolio assessment work? A portfolio, at its base, is a collection of products—actually, a selection of products. Therefore, portfolio assessment should fit nicely within a formalist context because the nature of the portfolio as a set of products readily accommodates formalism's product-based pedagogy. In addition, the criteria for judging the portfolio are as flexible as its construction. Thus, as long as the criteria for judgment center on the principal formalist objectives of conformity to specific rhetorical modes, of correctness, of elegance, and so forth, the assessment will promote outcomes that also conform to those objectives.

Besides being able to accommodate formalism, portfolio assessment should also help formalist teachers work more effectively within their constraints. For example, rule-bound grading tends to be rigid and unforgiving of error, and it does not easily accommodate the learners' need for space in which to learn how to do what they are being asked to do. Nor does it as easily credit growth as a writer because an emphasis on an objective application of rules most often produces a situation in which a learner's early, faulty performances are simply averaged in with later, more accomplished performances. This conflict between the teacher's theoretical and pedagogical approaches and the learner's need for time in which to learn, before judgment takes place, can be resolved if portfolio grading delays the moment of judgment, allowing learners time to perfect their products so that the contents of the portfolio can conform to formalist objectives. As a result, teachers can more comfortably insist on close adherence to announced standards, and students can become more invested in their writings over a longer period of time because the students perceive that they have some measure of control over their grades. The harder they work, the more closely they attend to their work, and the more time they put into improving that work, the better their portfolios will fare at midterm or at semester's end, when the teacher assigns a grade to the work.

Expressivism

Characteristics Available

- Collection
- Range
- Context Richness
- Delayed Evaluation
- Selection
- Student-Centered Control
- Reflection and Self-Assessment
- Growth Along Parameters
- Development Over Time

Most Prominent Characteristics

- Range
- Student-Centered Control
- Reflection and Self-Assessment
- Development Over Time

Expressivism emerged primarily from the writings of Murray (e.g., 1980), Britton (1982), and Elbow's (1973) *Writing Without Teachers.* Expressivism—the romantic counterpart to the classicism of formalist theory—focuses on "language that is close to speech, close to the self" (Young, 1987, p. 30). Expressivists, contending that the exact mental processes involved in writing are unknowable and hence unclassifiable, focus their instruction around the emergence of meaning from the self, and particularly from the way the writer responds to or feels about a topic. Out of these personal or emotional reactions will emerge the more rational, more objective, more generalized viewpoint where formalists would argue writing begins. Classes based on expressivist theory are more likely to ask students to react to readings, rather than to use readings as models. Expressivism rather naturally centers authority in the learner, whose reactions help define the tasks and dictate the criteria for judging the learners' performances. The pedagogy in such a class emphasizes first the thinking and then the writing processes, leading learners to focus, first, on expressing their thoughts in whatever way seems available—speech, writing, visual arts, and so on—and then on bringing those utterances forward, if necessary, as more formal expressions. As Gere (1981) said, the teacher's job is to help students use language to develop a more complicated view of the world. The underlying assumption of expressivism is similar to that of the New Testament Covenant: Inward conformation to spiritual development will eventually result in an outward, behavioral transformation—for the expressivist, the ability to find the forms and practices of "good writing" that will best express the writer's meaning and communicate that meaning to an audience.

The full set of portfolio characteristics is available for expressivist teachers, but given the expressivist assumption that writing and learning take place in a more organic manner, some of the characteristics of portfolio assessment will be more central than others for these classes or programs. For example, because expressivism begins with utterances that are as close to thought as possible, range takes on a heightened role. Expressivist portfolios might well contain a number of pieces on the same topic, each representing a development over the earlier utterance. Thus, expressivist portfolios may measure *growth along specific parameters,* but they might more effectively measure d*evelopment over time,* because each new version of a piece of writing would demonstrate the ways in which both the writing and the thinking had progressed. Finally, because expressivists tend to center authority in the learner, rather than in the teacher, that characteristic of portfolios enables expressivist pedagogy by allowing the learner both to present a fuller picture of his or her development and accomplishments and to take advantage of the lessons of expressivism in the process of reflecting on the learning represented in the portfolio. One would expect learners from expressivist classes to be more capable of reflection, more aware of their own development as writers and thinkers, than would be the case in other theoretical contexts.

The acid test of portfolio theory, however, lies in the degree to which it helps solve the dilemmas that naturally stem from the application of any single theory to writing or writing instruction. Expressivists constantly face, for example, the accusation that their teaching merely encourages an "uncritical effusion about the self" (Young, 1987, p. 30), or, put more broadly, it encourages students to center their writing on themselves, rather than focusing on the more objective, public discourse forms of writing that students must acquire if they are to be successful in the academy or, later on, in most careers. These criticisms stem from where expressivism begins, rather than focusing on the outcomes of expressivist courses. Portfolio assessment can trace those beginnings (in the personal) to their ultimate products—just the kinds of public discourse that academic writing courses are expected to produce. The portfolio can help expressivists defend their theory by demonstrating that outcomes serve students' and the academy's needs, thus validating the methods used in promoting those outcomes.

Cognitivism

Characteristics Available

- Collection
- Range
- Context Richness
- Delayed Evaluation
- Selection
- Student-Centered Control
- Reflection and Self-Assessment
- Growth Along Parameters
- Development Over Time

Most Prominent Characteristics

- Collection
- Range
- Selection

Cognitive psychology has inspired a writing theory that, in contrast to expressivism, claims that the cognitive processes of reading, understanding, and remembering a text, as well as the cognitive processes involved in conceiving, organizing, and writing a text, are not only knowable, but usable as the basis for teaching writing. Cognitivism's chief proponents, of course, are Flower and Hayes, the rhetorician-psychologist team that broke the ground for this approach at Carnegie-Mellon University in the late 1970s and early 1980s (e.g., Flower, 1979; Flower & Hayes, 1981). A cognitivist approach involves studying the minds of both readers and writers. In order to write effectively, writers need to know more about how readers process text, about the cognitive processes involved in understanding written text. In place of the study of classical rhetoric, the cognitivist focuses on what patterns of organization most readily communicate meaning to readers, what textual signals readers most easily perceive, and so on. This part of the study allows writers to incorporate these reader-friendly features into their texts; thus, cognitivism replaces Aristotle's art of rhetoric with a psychologist's science of rhetoric. This scientific approach carries over into the production of text as well, as cognitivists use techniques such as introspection and verbal report (e.g., think-aloud protocols) to "enter the writer's mind" and identify the ways writers plan their texts, the ways they write, the habits of mind and hand that lead to successful texts (i.e., effective communications).

Collection, range, and selection are the characteristics of the portfolio that most clearly and directly support cognitivist theory. As writers strive to develop a set of strategies, scientific *topoi,* and frameworks for organizing information so that it is most accessible to readers, the portfolio acts as a repository for their attempts and as a site where the writer can use selection to focus the collection on specific aspects of the writer's work. One of the criteria for judging a cognitivist portfolio might well be to inventory the number and range of strategies, *topoi,* and arrangements the writer has employed. Furthermore, peer review and grading could focus on how many of the strategies, *topoi,* and arrangements readers actually perceive, as well as on how easily readers can process and remember the texts in a writer's portfolio. Most important, writers themselves can use the portfolio to check on their own progress, to inventory the techniques they have incorporated into their texts and to reflect on the usefulness of those techniques within the demands of audience and purpose each writing task places on the writer. Furthermore, in reviewing their peers' portfolios, students can see how many other strategies and techniques their peers employ, and in what range of tasks, for what range of audience, and for what range of purposes. Each student can judge the effectiveness of these texts by how well he or she actually understands the texts and how easily that understanding develops.

In addition to supporting the main thrust of cognitivism, portfolios can help cognitivists solve some of the problems that confront them as they enact their theory in their classes. Ironically, because expressivism and cognitivism are in opposition over their basic assumptions about the degree to which the mental processes involved in reading and writing are knowable, these two theories share a common difficulty: Adopting either approach demands a leap of faith. In order to adopt either theory, a teacher must believe the central assumption that the mind is, depending on the theory, knowable or unknowable. Granted, cognitivism's assumption that the mind is knowable is backed by research in the field of cognitive psychology, but that research is hardly conclusive or definitive, the mind being an extremely complex phenomenon; and the application of cognitive psychology to writing is more in the nature of a metaphor than a direct relation. Thus, cognitivists need the portfolio to establish that their methods produce results that serve the writers' needs and that fulfill the institutional mission of the writing course. So, in addition to promoting learning that accords with cognitive theory, portfolios also aid cognitivists as they establish the effectiveness of their theory.

Collaborative Learning

Characteristics Available

- Collection
- Range

Most Prominent Characteristics

- Student-Centered Control
- Reflection and Self-Assessment

- Context Richness
- Delayed Evaluation
- Selection
- Student-Centered Control
- Reflection and Self-Assessment
- Growth Along Parameters
- Development Over Time

- Growth Along Parameters
- Development Over Time

Most classifications of composition theory and practice would list collaborative learning as a theory of learning or as a writing pedagogy, rather than as a theory of writing. However, if we think of theory as the explanation of an existing phenomenon or event, then we can see that collaborative learning, in its view of writing as an explicitly or implicitly collaborative activity, also fits into the category of writing theory. Like social construction, which is discussed later, collaborative learning assumes that writing and knowledge develop among individuals, not in the individual. Thus, not only is writing itself a collaborative act (see Lunsford & Ede, 1984), but so is learning to write. Learning, according to this theory, happens as a corollary to interaction, most often interactions among peers, though also in the interaction between learner and environment. Acts of communication convey information from a writer to an audience, and the information contained in the writing is the (knowing or unknowing) creation of individuals interacting, or in communication with each other. Collaborative learning, as defined by Bruffee (1973) and refined by Gere (1987), seeks to promote more rapid learning by having the learners share their opportunities. Having to negotiate over assignments brings the learning objectives into the foreground, rendering explicit that which is more often implicit. In addition, because collaborative learning also puts the learners collectively in charge of their experiences, collaborative learning classes tend to be learner-centered, rather than teacher-centered. Finally, in collaborative learning situations, students in groups can often take on larger, more significant projects than students working alone can accomplish, and the groups automatically incorporate a more complicated worldview into their work because no single learner's worldview can dominate the writing as it can and most often does when one writer writes alone.

Just as a writing class based on collaborative learning foregrounds learning objectives by sharing them among peers, so such a class foregrounds the characteristics of portfolio assessment. For example, collaborative learning seeks to place responsibility for learning into the learners' hands, and the fact that learners share responsibility for a written product means that they are more likely to accept that responsibility because each learner will rely on, and seek the reliance of, his or her peers. When these groups are working toward a portfolio assessment, the motivation to work harder and longer together in order to improve their written products—and thereby their grades—is even greater as a result of the fact that the moment of grading occurs at the end of the course. In addition, because collaborative learning brings the learning objectives out into the open, students can more easily measure their own growth along multiple parameters and their own development over time, thus making reflective writing or self-assessment a more powerful tool for inspiring or tracking learning.

The teacher's dilemmas in courses based on collaborative learning theory most often stem from some individuals' unwillingness or seeming inability to collaborate and from the basic inconsistencies between a class that is structured to be collaborative, but that exists within an institution that demands that the teacher assign each student a separate grade. Combining portfolio assessment with collaborative learning can ease, if not solve, these problems by increasing the sense of community in the class, and increasing the occasions for the learners to share their work with each other and to teach each other. Assessing learners' progress via a portfolio adds a level of sharing and peer review. As students share their developing portfolios, they get to see how their peers have solved problems common to the group, and they develop an appreciation for the range of strategies, modes, styles, and resources developed in the class. The crucial element in this heightened sense of community is the ability to use the emerging portfolios as a means for the collaborative development of criteria for the final course assessment. As students share their developing portfolios at regular intervals, the group or class discussions can center around developing criteria that accommodate the range of performances the class is producing. Near the end of the term, the class can formalize the criteria, field test it on their own and their classmates' portfolios, and revise it for use in the end-of-term grading of portfolios. Finally, teachers who wish to push this kind of collaborative learning to the limit might easily ask students to use those criteria in order to assess their own and their classmates' portfolios; factoring those assessments together with the teacher's assessment would create an ending for the course that is more consistent with the philosophy of the course.

Social Constructionism

Characteristics Available

- Collection
- Range
- Context RIchness
- Delayed Evaluation
- Selection

Most Prominent Characteristics

- Collection
- Range
- Selection
- Reflection and Self-Assessment
- Growth Along Parameters

- Student-Centered Control
- Reflection and Self-Assessment
- Growth Along Parameters
- Development Over Time

Social constructionism, a relatively recent entry in composition theory, emerges from the later work of Bruffee (1973), as well as from the writings of Bizzell (e.g., 1986), Swales (e.g., 1990), and Rorty (1982). Like collaborative learning, social construction focuses not just on the writer as the creator of texts and the interaction between writer and reader, but on the community within which and for which writers write. All knowledge, social construction says, is created by communities, negotiated by and in discourse communities; likewise, the means of bringing that knowledge into language are regulated, implicitly or explicitly, by those discourse communities. Thus, social constructionist classes focus on helping student writers acquire the characteristics of discourse within a target community. In college writing classes, this study focuses most often on the general characteristics of writing in the academy (Bartholomae, 1985) and on the specific genres employed in different discourse communities within the academy (Connor & Johns, 1989; Swales, 1984). This course of study invites learners to read works produced by a discourse community in order to derive the genres that community employs and the manner in which a specific discourse community has adapted those genres (Elbow, 1991a). As the learner has become familiar with the ways members of a particular discourse community create and convey new knowledge, he or she can begin to practice those forms, strategies, and tactics in order to join that discourse community. Finally, social constructionism involves students in learning how to detect and analyze discourse communities, acknowledging the fact that most of us belong to several, perhaps many discourse communities at once. Thus, the apprentice writer needs to learn how to join discourse communities, not merely how to join the one discourse community (i.e., academe) that concerns most first-year composition teachers.

Although the objects of study differ, social constructionism shares with formalism and cognitivism an emphasis on acquiring forms, strategies, and tactics by observing and analyzing successful discourse. Thus, social constructionist portfolios would be designed to help learners and teachers perceive the extent to which the learner has acquired the forms, strategies, and tactics of the discourse communities in which he or she seeks membership. Such a portfolio strongly supports social constructionist theory and pedagogy. Furthermore, as is the case in collaborative learning theory, social construction focuses on communities, locating knowledge production in the interactions among members of a discourse community. In courses based on social construction, then, writers naturally share their work extensively, providing for each other a set of readers who, like the writer, are in the process of entering a new discourse community (the academy, the class itself, a specific field of study or subdiscipline, etc.) and of learning the process of entering discourse communities. The ability to share an emerging corpus of work, in the form of a developing portfolio, extends this emphasis on interaction, as well as helping the members of a class see themselves as engaging in a common pursuit.

This emphasis on community, on creating knowledge collaboratively, puts the social constructionist writing class at odds with the institutional constraints of grading, creating the same dilemma here that teachers who employ collaborative learning experience. And portfolios help solve the problems for social constructionists in much the same way they do in collaborative learning classes. That is, no matter how extensively a class collaborates, how dominant the concept of shared creation of knowledge, the portfolio can act as the repository of each learner's work, each individual's progress in acquiring the forms, strategies, and tactics of academic discourse(s). Thus, out of extensive interaction and collaboration comes a collection of writing that each learner can identify as his or her own and that the teacher can use as the basis for assigning a course grade. In the alternative, in classes where social construction is so fully employed that the products are themselves collaboratively written, the portfolio's invitation for reflection and for self-assessment provides an occasion for individuals to describe or account for their own development and for them to assess their own work discursively in ways that allow teachers to make the judgments they need to make in order to assign grades. Finally, social construction, largely because of its relative newness and because it conflicts with Western culture's emphasis on the individual ownership of ideas, experiences a higher degree of resistance than do other, more established theories. Those whose practice is grounded in other theories question the validity of or the efficacy of social construction. These critics doubt the bases for the theory, in a similar manner as critics of the other theories attack them by attacking their basic assumptions. To a large extent, however, what matters in writing classes are the outcomes. In the end, what counts is whether the students have developed into stronger, more versatile writers and whether what they learn in writing courses serves their academic, intellectual, and career objectives. The fact that portfolios collect products—outcomes—of learning activities means that portfolios can help social constructionists examine and establish the effects of their practice. Just as portfolio assessment provided this ability for practitioners of other theories, it does so for this theory as well.

Process

Characteristics Available	Most Prominent Characteristics
• Collection	• Collection
• Range	• Range
• Context Richness	• Selection
• Delayed Evaluation	• Student-Centered Control
• Selection	• Reflection and Self-Assessment
• Student-Centered Control	• Growth Along Parameters
• Reflection and Self-Assessment	
• Growth Along Parameters	
• Development Over Time	

Like collaborative learning, process is more often thought of as a pedagogy than as a theory (Berlin, 1982, called it a pedagogical theory). But like collaborative learning, process theory describes an observable phenomenon—the processes writers use, on paper, at least, in order to create texts—in such a way that teachers can base their pedagogical practice on that description. Growing out of the expressivist movement and the writings of Elbow (e.g., 1973) and Macrorie (1970), process theory focuses on the writing behaviors that writers use to translate thought into language, and particularly into coherent, extended written statements. Characteristically, classes based in process theory begin as early as possible in the writing process, employing a wide variety of flexible invention techniques: freewriting, brainstorming, free association, prompted invention (such as Burns, 1984, *topoi*), and so on. Like the expressivists, process theorists encourage learners to "grow" their formal written statements out of their inner thoughts and feelings. Often, these classes involve students in keeping journals, partially for invention purposes, partially in order to ensure that writing becomes part of a student's daily life, and partially as a source or trigger mechanism for public discourse. After invention comes drafting, as the writer continually works to improve a piece of writing, to take it through a set of drafts in which ideas are developed more fully, issues are considered in their full complexity, the writing is connected with readers, and so on. This extensive drafting process also enforces a "learn-by-doing" philosophy that assumes that the only way to learn to write is by writing and the only way the learner will improve his or her writing is by working to make the actual written products better. This learning process most often involves a recursive writing process, so that writers move from one stage to another, return to an earlier stage, jump to another, and so on, rather than moving systematically and sequentially through the stages.

Because portfolio assessment of writing originally grew out of the process writing movement, its support of process-based classes comes as no surprise. Portfolios incorporate the range of writing that learners do in their studies, so process portfolios are more likely to include multiple versions of a single text, for example, or perhaps a wider range of writing—free writes, journal entries, drafts, finished products, written peer reviews, and the like. In a class grounded in process theory, all the writing counts, so samples of all the writing tend to find their way into process portfolios. Thus, range is a key characteristic for process-based portfolios, and writers in those classes need to be able to display a broad range of writing in order to portray their work and their progress as writers.

That same range creates the process teacher's greatest difficulty: deciding how to assign a single grade to or make a single evaluation of such a range of outcomes. But the portfolio, acting as an extension of the premise that writing develops continually along multiple dimensions, allows students to assemble a collection that they feel best represents the scope of their abilities as well as the quality of their work. Out of the full context of the course comes a portfolio that students continually develop in order to portray their development as writers. Thus, selection and student-centered control work together to solve the teacher's dilemma and to prompt students to see their development as writers as centered in themselves, rather than centered in the teacher or the class. The portfolio belongs to the student, and it acts as a mechanism that allows the student to show what she can do by revealing what he or she has done.

This discussion of the ways portfolio-based assessment accommodates the major theories of writing leads us to several conclusions. First, the chart of characteristics and theories, in Table 2.1, shows the extent to which portfolios support the full range of writing theories and the pedagogies that flow from those theories.

As Table 2.1 demonstrates, every characteristic of portfolios is available in all but one of the existing theoretical bases for writing classes. Formalism is the only theory that reduces the set of characteristics, and that reduction is hardly problematic, because the limitation comes from formalism itself, not from portfolios. Because formalist pedagogy centers authority in the teacher, student-centered control is not an attractive characteristic for formalist teachers; similarly, formalism's emphasis on written products limits the ability to attend to growth. In a formalist writing course, what matters is the destination, not the journey, so although growth is assumed, the pedagogy neither invites teachers to attend to it nor provides tools for tracing it. The characteristics of student-centered control, reflection and self-assessment, growth along parameters, and development over time could be incorporated into a formalist portfolio, but, because of the pedagogy, they are unlikely to be. What they measure

Table 2.1. Portfolio Characteristics and Theories of Writing.

	Formalism	Expressivism	Cognitivism	Collaborative Learning	Social Construction	Process
Collection	X√	X	X√	X	X√	X√
Range	X√	X√	X√	X	X√	X√
Context Richness	X√	X	X	X	X	X
Delayed evaluation	X√	X	X	X	X	X
Selection	X√	X	X√	X	X√	X√
Student-centered control		X√	X	X√	X	X
Reflection and self-assessment		X√	X	X√	X√	X√
Growth along parameters		X	X	X√	X√	X√
Development over time		X√	X	X√	X	X

Note. X = available characteristic, √ = prominent characteristic happens, nevertheless: Students do have some measure of control, if only due to delayed grading; students will reflect on their progress, and assess their own abilities, in order to make an advantageous selection of their writings for the portfolio; students will make progress along the parameters of the curriculum (or fail); and students will develop their overall writing abilities as the term progresses. A formalist portfolio, however, will not necessarily seek to measure those characteristics.

This dynamic holds true across theoretical bases and pedagogical practices. Portfolio-based assessment offers a range of potentially useful characteristics to teachers generally. Not all courses or programs take advantage of all the characteristics, but the constraints on portfolio assessment come from the context of the class. The theory, together with the ways individual teachers and programs interpret and apply their theories, limits what portfolio assessment makes available. Portfolio assessment itself places no constraints on writing theory or practice. In theoretical or pedagogical terms, portfolios are neutral.

PORTFOLIOS IN BROADER CONTEXTS

Our descriptions and analyses of portfolio assessment and writing theory, so far, have focused primarily on the context of the individual class. Increasingly, however, portfolios are being used more broadly—across writing programs, university curricula, even as students move from one institution or one educational level to another. As we move into a consideration of these broader contexts, we need to look at how the theory of portfolio assessment we have begun to develop can account for and enable these larger efforts. As the context for assessment extends beyond the single course, portfolio theory prompts us to retain as many as possible of the characteristics of portfolios, in order to preserve a rich, flexible, robust, effective assessment. Each characteristic accounts for a portion of portfolio assessment's greater value, of its advantages over other methods of assessment. Additionally, each theoretical characteristic comes with a practical cost in time, effort, and money. With each enlargement of the context for assessment, the process becomes more complicated, requires more time for conceiving, planning, and executing the assessment, and raises new issues about resources. All these concerns mean that each time the context expands, the temptation to drop a characteristic or two is present—perhaps even great—and each time the context expands, the stakeholders have to make conscious choices about which characteristics they will bring forward, how to define the characteristics at the new level, and whether certain characteristics are worth the time, effort and money required to retain them as meaningful factors in the assessment.[1] The more we resist the temptation to limit the characteristics we measure, the more likely we are to achieve the direct objectives of the assessment and to reap the kinds of unanticipated benefits that accompany any portfolio-based assessment and that we discuss further in chapters 3 and 4.

PORTFOLIO ASSESSMENTS IN WRITING PROGRAMS

When assessment of any kind expands so that it is applied to a context larger than a single classroom, the assessment necessarily becomes more complex; the greater the expansion, the greater the complexity. Basically, all the concerns that applied to the limited context apply in the larger one, more or less in the same ways they applied to the individual class. The added complications stem from having more stakeholders—more teachers and students, with the added layer of administrators. In the larger context, portfolio or writing theory applies in just the same ways it did in the single class, but the definitions, applications, weights, criteria, reading and scoring processes, even curriculum, have to be negotiated among many teachers and receive a stamp of approval from whoever bears administrative responsibility for the program in which the assessment occurs. In program portfolios, teachers from outside any one class will read and judge the portfolio. They may assign a placement to it, as they do in Michigan's English Composition Board Writing Practicum (Condon & Hamp-Lyons, 1991); they may simply rate it pass/no pass, as in the program at SUNY-Stony Brook (Elbow & Belanoff, 1991); or they may actually assign the portfolio a grade, as in the program Hamp-Lyons instituted at Colorado University (CU)-Denver. In any case, program portfolios operate from an agreed-on context—a set of consensuses about the characteristics that, once reached, bind all the teachers and students to certain parameters.

In negotiating these parameters, usually during the process of agreeing on what to put into the portfolio, teachers and administrators implicitly or explicitly focus on the characteristics of portfolios described earlier in this chapter. (In practice, students have only indirect impact—through their eventual success or failure—on the contents of the portfolio. Involving students earlier in the design process, through pilot projects,

---

[1]Everyone involved in the assessment should remember that no characteristic can really be discarded. All are present, and all affect the assessment in one way or another. What we are really discussing here is the degree to which the assessment will acknowledge and take account of each characteristic—in effect, which characteristics will be funded.

interviews about their experiences, even focus groups about portfolios, would strengthen the assessment by giving all its stakeholders a substantial voice.) In the expanded context of a writing program, the characteristics of portfolios remain the same, but they have to be understood more broadly, and the fact that they will apply across class lines, across teachers and methods, means that those teaching in the program must develop and maintain an understanding of how the characteristics operate in that larger context, and that the negotiated definitions must be expansive enough to allow teachers the flexibility to employ a variety of means to achieve the ends specified in the portfolio. For example, collection (the fact that portfolios collect multiple samples) needs no particular elaboration in a single class because all students will have had the same opportunities to write, and the teacher will decide how many of those opportunities she will read. However, in the context of a writing program, faculty have to arrive at an understanding of how many samples are enough, and how many are too many. Once reached, that consensus is binding on the program. Portfolios that violate the consensus that a portfolio should contain four items, for example, are likely to suffer some sort of sanction from, at least, external readers. Similarly, in individual classes range will vary according to the set of tasks the teacher sets or the students generate. Once portfolios are shared across classes, however, teachers have to negotiate range. Will they specify the portfolio's contents only by the number of pieces, leaving genre open? Will the requirements specify that the portfolio must contain a piece or pieces of a particular genre? Will the portfolio contain drafts—evidence of a different sort of range? Again, once faculty reach these consensuses, the decisions become part of the course materials, part of the commitment that faculty make to students. For a period of time (at least one term, in practice more), these decisions are binding. The stakes for violating the consensus can be high because portfolios that do not meet the readers' expectations can receive a lower rating than portfolios that do meet those expectations.

The same conditions apply to the rest of the characteristics, too. Everyone teaching the course has to agree on how selection will work, for example. How much control will students have over the contents of their portfolios? To what extent might students have a voice in or an impact on the assessment? Decisions about selection will also determine what evidence readers will see relating to growth and development, and that consensus, in turn, will affect how those characteristics are measured. In all these decisions, the weighing process involved affects the ease and the reliability of the assessment. Portfolios that are closely defined and rigidly enforced will put constraints on individual teachers, but the portfolios will be easier to compare because the resemblance from one student or one class to the next will be great. Readers will have an easier time agreeing about scores, grades, or placements. Allowing more freedom for teachers and students to decide what to put into the portfolio eases the constraints on the classroom, but it adds a degree of difficulty to the reading because portfolios might vary widely in what they contain, as well as in the quality of the work. If portfolios vary widely, then readers might disagree more, and the managers of the assessment will have to find other ways to induce reliability.

All these consensuses demand attention, and working them out can be exhausting and frustrating work. The advantage is that in working toward consensus, teachers articulate, share, and negotiate virtually every aspect of their classes, from the basic theoretical underpinnings to the criteria for final judgment. Just as collaborative learning techniques force students to bring their assumptions about writing out into the open and share them with each other, so this kind of collaborative assessment on the part of teachers brings hidden assumptions out where everyone can see them. Once shared, these assumptions can be accommodated in the consensus or excluded from it. Either way, the course design that emerges needs to provide teachers with a sound and consistent theoretical basis, a set of tasks around which to build a curriculum, a set of criteria for compiling and judging outcomes from the course, and a strong sense of community, of common purposes and objectives. Taking care in designing, initiating, and maintaining a portfolio assessment requires more time and effort, sometimes, than anyone can anticipate. However, all the benefits, in the end, are worth the hard work of arriving at all those consensuses, and the set of consensuses provides the extended, often unanticipated benefits we describe in chapter 3, and that others, beginning with Elbow and Belanoff in 1986, have also noted (see Roemer et al., 1991; Sheingold, Heller, & Paulukonis, 1995; White, 1991).

PORTFOLIOS AND WRITING ACROSS THE CURRICULUM

Introducing portfolio assessment into contexts broader than or different from the first-year writing program may not always bring with it all the complications mentioned in the writing program section, depending on who is to perform the readings. For example, in the program at Washington State University, portfolios contain writing from across the disciplines, and more than 80% of the raters (a cadre of about 40 faculty members, at any given moment) come from across the university. Criteria are established by the program administrators, in consultation with raters, faculty, and higher administration. This system has resulted in a high level of consensus among readers, who in turn make a diagnosis that identifies rising juniors who need more help with their writing as they head into "Writing in the Major" courses, and the assessment provides the certification required by the institution and the State of Washington (Haswell & Wyche-Smith, 1994). Similarly, at Eckerd College in Florida, a much smaller school, faculty at large share the task of reading WAC portfolios, out of much the same sense of duty they exercise in acting as advisors. Here the existing sense of community and common purposes among a small faculty in a small liberal arts college have served to make the consensuses easier to achieve. In agreeing to institute a WAC certification via portfolio assessment, the faculty, who already used writing extensively in their uniformly small classes, also assented to a process of working out the characteristics, of negotiating contents, standards and criteria, and so on (Harrison, 1995).

One way or another, the same negotiations must take place, and if comparing Washington State with Eckerd College tells us anything, it tells us the benefits of confining the negotiations, if possible, to a small group of stakeholders who share a central, common mission. Trying to apply the Eckerd method at a very large institution, for example, where the faculty is divided into schools, colleges, departments, centers, and programs, would involve entirely too large a set of stakeholders, most of whom would lack the expertise in writing to allow them to participate usefully in the negotiations. Luckily, in larger institutions, most faculty outside the writing program are happy to leave the negotiations to others, and the few faculty in the disciplines with enough knowledge about writing in their own fields and a sense of the breadth of writing across the university are often the most valuable participants in the discussion surrounding a portfolio-based WAC assessment. These few possess enough knowledge about writing to participate fully as the characteristics are negotiated, and they also bring a sense of *realpolitik* to the table because they know what will and will not work for faculty in their home departments. Thus, these faculty from disciplines other than writing can rein in the sometimes overreaching enthusiasm of faculty in writing. In effect, then, this form of negotiation, carried out by representatives of the various stakeholders, takes the place of the kind of full involvement of stakeholders that is possible in smaller contexts such as writing programs or smaller institutions.

Whatever the context, the characteristics apply; however, expanding the context alters the characteristics, altering the kinds of product that can go into the portfolio and the kinds of evidence writers can present to establish their competencies. In practice, the descriptions of items for portfolios become more general as the context for the assessment expands. Thus, in a single class the definition of a particular task results in a specific notion of what the item in the portfolio will be. Broaden the context to the level of the writing program, and the specifications of collection, range, and selection take on the nature of categories, often centering on genres that the underlying philosophy of the program endorses. An argumentative essay, for example, is one of the requirements for the exit portfolio from the ECB's Writing Practicum, a requirement that responds to Michigan faculty at large, who identify critical analysis and argument as the primary genres for academic writing. Broaden the context again, and the characteristics broaden as well, so that a WAC portfolio, of necessity, must define items broadly—perhaps specifying an item that builds an argument from source materials, or an item that demonstrates the writer's ability to use writing as a tool for learning, or, at the broadest level, simply a piece of writing that was produced in any class the student has taken. Collection, at this level, becomes a constraint because, presumably, the writing samples a student amasses over 2, 3, or 4 years are far more numerous than a portfolio can accommodate. Selection, in turn, becomes a more critical factor for the writer, who must choose from a large corpus a few pieces that represent her well. Other characteristics, such as range, are almost inevitably significant, as long as the portfolio contains enough samples for the writer to include a range of writings.

For WAC portfolios, characteristics like growth along parameters or development over time naturally play a part in the assessment because the samples come from a wide range of classes, including both those that are writing-centered and writing-intensive. The assessment will definitely be more responsive to the students' needs when such evidence is present. When the portfolio can reveal a student's development over time, the assessment can more surely help the student determine his or her needs for the future—the sense of where the student has been and where the student is helps in making decisions about where the student needs to go. Here we have an example of characteristics that appear in a different form—across multiple texts, as opposed to existing in drafts of one text— as the context expands. All the characteristics are still operative, of course. Students grow, whether or not we measure that growth; they improve, given opportunities, along the parameters defined by the tasks they perform, whether we measure that development or not. If the assessment has broad support in the institution—from faculty and administration, as, for example, at Washington State—then its designers can make it sufficiently elaborate to account explicitly for most or all the characteristics of portfolios. However, when institutional support is slight—the Minnesota example comes to mind (Anson & Brown, 1991)— then the assessment can only take into account those characteristics that are endemic in the fact that the portfolio has been collected: *collection, range, selection* and, to some extent, *reflection and self-assessment.* In other words, if, as at Minnesota, the portfolios are collected, but institutional support is so slight that they are never actually assessed, then the only benefits accruing to the students stem from the existence of a curriculum that leads students to develop the kinds of samples that they will include and the act of assembling the portfolio. In any event, as the portfolio assessment develops, the institution will make choices about which characteristics it will account for. That fact is a natural part of assessment—part of any assessment is deciding what features to test, what to rate. Such decisions often stem from logistical, personnel, and financial constraints, as well as educational ones. Realism dictates that this will be so. As far as possible, however, decisions about characteristics should be made consciously and should be based on educational needs.

CROSSING INSTITUTIONAL BOUNDARIES

As the context expands, the potential for controlling all the aspects of an assessment decreases. In the years following World War II, as educational assessment grew in importance, the response to this lack of control over the contexts within which learning takes place was to establish strict control over the tests and neglect the learning contexts—hence, the advent and, for more than two decades, the absolute ascendancy of standardized tests. Now, however, as portfolio assessments succeed holistically scored timed essays, we are finding ways of mounting large-scale assessments that accommodate local contexts. Thus, we are beginning to be able to assess writing as students move from one institution or one level to another—transfer students between universities, for example, or high school graduates moving into college. The combination of the portfolio's *range, collection, selection*, and *student-centered control* allows students learning in one context to compile selections of their work that enable teachers or assessors in another context to learn what they need to know about the student's writing experiences and competencies.

Still, portfolio assessment across institutional boundaries is a difficult process. Because no single institution can control all the elements of the context, no single authority can either compel or assure compliance. Universities—or testing agencies such as ETS or ACT—can require students to submit a portfolio, but unless the schools have provided the kind of curriculum that allows students to develop the samples, the demand will cause more problems than it solves. Experience at the University of Michigan has demonstrated that the institution that demands the portfolio must predicate that demand on the kinds of writing students do in the schools, rather than on the kinds of writing the assessing institution values most. In the early stages of development, Emily Decker, the designer and first director of the ECB's entry-level portfolio writing assessment, quickly discovered that Michigan could not ask students to place an argumentative essay in their portfolios, even though students' success in writing at Michigan hinges to a large degree on whether they can argue in writing. Teachers across the state told us that students were not routinely—or even often—asked to write arguments in high school, so testing them on their ability to write an argument made little sense. Instead, Michigan had to relinquish its control over *range* and *selection*, and design a portfolio that incorporated writing students would have on hand.[2] In addition, Decker decided to focus attention on the reflective piece, asking for many details about the assignment, the student's writing process, her sense of audience and purpose, and so forth. In this way, she hoped to gain information about students' development as writers and their attention to various parameters, in lieu of requiring students to submit drafts—which she was fairly certain they would not have. From this complex set of decisions, we can see that expanding the context for assessment beyond a single institution leads to a different set of negotiations before the assessors can arrive at the set of characteristics they would like to—or can—incorporate.

It also involves some explicitly political decisions. Portfolio assessment is invasive. It takes materials from a classroom context and places them in the harsh light of judgment. Judgments of the portfolio also apply to the curriculum that provided the opportunities from which the students drew samples and to the teachers who guided the preparation of the samples. In effect, in attending to as many characteristics of portfolios as possible, the assessors must also pay attention to *whose* characteristics they are judging. *Collection* and *range*, for example, are shared characteristics. They are part of the assessors' context (otherwise, why look for them in assessing students' writing?), but they are also part of the context in which the writing was produced. The characteristics, as well, provide evidence of the range of experience a student has had. They also describe the instructional context in which the student had the experiences and from which the student has selected the samples. If the genres are uniformly simple, then, probably, the curriculum provided few opportunities to think or write in more complex forms. Uniformly short pieces may reflect heavy teaching loads and large class sizes where the student attended school; that is, the teachers may have assigned short pieces because there was no time to work with students on longer ones— or to grade longer ones. The moment an assessment asks for actual samples of students' work from a former educational institution (or other setting), then the assessment is also, to some extent, assessing the effectiveness of the student's education, of the learning opportunities with which the student was presented, and even of the resources a local school district brought to bear on the student's education.

---

[2]This decision was also made as a disincentive toward plagiarism. If the portfolio requires writing samples the students have on hand, then the motivation to plagiarize is low.

Broadening the context for assessment beyond the boundaries of a single institution, then, involves even more complex negotiations—in which, inevitably, not all the stakeholders can participate. Even if one could call together all the teachers, principals and headmasters, and school superintendents from all the schools that send students to the University of Michigan (and that would include teachers and administrators from 110 countries!), the group would be so large that it could accomplish nothing. In this context, not even the representative process that works for WAC portfolios is fully effective. Of course, a process of discovering common ground between the assessors and the teachers is necessary. If the assessment can proceed out of common interests, then the assessors can gain the support they need from teachers, and teachers can gain support for their initiatives as well. As Michigan developed its entry-level portfolio assessment, Emily Decker and George Cooper traveled all over the state to talk with teachers, to find out what Michigan could reasonably ask students to include and to find out how that demand might be used to support objectives that teachers valued. In the process, the portfolio's contents changed. From a set of requirements that were, in effect, genre-centered, Decker moved to asking for more broadly defined items that would employ *selection* in order to give students more *control* over the contents of their portfolios, but would also assure that students could include work they would more likely have already done. Thus, instead of an argument (ECB's original preference, negated by the high school teachers), students must include a piece that responds critically or analytically to something the student has read. And, in direct response to the teachers' desire to promote WAC in the high schools, students are asked to include a piece from a class other than English. Finally, to invite students to select broadly, the portfolio solicits a piece the student identifies as her best, favorite, or most representative. All this, together with a two- to five-page reflective piece and a table of contents, comes to the ECB for assessment.

Again, the important factor here is not the outcome—the description of the portfolio in this particular instantiation—but the way the characteristics have to be negotiated and the way they expand with the context. In the single class, a teacher can dictate. In a writing program, a high level of shared values makes negotiation relatively easy. In a WAC context, the stakeholders are sufficiently diverse and, often, sufficiently divorced from the assessment process that negotiations become more difficult, more protracted, and the temptation to allow some characteristics to fall away becomes great. In the cross-institutional context, the side asking for the portfolio has to find ways to listen to the people in charge of what we might call the *source context*. As long as the portfolio's characteristics can accommodate mutual interests and as long as the portfolio asks for products that the source context can be reasonably expected to produce, then the assessment is likely to succeed—in both the logistical sense and the larger, theoretical sense. The portfolios will come in for assessment, and the assessment will yield information that will help students come into the new context more easily and help the institution know more about how to address those students' needs. The key is to remember that, although the *destination context* sets the requirements and accounts for how the characteristics will be counted and weighed, the portfolios come from the source context, and the characteristics belong to that context too. In effect, the destination context will know what it wants—what it needs to see in order to make sound decisions about students' competencies in writing—but the source context will know what the destination context can get. Without communication between these contexts, the assessment is doomed.

PORTFOLIOS AND NONNATIVE WRITERS

As we have moved from judging competence in writing by multiple-choice test to using timed writing tests on uniform prompts one of the arguments that has been used is that asking students to perform actual writing is a better way of allowing them to show what they *can do* than requiring them to submit to an indirect measure. Going further, it has often been claimed (Hamp-Lyons, 1996, 1997) that portfolios offer a special benefit for nonmainstream writers. And yet, there is so far little available evidence of whether and how far those claims appear to be upheld, in either classroom practice or testing practices and results (Hamp-Lyons, 1993, 1996).

According to the 1992 Census Bureau report, more than 31.8 million Americans (i.e., one in seven) speak a language other than English at home. In community colleges and universities all across the United States, "freshman" composition classes contain second-language and bilingual users of English who struggle in the courses, and "basic" writing classes often contain 50% or more nonnative or bilingual users of English.

It is often argued that nonnative students are inexperienced in using the formal, conventional genres that are expected on writing tests. This concern has also been raised for Black students and for other minority groups within U.S. culture, such as Hispanic students. We might expect that international students, who are penalized in the academy by having to write outside their dominant language, would be even more severely handicapped on tests, especially essay tests, which demand the use of the full gamut of written language skills under stressful circumstances. Essay tests have an especially threatening nature. Not only are they conducted under depersonalized conditions and time pressure, they are, from each individual's perspective, high stakes—grades, permission to enter a major or special program, the obligation to take (and pay for) remedial courses all hang on the outcome. In a small study of nonmainstream writers' ways of handling the stresses of an essay test Hamp-Lyons (1997) found that students from different cultural and educational experiences brought different expectations and strategies to the essay test, and thus, responded in different ways with varying levels and kinds of success, or failure. But she did indeed find indications that minority writers were failing at a higher rate on essay tests. This should mean that for all these students, a portfolio-based assessment would be less intimidating because students have much more latitude to choose the kinds of writing they do, the subjects they write about, and the conditions under which they write.

Portfolios are thought to be especially suitable for use with nonnative English-speaking students because portfolios provide a broader measure of what students can do, and because they replace the timed writing context, which has long been claimed to be particularly discriminatory against nonnative writers. After portfolios were introduced into the exit assessment from the University of Michigan's Writing Practicum, more English as a Second Language (ESL) students tested out of Practicum on the first try than had been the case when the exit assessment used a timed essay. Common sense suggests two reasons for this: First, in portfolio assessment, students have significant amounts of time to revise. They do not have to turn in papers that are full of fossilized errors that pop out when time pressures are on. Instead, writers are able to take the time to find and correct their own errors, to go to the writing center and get tutorial help with problems of expression, to write with the computer and use the spell checker, and so on. These are all strategies that any writer is free to use in normal writing environments, and that are denied them in the setting of a timed impromptu exam. The method of evaluation is more realistic and in its realism it appears not to penalize ESL students relative to other students as much as timed writing tests do. A second reason may be that ESL students are encouraged to try harder, not just zip out a quick short skinny text and work on correcting their language. They know that papers may come around again, that any paper may be one they choose to put in a portfolio, to represent them to outside readers. They are able to see the paper in layers, and work on different layers at different times. Often, the need to focus on competing textual needs at the same time overwhelms uncertain writers, nonnative or native speakers, in timed situations. In the portfolio assessment context, ESL writers can be convinced that concentrating on ideas, on content, support, text structure, and so on, are worthwhile because they need not fear the cost of such attention to achieving technically correct language—which most of them have been conditioned to believe teachers value first and foremost.

An overlooked potential of portfolios, especially for nonnative and other minority writers, is their ability to reveal the differences between "novice" and "skilled" writers. In narrow writing contexts, novice writers always have the excuse of time pressure to account for their single-draft writing approach, for sticking to simple ideas and simple sentences, for editing instead of revising: all those features of novice writing identified by Perl (1980), Emig (1971), and others in the first language are confirmed by Zamel (1982), Raimes (1985), and others in the second language. These "excuses" do not hold water in a portfolio assessment. Novice writers, or experienced ESL writers who have chosen novice strategies for their ESL writing survival, have time to see that their teachers expect more, and that those expectations are reasonable given the time available. Thus, when we find a portfolio that displays novice writing skills, we know that the writer is truly there, at that point in growth toward writing excellence, rather than driven there by time and context pressures.

For long-term residents even more than for international students, the portfolio, once they understand it, provides a motivation, or at least a pressure, they have not had before. These students often need to be motivated; they often have developed ways to survive in the society, in jobs, and even in most courses in college, with very poor writing skills. But faced with a portfolio assessment they begin to realize they will have to become skilled, for this assessment mode does not allow them to pump out the same old barely acceptable formulaic, extremely short writing that has got them through high school. In theory at least, the expectations are higher because there are no excuses for weak writing, no "well, it isn't that bad, he is ESL after all." Failure to work, failure to listen to peer input and revise to meet it, failure to put the teacher's comments into practice in the revision, failure to go to the writing center and get special help when the teacher asks—all these failures can be seen in the portfolio that results. Questions such as "Did the writer follow through?" "Did the writing really get better?" can play an important part in deciding pass/fail or grades. Improvement, the ability to act on input, can be expected of every writer, however weak at the outset.

However, in a classroom-based observational study of ESL writers working on portfolios throughout a semester, Hamp-Lyons (1995) found that some ESL writers were not particularly motivated and did not take advantage of the opportunities offered by a portfolio-based assessment to create highly accurate and fully developed texts; some did not even produce collections that fully conformed to the requirements of the portfolio. And as troublingly, she found that some portfolio readers were inclined to make the same kinds of allowances for nonnative writers that some essay readers have been found to make. Clearly, then, we must explore the questions of how portfolios operate for minority and nonnative writers much more fully than we have to date.

PROBLEMS THAT ARISE IN PORTFOLIO ASSESSMENT

These early experiences of using portfolios that, in effect, cross institutional boundaries highlight an interesting pattern. First comes a fairly limited goal, usually one that stems from an attempt to apply new theoretical developments about how writing should be taught, how it should be evaluated, how writing teachers should be prepared for teaching writing, how a whole writing program needs to develop internal consistency or even how a university as a whole should be fulfilling its obligation to help students acquire the intellectual tools they will need in order to succeed in their careers and their lives. Then, as the new initiative proceeds, one of two results occurs. First, and most happily, when a program is fully grounded in theory and when the teachers in the program consistently put that theory into action in thoughtful ways, portfolio assessment can merge with a theoretical basis in place, and the portfolio will be consistent with the theory that already informs the writing program, WAC program, or an entry or exit assessment program. This merger reinforces the program's theoretical basis, bringing it out in ways that allow those inside and outside the program to see the bases for the program, the internal consistencies, the standards and criteria on which judgments of competency are rendered, and so forth. Introducing a portfolio-based assessment into an already strongly theorized program can even highlight the need to change theory and practice in some way that is desirable in the light of the portfolio assessment. In particular, well-theorized programs will find that portfolio assessment provides a powerful engine for faculty development (or, in other situations, graduate student training), that the assessment acts as the focal point for strong community building within the program or among the instructional contexts the program serves, and that curriculum will constantly change and grow in response to what teachers see students doing in portfolios. We have made this point before, but it is worth making again: portfolios are always usable for more purposes than grading or placement. As teachers or administrators design portfolio-based assessments for their classes and programs, they will do well to consider the ancillary uses for those portfolios because the value of those ancillary uses often—we are tempted to say always—outweigh the primary uses.

However, when a program is not adequately grounded in theory, not perceived as a coherent whole, the second result is likely to occur and the portfolio reveals these weaknesses and forces a sudden effort to theorize the program, often in painful ways that make the job seem many times more difficult than one would expect. In effect because a collection of portfolios from a program describe that program, portfolio assessment reveals weaknesses, leading to attempts to solve many problems—often long-standing ones—at once. In a program where there are rich possibilities, portfolio-based assessment reveals weaknesses, but it also points the way for reform and improvement, for exploiting the rich possibilities. In a program that is undertheorized, however, a portfolio assessment reveals both the existing problems and the difficulty or impossibility of solving those problems without changing the very bases—conceptual, political, economic, even social bases—on which the program is founded.

   Portfolios are by their nature collaborative instruments, and assessing portfolios in any context changes the locus of control. Teachers share control with students and with each other. Writing faculty and faculty from other disciplines share control over the WAC program and, inevitably, over the WAC portfolio. The source and destination contexts, knowingly or unknowingly, share control of the cross-institutional portfolio assessment. Furthermore, portfolio assessment leads to more collaborative grading practices, from the individual course right up to the level of the program as a whole. In fact, we contend both that portfolios are by nature collaborative and that there is no collaboration until there is shared control. Portfolio assessment cannot be fully effective in a top-down model. The teacher who designs a portfolio assessment for his or her class and takes only his or her own needs into account, the writing program administrator who designs a portfolio assessment for his or her program without involving students and teachers in the design, the assessment director who designs a portfolio solely from the perspective of the destination context and refuses input from the source context, all will find that their assessments provide little useful information, excite a high degree of resistance and various forms of noncompliance, and cause limitless problems. Taking account of the needs of *all* the participants in an assessment, and taking the time and trouble to negotiate and include as many of the portfolio's characteristics as possible, will lead, instead, to a broadly conceived, responsive assessment in which all the stakeholders can feel invested. Those who are in charge of portfolio-based assessments need to understand the collaborative nature of even the largest of the large-scale programs, and they need to understand—and take advantage of—the fact that portfolio assessment promotes a different understanding of and different roles for students, teachers, texts, courses, even the writing program itself.

   In short—and this is a focus of chapter 3—the portfolio is a change agent, in and of itself. Those who take the time to ensure that their programs are fully theorized, fully coherent, will find that the changes amount to a series of significant benefits. Those who ignore theory and simply charge into the assessment may find that the only significant change is the abandonment of the project. Portfolios highlight the degree to which a class or a program is coherent, the degree of input that each participant in the program has, and the degree of investment. They bring the curriculum out into the open and include it in the process of judgment. They expose the learning (or lack of learning) that teachers promote via the curriculum. They force consensuses—or point out where lack of consensus is causing problems. They affect the entire context that the assessment encompasses. Those who enter such an endeavor without accounting for all these effects, without being prepared to develop the theoretical underpinnings that allow both successful learning and successful assessment, had better be prepared for failure. Those who enter the endeavor willing to account for all these effects—their fates are described more fully in the next chapter.

Chapter 3

PORTFOLIOS:

PRACTICE

IN PRACTICE: PORTFOLIOS IN THE WRITING CLASSROOM

Although portfolios exclusively serve no single writing theory nor pedagogy, the use of a portfolio approach to writing assessment strongly supports certain features of writing pedagogy (which may or may not be embodiments of theory). In this chapter, we take a look at some of those practices, as we have observed them in our own classes, in the writing programs in which we have worked, and in the literature that has appeared to date using portfolios in writing classes and writing programs.

Drafting

The use of multiple drafting is common in many writing classrooms; students write their way to richer perspectives on their topic through successive drafts accompanied by peer and teacher feedback. At the same time, students improve the language control evidenced by their writing as a consequence of clarifying their own thinking and in parallel with higher order operations on their drafts. In this context, learners can take advantage of the portfolio's characteristic of delayed evaluation in order to decide which texts in progress they like best, which have the most potential or the most meaning for them, and which ones to rework. Portfolios containing "final" papers accompanied by their drafts can help teachers or assessors trace a student's progress more fully and reliably than can be done by simply averaging the grades from assignments handed in at different points in a semester. Such portfolios also help teachers or assessors see how much effort students have expended on their writings. Basically, the portfolio can be designed to provide a detailed record of a student's progress, and both teacher and learner can make use of such a record.

Deep Revision

Teachers who teach deep revision (Willis, 1993) will find that portfolios can work to their students' advantage, as long as the portfolio is structured to let in the evidence of the drafting processes in which writers have engaged. In deep revision, students are taught to look below the surface of their text and to see it as multilayered and multipotentialed. They might write the same story from two vantage points; or take a real place and write it to unreality before rewriting it to a richer viewpoint on reality than they had seen before; or they might work as a group to build a description out of multiple viewpoints on one thing, place or person: Central to the range of ideas that Willis offered in her book is the concept of revision as both a writing improvement or enrichment strategy and as a way for a writer to understand more of what he or she wants to say. No assessment that looked only at final drafts would be able to give full credit to the writer for the growth he or she went through while revising, for it would close out the evidence of successive and alternative drafts. If the writer is to receive credit for the intellectual work he or she has done in arriving at the final draft, then the portfolio must contain, at least for one paper or writing project, what Willis called the writer's pretexts.

Writer's Workshop

In a writer's workshop approach, one student reads a draft aloud to the class or to a small group of class members, after which audience members discuss the paper on several levels. This approach—excellently illustrated in the videos produced by Hale, Mallon, and Wyche-Smith (1988, 1991) and colleagues—is beneficial for both writer and audience. Among other benefits, it develops self-assessment faculties in learners. As writers listen to readers' critiques, they gain information about where they have effectively addressed their audience and where they have not. The writers thus have the opportunity to learn which of their writing habits work well and which they should begin to change or avoid. Thus, the workshop helps them recognize these features in future drafts and implement changes before the draft is handed over to the workshop. In addition, the students in a writer's workshop gain experience in recognizing and accommodating to the standards of one discourse community—the class—so, by using the knowledge gained in that one experience, the students are more likely to be able to recognize and accommodate to the needs of other discourse communities. During the workshop, the writer focuses on the audience response to his or her text and thinks directly about how to take account of this response in the revision. This is another facet of writing pedagogy that encourages students to assume responsibility for their own learning. This setting also asks students to reflect on their writing and their writing practices; thus, these writers can more easily produce the kinds of reflective pieces or self-assessment called for in most portfolios. Students who have worked in writer's workshop classrooms have already had a preview of the kinds of processes portfolio readers are likely to undergo as they read and talk together about a portfolio: A writer's workshop approach puts the writer on the other side, the side where the reader is—an important place to be in preparing a portfolio for assessment.

Peer Critique

Classrooms that use peer critique, or peer feedback as it is also often known, also provide opportunities for writers to become aware of an audience's response to their text in progress and to take account of that response in revision. Because the ability to write for an audience is stressed in many writing pedagogies, and especially in social-constructionist theory, teachers often have students include among the supporting documents for any particular "final" paper the notes of the peer critique session(s) that he or she participated in while working on the paper. This enables the reader to see how the writer was influenced (or not) by the peer feedback. Many of us stress that peer feedback is available input for the writer, not something the writer *must* alter the writing to accommodate. We therefore ask the writer to write a reflection on the peer feedback, which will include indications of what feedback the writer *won't* respond to, and why not. These kinds of exchange help writers understand more about the context and process of reading portfolios because the reviews demand that writers function as readers or evaluators. The process also fosters the writers' responsibility for their own learning and their own texts. The presence of notes from and on peer feedback help the portfolio reader understand whether the writer has had rich or poor input to the revisioning process, and such context-rich information can help the reader make a more informed judgment.

Collaborative Learning

The classroom techniques described here all share a common thread: collaboration. Increasingly more writing teachers see writing as in large part a social process, not only because they value the notion of *audience* for their writing students, but because so much of the text-making we all must do in the world is done with or around others. Collaborative writing takes place in many forms and in many writing classrooms. Groups work together on a project that culminates in a single shared text, or students work collaboratively on a text until a point at which they break away and create their own texts—perhaps a personal viewpoint on the work done in the project. In even more classrooms, collaborative learning activities are important. When writers talk together, about ideas and about their texts, they learn together about what works for them and what works for others. They hear themselves, and they hear others. Writer's workshop, peer critiquing, peer revising, peer editing, engaging together in action research to be written about from a personal standpoint are all collaborative ways of learning that are valued in many writing classrooms today.

A portfolio assessment can permit students to include in their portfolios the traces of the learning they have done, singly and together: They can offer portfolio readers evidence of the learning the student has done that lies behind the finished writing. Neither the portfolio as an artifact nor the mere fact of portfolio assessment legislates how teachers or readers will read the portfolio. The individual class' teacher, or the teachers and administrators of a writing program, will decide this; but the portfolio assessment *permits* them to decide to value these kinds of records of learning together.

Reflective Writing

Portfolios demand either implicit or explicit reflection and self-assessment on the part of the writer. Reducing the collection of writing to a selection that displays particular characteristics involves the writer in reflecting on the corpus of work he or she has produced and assessing it in order to make a purposive selection for the portfolio. However, portfolios do not necessarily contain evidence of this reflection. Portfolios that do require or permit reflective writing provide a look at a student's metacognitive knowledge, an aspect of learning that is difficult, if not impossible to trace using conventional methods of grading or assessment. The writing classroom is the ideal place to provide opportunities for writers to activate and extend their metacognitive skills, and reflective writing is an appropriate vehicle for this. Although reflection occurs most commonly and obviously in writing the "reflective piece" for the portfolio at the end of the semester, many writing teachers bring other opportunities for self-reflection into their courses. *Journaling* is one obvious and popular form of self-reflective expression; some portfolio programs have experimented with the inclusion of journal entries in the portfolio; the Composition Program at UC-Denver found them a helpful addition, although not a replacement for formal papers. The journal entries provided information that the formal essays did not, information that supplemented the evidence found in the more formal writings. Often, teachers want to know what writers think or know about themselves as writers or about the writing they have done.

In point of fact, the rise of portfolios as an assessment tool has occasioned a rise in the importance of reflective writing in composition curricula.[1] This genre received an initial boost from the fact that in publicized models for portfolios, from SUNY-Stonybrook to Cincinnati to Miami to Michigan, reflection plays a central role in students' learning processes and in the way readers approach the portfolios. We have already referred, several times before, to the role of self-reflection in both

---

[1] Today, we find a whole literature arising about reflective writing. Yancey and Huot have both written influentially about this genre, and the first 2 years of the journal *Assessing Writing* feature several articles that focus, in whole or in part, on reflection. Finally, in June 1996, NCTE sponsored a well-attended conference devoted solely to reflective writing in all its forms—not solely as it appears in writing portfolios.

the learner-writer's personal growth as a writer, and in the reading of the portfolio by the teacher and other readers. In the *self-reflective letter* (other terms such as *cover letter* or *self-assessment* are also used, often but not necessarily interchangeably) the students are able to show most clearly their growth as writers, their sense of themselves as individuals who write, who use writing for personal purposes, as individuals and as members of the academic community. Increasingly, the value of the reflective letter is being recognized, and increasingly portfolio programs require writers to compose a reflection at the conclusion of the course, after they have put the portfolio artifact together, to share with readers their reflections on their writing experiences and their own perspective on the portfolio the reader will see.

Yancey, in her opening remarks at the NCTE Conference on Portfolios and Writing Across the Curriculum in Scottsdale in June 1994 described the reflective letter as the point at which the portfolio becomes a "site of learning." The reflective letter has tremendous potential to reveal the student's own voice, to let the reader through into what is really important to the writer. It also has the potential to show the reader a greater learning than "just" writing skills. Often, students' remarks move beyond the objectives of the class to include revelations of personal growth, insights into their world views, and musings about future goals. At its best, the act of composing the reflective letter encourages reflection and candid self-assessment in the writer, and the letter itself can highlight for the reader the important issues the writer has engaged during the course.

There are problems too with the self-reflective letter: Some students learn the rhetorical "moves" of this genre and trot them out without reflecting on growth or development, and without reflecting on what the student has learned about writing or about herself as a writer. Some people argue that the self-reflective letter can overly influence portfolio readers' judgments; indeed, the weight readers place on the reflective piece presents a particular concern when readers are evaluating mixed sets of portfolios, some of which are from majority English/White writers and some of which are from nonnative and minority writers, where the self-reflection may reveal a weaker command of basic syntax and morphology than do the revised pieces in the portfolio. We already raised some of these issues in chapter 2, and we return to them later in this chapter and in chapter 5.

In summary, many writing assignments—besides the reflective piece for a portfolio—stimulate reflection in students, and many activities writing teachers use extend students' metacognitive knowledge in preparation for or as part of a writing project. An activity especially popular with teachers and students at CU-Denver, which is an urban commuter campus set in a green oasis in the heart of downtown Denver, is a "field trip" to the 16th Street Mall, a pedestrian mall that is struggling for credibility as a "city center revival": The mall is inhabited at various hours by large numbers of homeless persons, street artists, drunks, the physically disabled, as well as city workers in running shoes on their lunch hours, state senators, attorneys, and tourists haunting the cut-rate souvenir shops. Students, in small groups, must strike up conversations with people on the mall and learn enough about them to raise a series of questions in their minds (and later, in their writing) about the individuals, their "groups" (social group, class, profession, whatever), and the wider context. One group talked with mall police officers and went on to learn a great deal about the city center crime rate, safety procedures and provisions, and the safest places to hang out. Another group became so involved with a street musician that they took him to lunch; and one of them later went to visit the shelter where he had been staying, and learned a great deal about the state of the less fortunate citizens in the city. Social action projects such as these provide opportunities for reflection on many issues, and this reflection is both a stimulus for and substance of writing that demonstrates reflection. Doing these projects in groups not only makes students a little more venturesome than they might be alone, it is also, as suggested in the previous subsection, a valuable site for learning collaboratively.

IN PRACTICE: PICTURING THE PORTFOLIO PROGRAM

As the previous section demonstrates, portfolio-based assessment provides strong support for many of the most effective teaching and learning strategies in composition. However, this potential for support is even greater in circumstances that allow teachers to share responsibility for grading and evaluation in teams and in writing programs in which faculty teach a given course a number of times. In such a setting, each iteration of the planning, teaching, assessing cycle increases the teacher's expertise. Each iteration adds to the teacher's awareness of curricular goals, of methods for achieving those goals, of the kinds and variety of possible assignments, of what activities most effectively promote students' learning, and so on.

The best systems organize faculty into portfolio reading groups and provide several opportunities throughout the term for group members to meet in order to share syllabi and assignments, to discuss issues of theory and practice as they relate to the events that are developing in their classes, to share the joys and the challenges that individual students present, and to lend each other aid and comfort as the semester passes (see, e.g., Elbow & Belanoff, 1991; several of the essays in Belanoff & Dickson, 1991; Condon

& Hamp-Lyons, 1994). Members of portfolio groups can visit each others' classes in order to see how the plans different teachers have shared are working out and in order to become acquainted a little with the students whose writings the teachers will assess—and to allow the students to know who their assessors will be. Together, teachers become expert readers and knowers for their shared context. Of course, it is possible to provide this level of contact without initiating a portfolio-based writing assessment, but the effort required to do so outside that context would be so great that it would be unlikely to occur. As the iterations pass, evidence of excellence accumulates and is shared in by all participants; thus, teachers' motivation to participate—their investment in doing so—increases as well.

The general features of excellence in a portfolio-based program have probably emerged intuitively from reading the book so far, but we pause a moment here to draw more explicitly the picture of the portfolio program as we have experienced it and as we have observed it in other programs we have visited and as people in other portfolio assessment programs have described it to us. These features, which we call the seven Cs, seem to us to be as follows:

- Development of a teacher *community.*
- Shared *criteria* and standards.
- Shared locus of *control* (teachers, students, administrators).
- Responsiveness to the needs and goals of the *context* (including all parties to the assessment), and to all of its restrictions.
- Valuing of the process of reaching *consensus.*
- *Care* in all aspects and phases of the development, application, maintenance, and validation of the assessment.
- Emphasis on *conversation,* talk over and about texts and processes, in all of the above.

We argued, what seems a long time ago now (Condon & Hamp-Lyons, 1991), that the messy processes of negotiating ways of constructing a portfolio program, of making decisions about what is to go into a portfolio, how it is to be judged, and by whom, and so on, are not an irritant interfering in the straightforward delivery of a professional assessment program, but an absolutely essential part of portfolio program development and success—we call this messy essential process the development of a teacher community. This community must work out many elements, but two vital ones are criteria and standards that the community as a whole can uncover and agree to invest in; and an appropriate amount of sharing of control among teachers and their students, and a realization that some control (but not necessarily as much as had been previously passively assumed) resides with the program's administrators. Underpinning the part played by every member of the teacher community must be responsiveness to the *needs and goals* of the context and to all of its *restrictions.* Different members of the community will respond to different facets of the context, so the sharing of perceptions plays a vital role in remembering the needs of *all* those involved in the context-rich, long-term act of assessment. In drawing a realistic yet optimistic picture of where the restrictions exist and where the potentials and opportunities lie, teachers or readers must think of the right kinds of responses to fit this unique (even if not entirely dissimilar from others) context. This is often a long-drawn-out, frustrating, and even upsetting process for some community members. Yet if everyone can keep in mind the value that resides in the very *process* of reaching consensus, it can become the most rewarding part of establishing a portfolio program.

So far, then, our central premise has been that all parties to a portfolio program will care about and take care in all aspects and phases of the development, application, maintenance, and validation of the assessment. Although care was always necessary in approaching any kind of assessment, the need for it has become more obvious as we have tackled complex assessments such as portfolios, and teachers have more readily understood that they need to invest care in the portfolio assessment because their role as stakeholders has become clearer to them and everyone else. Our final "C" is also an overarching one: an emphasis on conversation, on talking it through (whatever "it" might be), on talk over and about texts and processes. Valuing our conversations on and around the topics of the portfolio assessment means opening spaces in which to think about that aspect of our work, and to see that aspect as part of the whole fabric of our lives as teachers and colleagues.

Of course, these features play out in different ways within any particular writing program, depending on the use the portfolio is put to, the level of stakes assigned to it, the number of interested parties, and so on. Nevertheless, they are important *as generalizations*, as part of the theory behind portfolio-based writing assessment. In each context, portfolios alter both instruction and assessment in significant ways. They do not of themselves change an instructor's pedagogy, of course; as seen in chapter 2, portfolios can just as readily support the most conservative formalist pedagogy or the most radical expressivist one. But they do introduce many new possibilities to the thinking of each individual teacher, and from all such possibilities and changes may come other changes; in theoretical positioning, in the teacher's perception of what it means to be a teacher, in her understanding of her role in the college, and more. Finally, implicit in all these features is the interlinking of teaching and assessment in interesting and productive ways that the rest of this chapter explores.

In what follows, we first describe two examples known best to us, of the most common use of portfolios in writing programs: for assessment at *exit* from a writing course. We then look at the use of portfolios at *entry* to a writing program or sequence; at portfolios for WAC *assessment;* at *graduation* portfolios; at the use of portfolios for staging dialogue between faculty *across institutions;* and finally, at the role of portfolios in *articulation* (i.e., to ease movement across school, college, and university boundaries). This does not exhaust the uses to which portfolios are being put: graduate student portfolios and teacher portfolios come immediately to mind. But these uses connect most strongly with writing, which after all is our focus; and because these programs exemplify the generalizable features of all portfolio assessment programs, the seven Cs, the stories we tell for each of them serve wider purposes.

Portfolios for Exit From the Writing Program: Two Examples

To talk about the many interwoven themes of the practice of portfolio-based writing assessments in writing programs, we first discuss portfolios as exit assessments, and use our experiences at the University of Michigan and CU-Denver as concrete examples.

From 1978 through 1997, the University of Michigan's ECB offered a course called the Writing Practicum.[2] The course was originally designed with a classic pre- and posttest feature: During summer orientation, students wrote a timed impromptu argument, by means of which approximately 12% were placed into, and required to take, the course (84% were placed into Introductory Composition, and approximately 4% exempted the first-year composition requirement). At the end of that half-term intensive, conference-centered, ungraded course in academic writing, students wrote another timed impromptu argument. On that basis, they could place out of or back into the practicum course (they could also, as in the entry assessment, exempt Introductory Composition). As the years passed, and teaching methods became increasingly process-based, the fact that the exit assessment was undermining instruction became more apparent. We taught our students the value of revision, but on the posttest we allowed them no time to revise. We taught our students that their professors would value a carefully thought-out response to a topic, but the posttest allowed them no time for careful development of their ideas. We even taught them that their professors would demand carefully edited and proofread essays, but the

---

[2]The Writing Practicum is still being offered as of this writing, but it is now taught in Michigan's Department of English Language and Literature, which in 1997 absorbed the ECB, ending any significant presence of composition studies at that institution.

posttest allowed no time for anything but the most cursory editing. In short, almost everything faculty taught in the Writing Practicum was undercut by the timed impromptu instrument we were using for exit assessment. Not surprisingly, the students noticed. Although many of them took advantage of all the learning opportunities the course provided, most felt free to put in the minimum of effort on revisions because they knew that they would not be tested on that skill. They also felt free to ignore most of the attention faculty paid to the writing process and focus on the one or two opportunities the class offered to practice timed, in-class writings. They realized, understandably, that they could save time in this course by ignoring most of what was going on because all they had to do to get out was perform well for 50 minutes on the last day of class.

In 1987, the ECB's faculty introduced a pilot portfolio program, using it as a backup to the existing exit assessment by timed impromptu essay. A validation study of the exit portfolio results compared to the exit essay test results (Hamp-Lyons, 1988) revealed that in 60% of cases the scores on the two kinds of tests placed students exactly the same; in the majority of the other cases, the portfolio score placed the student higher. We learned a great deal else. All could see, for example, that the contents of the portfolio far more accurately reflected both what the students had been asked to learn in the practicum and their overall ability as writers. And practicum teachers reported that students placed a great deal more faith and credit in the portfolio—and worked harder toward completing it—than they had in the previous method, the timed essay. Finally, we were able to demonstrate that practicum faculty could read and score the portfolios as reliably and almost as efficiently as the timed essays, using standard assessment methods (two readers, with a third reading in case of splits; a reading process resembling W. Smith's, 1994, "expert rater" system, and so forth). As a result of these studies, we were able to gain approval from a very conservative (and, where writing instruction or assessment is concerned, extremely ignorant) college curriculum committee to go ahead with a portfolio-based exit writing assessment system, backed up by an impromptu, in 1988.

The process of introducing the portfolio system, and particularly the initial design, development and implementation of it, required a great deal of work. And yet, our experience was that adopting such a system brought the benefits we have already asserted. Our development work, following the seven Cs (although we did not think of them as such at that time: Like everything we have done with portfolios, our clear view of them has emerged gradually) resulted in a portfolio assessment that exhibited the traditional psychometric quality of reliability, in terms of the decisions raters made in reading the portfolios, and it was a far more valid instrument for assessing the students' academic writing skills than a timed impromptu, or even a take-home writing test. What was clear to us from the start was that the writing in the portfolio had to be writing that was accomplished in the course itself, and therefore that the content of a portfolio had to be limited to the kinds of writing taught in the course. In this first version of the exit portfolio, for example, one of the revised essays had to be an argument; the other revised essay could be any three- to five-page essay identifiable as academic in nature and the third piece was a timed, in-class writing of an argumentative nature. Finally, the reflective piece addressed the other pieces of writing in the portfolio and drew heavily on the student's experience in the course. The fact that two pieces were revised essays, pieces that the students had time to work on, revise over and over, and perfect, meant that readers saw the kind of work a student was capable of, given time and guidance. The two in-class pieces, the timed essay and the reflection, revealed what the student could do under less optimal conditions, and acted to validate the portfolio as the student's own work: if the writing in the in-class pieces was very different from the writing in the revised pieces, then the reader might suspect, for example, that the expertise in the revised pieces came from support the student received in conferences, in-class workshops, and peer review sessions. Similarly, the portfolio could only contain writing from the practicum, that is, writing that had actually gone through the drafting process under the instructor's eyes. Thus, readers could trust that a student's portfolio contained her own writing. Most importantly, however, the portfolio was both a product of the course's curriculum and an expression of it.

These are, more or less, the benefits we had looked for when establishing our portfolio-based assessment. We were surprised, in those early days, by the other, unlooked-for benefits that came to us as teachers as a result of having to define the contents of the portfolio and as a result of the recursive process of teaching, reading portfolios, learning from the reading, and going back into the next practicum.

We had not realized before we began how the portfolio reading groups, for example, would act as an important medium for exchanging ideas and methods. The groups had been set up in order to provide a way to let the second and third readers know what to expect in a portfolio. Our teachers had rightly felt that to judge a student's writing without knowing what the assignment had been and something about what and how a teacher has taught would be unfair to the student. The groups did serve this necessary purpose well, but their value, as we learned, reached far beyond fairness to student writers. We saw that instructors were using these groups as a source of new ideas, as a sounding board in which to discuss possible reforms in assignments or methods, and as a place to test out with others their thinking about how well what they were teaching addressed the curriculum.

The standards-setting session we introduced, where practicum faculty gave a very small number of portfolios a close reading, not only allowed readers to calibrate their score levels with the group, but also provided a forum for modeling reading and teaching behaviors, for extending the reading group's discussions of assignment types and teaching methods to the whole faculty. The sessions also created an opportunity for individual teachers to assess, publicly yet privately, how their own performances measured up to what colleagues were doing in and with the course.

Finally, the portfolio reading itself gave teachers a chance to see in detail what students in other sections were doing. Teachers often reported that all of this conversation led them to change some aspect of their course in order to make it more effective in addressing their students' needs. Perhaps the most important benefit for our program, which we had predicted but underestimated the power of, was that portfolio-based assessment raised the status of process-based teaching.

The first stage had gone well, providing a sound method for writing assessment and many benefits. But problems were arising, problems that we now see as part of the maturation process for a portfolio system, as what happens when the system becomes routine. As we worked and lived with our exit assessment longer, it became part of the landscape, a regular set of activities and routines that had their time and space in our program. We didn't feel ourselves doing it, but perhaps we all—associate directors of instruction and assessment respectively, and teachers of the courses too—relaxed a bit. The time came when we began to question whether the well-being we were feeling, the sense that things were going along smoothly, was perhaps a little too good to be true. We decided to look more closely not only at the system but at the acts that made it up. In hindsight, it was that littlest "C," that vital care (or perhaps another "C" not listed, "conscience," that still, small voice), that impelled us to look within in this way. When we looked, we found the act of reading was not being carried out with the care we had assumed. As reported elsewhere (Hamp-Lyons & Condon, 1993), readers were paying less attention to the portfolios. As reading became routine, readers' confidence in their ability to make fast judgments grew, as did a tendency to listen less carefully to the other members of their portfolio reading groups, or to their colleagues' reasoning in standard-setting sessions. Clearly, some kind of procedural change—at least—was required if the assessment was to remain fair, consistent, and useful.

In the work that we did to remedy matters we put into practice not only the belief that the reading of portfolios for purposes of assessment *must* be done with care, but another belief: that lack of care in one area could be a symptom of, or else turn to be a cause of, lack of care in wider areas

(Condon & Hamp-Lyons, 1994). The process of finding ways to focus readers' attention on their readings of portfolios itself stimulated new energy within the faculty for thinking about the work of portfolio-based assessment. Out of that thinking came a new set of discoveries about the richness that lies within a portfolio-based writing assessment program, if only we are willing to mine it. If we had not become a little lazy, if we had not then questioned our assumptions and our "good fortune," we might not have confronted the tougher side of program-wide portfolio assessment. Confronting the tougher side, we learned as much again as we had in the first implementation. This process of investigation taught us an important lesson, one we want to share with everyone who is setting up a portfolio-based writing assessment program—you are never finished: the program can never look after itself. It can always be disrupted by ill will, failure of community, holding to outdated criteria or standards, assumptions about consensus that below the surface does not exist, and more.

On the other hand, what happened in the second stage of our program's development reveals the benefits to be gained by working through the problems that arise along the way. Just as, in the beginning, a sometimes painful process of negotiation and a slow process of collaboration resulted in high levels of consensus and shared values on the part of practicum faculty, so this second stage was marked by rapid faculty and curriculum development, which in turn resulted in improvements in the course.

By 1991 (Hamp-Lyons had moved on to CU-Denver by then), we had gathered enough data to convince the college's curriculum committee to allow us to abolish the exit impromptu (it had been written into the Faculty Code, so we could not take that action unilaterally) and rely solely on the portfolio. The ECB's exit assessment program now collects a portfolio that contains one revised argumentative essay, one other revised essay of the student's choosing, one in-class timed writing, usually based on readings done outside class, and a reflective page that is also written in class, during the final class meeting. Using this system, the community now both teaches and tests revision. We also both teach and test for development of ideas, the ability to treat a complex issue in a complex manner, even the ability to edit and proofread with care and precision. In summary, the portfolio supports what the practicum teaches, whereas the former impromptu-based exit assessment undercut both the curriculum and our various pedagogical approaches.

Practicum teachers read and scored their own students' portfolios, acting as the first of the two readers for each portfolio. Being the judges of their own students' portfolios placed teachers in a valuable advocate or adviser role that was balanced with the need to speak honestly with students about how their writing was shaping up. Faculty worked in groups of three readers or teachers (typically, one veteran, one newcomer, and one with middling experience in the course); the groups met early in the term to exchange syllabi, assignments, and materials; set up a schedule for group members to visit each others' classes; and decide what form or forms the in-class and reflective writings will take. About 2 weeks before the end of the practicum, the faculty as a whole met to standardize on several anchor portfolios. Then, as soon as the classes' portfolios were collected, the groups met and standardized on at least one portfolio from each teacher's practicum. Teachers then read and scored the portfolios from their own classes, whereupon they exchanged portfolios with the other members of the group and acted as second readers for those portfolios. In cases of disagreement, the two readers conferred, but if they were unable to agree on a placement, then the third member of the group acted as third reader. This sequence of activities constituted a single iteration.[3]

Taken by itself, each iteration provided opportunities for teachers to meet and discuss their plans; to observe each other in class; to see each others' assignments, together with the products that come out of those assignments; and to observe the connection between theory and practice in their own and two colleagues' classes. They also spent a considerable amount of time, both in the reading groups and in the whole-faculty standardizing session, analyzing extensive samples of students' writing, exploring that writing for evidence of competence and excellence, and discussing criteria for advancing through the writing program. However, it was rare for any teacher to pass through only one iteration. Even the adjunct faculty member who only taught half time in the ECB passed through two iterations of the course. A full-time faculty member passed through at least three iterations in a year. This cyclical process acted as a powerful tool for faculty, curriculum, and program development, and the fact that faculty passed through iteration after iteration means that faculty passed from their teacher roles into their reader roles and then back into their teacher roles, each stage informing and enriching the other. Repeatedly, as teachers left our program, they cited the portfolio groups as their most valuable professional development, and they took with them a view of the possible into new contexts.

Anyone reading the previous account of the exit assessment from Writing Practicum will recognize that the course improved in manifold ways. Teachers appreciated the greater fairness the system brought, and

---

[3]At this writing, ECB faculty are experimenting with a different order. Specifically, they are trying out a system in which the teacher acts as third reader. Thus, if the first two readers disagree, the student's own teacher will make the ultimate choice. We have retained our description because it accounts for the system we set up as associate directors for assessment and instruction. As changes occur, the people who fill those roles can describe their systems.

especially liked the many opportunities to discuss their teaching with colleagues and improve their practices as a result of those exchanges. The final payoff was that the students, too realized the impact of the portfolio on the practicum. In 1990, when the system had achieved some stability, we began to track students' responses to two items on the standard course evaluation form:

- "Overall, this was an excellent course"
- "Overall, my instructor was an excellent teacher"

and have continued to do so every semester since. The results for fall 1990 and winter 1994—and a comparison with similar courses across the university for the same semesters, are shown in Table 3.1.

Table 3.1. Student's Evaluation of Writing Practicum.

Medians for:	Fall 1990	Winter 1994
Writing Practicum		
Excellent course	3.41	4.40
Excellent teacher	4.08	4.63
Similar Courses Across University		
Excellent course	3.99	3.96
Excellent teacher	3.94	4.02

As the table indicates, students' perceptions of the course and of the teachers rose markedly over this 4-year period. A course that was rated in the 50th percentile according to student's responses on a five-point Likert scale in 1990 rated well into the top quartile by 1994. And teachers, who were rated only slightly higher than their colleagues in 1990 rose far into the top quartile by 1994. We attribute the change in rating to two factors: first, students responded to the opportunity the portfolio gave them to assume control over their fates, so that students perceived the greater fairness of the assessment; and second, teachers took frequent advantage of the opportunities to improve their syllabi, their assignments, their teaching methods, and so on. Such a shift in ratings would be remarkable for any course. That it occurred in Writing Practicum—a course Michigan students adamantly resent being placed into—is strong testimony to the effectiveness of the teachers and of the portfolio system of exit assessment.

The Michigan story is one of progress through problems to multiple benefits. But our story should have made clear by now that the benefits of portfolio-based writing assessment do not occur automatically, or even easily. The story of the introduction of a portfolio-based exit assessment to the first two levels of the Composition Program at CU-Denver is more a mix of positives and negatives, and is therefore perhaps more typical of portfolio programs in development across the country. Without a stable and highly experienced faculty, without even a core of full-time writing instructors, but instead with mainly pre-master's teaching assistants (TAs), poorly paid and often early in their course of preparation as writing teachers, the course of portfolio assessment was far less smooth. Because of their less certain foothold in the academy, and because they have read less in the field, and had less experience of the different ways of "doing comp" that exist across the country, the part-time instructors and TAs at CU-Denver were understandably more suspicious of the concept of portfolios. Furthermore, in contrast to Michigan where the basic writing courses that were the site of our first portfolio assessment were both ungraded (pass/fail) and assessed on the basis of a formal timed, impromptu essay test, instructors in the CU-Denver composition courses had always been free to assign their own grades, with no shared assessment playing any part at all. Therefore, introducing a portfolio increased rather than decreased the assessment stakes.

The idea was introduced and discussed for a semester before any attempt was made to establish a portfolio-based assessment, and a small number of readings about portfolios (small because of the extreme time constraints on graduate students and part-time teachers who may be teaching on three campuses) was distributed. In a series of meetings and professional development sessions, the group of teachers at that time discussed different models for setting up the portfolio. They agreed that the portfolio could not replace the grading process (nor could it without administrative changes several levels above) but would become a piece of the grade. After a great deal of negotiation this was resolved as a minimum of 10% of the grade, which could be more at the teacher's discretion. In later years, as the portfolio program has continued, and increasingly more teachers see that the assessment is not threatening their students or the teachers' right to develop their own curriculum, confidence has grown, and teachers have begun to use portfolio meetings as an opportunity to bring forward problem portfolios in progress, or stories about classroom and student scenarios. The portfolio discussions have become the site for teacher development, less consciously and more modestly than at Michigan, but nevertheless it did happen, and these portfolio discussions provided the only formal opportunity for talk about teaching writing outside of required graduate work (hence, for adjunct teachers, the only formal opportunity). As confidence and investment in the portfolio system has grown, this minimum element of the grade assigned to the portfolio has increased to 25%, and in most cases teachers assign much greater weight to the portfolio—a range of 40% to 90%.

At the same time, a curious problem emerged. Most teachers established some system for grading individual essays, in addition to the portfolio. Most frequently, students would assemble a kind of mini-portfolio for each paper they produced in the course. Into this mini-portfolio would go all the materials that the student had generated in writing the essay: notes, drafts, reflections, peer reviews, and so on. The teacher would grade that paper at one point in the semester and then see it again, as part of the course portfolio at the end of the term. This process subverts the characteristic of *delayed evaluation* because a major portion of a student's grade still depended on an average of the grades for each assignment and because, at the end, the teacher's judgment of the portfolio was often constrained by his or her awareness of the grades awarded on each paper—and the teacher might be heavily invested in seeing the portfolio receive the same grade from the outside reader. In many cases, no conflict arose—although the potential always existed. But in a worrisome number of cases, conflicts did arise. Consider, for example, a student who consistently earns A's on individual essays, but whose portfolio contains only one kind of text—only one genre, perhaps. Does a portfolio that contains only one kind of text deserve an A in a writing course that asks students to write a variety of texts? The outside reader could well award such a portfolio a B, yet the class teacher, who has consistently awarded A's on earlier papers, can scarcely award anything less to the portfolio without raising some very sticky issues of fairness. This instance demonstrates the degree to which neglecting a characteristic of portfolios can create serious problems for teachers and for students.

Another problem, logistical but having much more broad-ranging effects, concerns the nature of portfolio groups. In the first year, portfolio reading teams were organized so that more and less experienced teachers were grouped together. But this meant that teachers on conflicting time schedules were grouped together, and finding time to meet became extremely difficult. It also turned out that the long-term part-time teachers were quite resistant to the extra work involved in doing portfolios, whereas the TAs were excited by it and realized the kinds of benefits we have written about encountering as we introduced portfolios to Michigan's ECB. In later years, we grouped portfolio reading teams by the time their classes met, which meant that sometimes new TAs were grouped together. Although this problem could be overcome by using the in-service practicum (TA training) to continue teacher development in portfolio theory and practice, it meant too that group members could not visit each other's classes, a practice we have found extremely valuable in a portfolio program. At that time, some of the teachers established the practice of not holding class in certain weeks, once or twice in a semester, and using class time to meet students individually or in small, focused groups. We were able to take advantage of the flexibility this created in the teacher's day to have *new* teachers visit the two classes of their teammates. Although this process added a major burden for teachers, the teachers reported that the experience was valuable as general professional development, and as a mechanism that allowed them to understand important aspects about that class and the teacher's approach. New TAs, through their practicum, also visit two other classes, although not necessarily with an eye to portfolio-related aspects of the class or teaching, and this too enriches their awareness of the context outside their own discoveries in their own classroom.

Although the system as described here is of necessity a minimalist one, it nevertheless produced changes in teaching and assessment practices in the classrooms: Most of the teachers adopted a "portfolio approach," where they collected students' work as a portfolio containing prewritings, drafts, peer critique reports, and so on, as well as the "final" paper. Once these paper-portfolios had been graded, students could revise the "final" paper (final no longer) if they wished, for inclusion in the semester portfolio. In that portfolio they placed three papers, for one of which they included all their work (i.e., the full paper-portfolio, as well as a reflective letter). Even though the turnover of both TAs and part-time instructors operates against building a stable system with shared, common standards, we found that the work of portfolios had a similar effect, slower than at Michigan but positively cumulative, in developing such a system. In this kind of context, the portfolio system requires even more care and maintenance because so few people have a long-term investment, and more initial training is required every year; but the ethos of the program has changed to one in which the portfolio is accepted and discussions now turn on the ways to improve the system.

Among the implications of this system, the "underlife" of the TA group contains a strand of discussion about how to "do" portfolio assessment, talk about the kinds of assignments TAs have seen in other teachers' portfolios, the informal swapping of essays via mailboxes with appeals for advice on how the student would "shape up" in the colleague's class—a range of small but positive signs that the composition program is developing a portfolio culture, and that the culture is having its impact in professional development. In this ethos, many of the teachers are now comfortable assigning more than 25% of their course grade for the portfolio; many assign 50% and one or two assign 90% (reserving 10% for attendance or effort). Small gains, perhaps, but important ones for the

TAs as future professional writing instructors and faculty members, and most importantly for our students, who are much likelier to receive an equitable reading of the writing than in the isolated classrooms they would have inhabited before.

An important argument supporting the use of portfolios for exit assessment is their role in contributing to student retention. A college or university must work to *keep* the students it admits and eventually to graduate them. The use of portfolios at exit from courses has the positive effects we have already described in detail; it also provides even more opportunity for writing teachers to work closely with their students, as they consult on drafts and revisions of papers to go into the portfolio. Students' evaluations of courses at CU-Denver have consistently shown that the close attention they receive from a teacher is one of the things they value most about their writing courses, and their comments show that they do not often get such personal attention in other classes. Feeling valued as an individual is an important factor that keeps students in college.

Portfolios at Entry to the Writing Program

In recent years several universities have begun to use portfolio assessment for determining student placement into a suitable level of a multilevel writing program, or for exempting superior writers from the writing requirement. At Miami University of Ohio, for example, an optional entry portfolio assessment has been in existence since 1989 (Black, Daiker, Sommers, & Stygall, n.d.), and Miami has published several issues of the *Best of Miami's Portfolios.* The guidelines for portfolios are carefully laid out, as are the scoring procedures used. Portfolios are scored holistically on a 6-point "relative" scale ("relative" means the scoring is not directly tied to placement decisions, which may move from year to year). The Miami team reported the same kinds of benefits in this context that we have reported for exit portfolio assessments, as well as positive impact on teachers and students in participating schools.

The University of Michigan, through its ECB, instituted an entry portfolio-based writing assessment in 1994 (after a large pilot program in 1992 and 1993). Each year now, approximately 5,000 entering students—both first-year and transfers—submit writing portfolios containing the following:

- A cover sheet containing the student's name, social security number, high school, city, and state, and a list of the items the student has included in the portfolio.
- A two- to five-page reflective statement that introduces and describes the writing in the portfolio. In the reflective statement,

students tell the readers what is included in the portfolio and why, the occasion and the intended audience for each paper, and so on. Students also have a chance to write about themselves as writers— about the processes they use, about how they feel about their writing, about what concerns them in that writing, how they hope to develop as writers, and so forth.

- One piece of writing from a class other than an English class.
- One piece that responds critically or analytically to something the student has read.
- One piece that the student identifies as her or his best, favorite, or most representative piece of writing.

Students who cannot send one or more of the specified pieces are asked to send a substitute piece and to explain the substitution in the reflective essay. In addition, Michigan places a 25-page maximum on the portfolio's length (there is no minimum; the shortest portfolio on record was 2 pages long).

The readings themselves progress in a fairly standard way. The day begins at 9 a.m. with a norming session in which the day's 15 to 20 readers read, place, and discuss two portfolios at different placement levels that were chosen because readers agreed on their placement levels, or because the portfolio exhibits some difficulty or complication that readers need to discuss. After this calibrating session, readers adjourn to their packets: five portfolios per packet, and an expectation that each reader will finish at least six packets before 4 p.m. Each portfolio is read by at least two readers, each of whom spends from 6 to 12 minutes on the average portfolio. If the first two readers disagree about placement, the portfolio is usually given to a third reader for the deciding vote; however, if two readers consistently disagree, they may be asked to recalibrate by consulting over their disagreements. And if a reader consistently splits with other readers, that reader can recalibrate by reading a packet of sample portfolios selected to exemplify one placement level. Thus, a reader who too frequently places "composition" portfolios into practicum could read a packet of practicum portfolios to rediscover the boundary between those placements.

This system has not resulted in a change in the proportion of students placed into practicum, although it has slightly reduced the number of students who exempt the Introductory Composition requirement. However, portfolios have increased the likelihood that students will be placed into the most appropriate course for them. Before portfolios, for instance, 20% to 25% of practicum students exempted Introductory Composition *on exit from Practicum.* Although we would expect that Michigan's select student body might contain a number of less experienced writers who were capable of rapid progress, that percentage seemed too high. Some of those students had probably been misplaced; they might just as well have started off in Introductory Composition. The portfolio results bear out this feeling. As students who were placed into practicum via the portfolio assessment exit the course, only 13.5% exempt Introductory Composition, and when we factor out the students who self-placed into practicum (because they were unwilling or unable to assemble a portfolio), the exempt percentage falls to 8%. Of those, some were fast learners who came from schools that did not require them to write very much or very often. The rest made poor choices for the pieces in their entry portfolios: Trying to be considerate, they sent only their shorter pieces, for example, so readers assumed that these students were only capable of writing two or three pages at a time. Thus, although the proportions placed into the three levels have not changed significantly, the accuracy of the placements has increased markedly. This increase was confirmed by surveying teachers of courses that fulfill the Introductory Composition requirement. These teachers reported that only 10% of their students seemed misplaced—might have been exempted or should have been placed into practicum. The teachers were happy to have the former in their classes. Of the latter, most students who performed poorly were just not trying very hard—an attribute the students' portfolios simply could not portray.

After 3 years of experience reading more than 5,000 portfolios each year, Michigan can declare its entry assessment an unqualified success. A survey of entering students in 1994 indicates that students spend between 2 and 4 hours assembling their portfolios and writing their reflections. They consider this a reasonable investment, and they trust the assessment results as fair. In fact, they are impressed that such a large university will lavish so much attention on so many individuals. Secondary-level teachers indicate that the portfolio is already affecting their curriculum. Whereas before they had taught to Michigan's 50-minute impromptu argumentative essay assessment, now they teach to the portfolio—a much more positive prospect. And many schools have established writing centers to help students put together their portfolios or appointed one teacher as the portfolio consultant. Both these measures increase the amount of writing instruction available to students in high school. In addition, a few schools have established their own portfolio requirements, so that every student, Michigan-bound or not, assembles a portfolio like the one Michigan students submit. Finally, the portfolio readers, most of whom are graduate students who teach writing, testify that the assessment experience has helped them in a number of ways. Readers learn what their incoming students are like, so as teachers they can plan courses that more closely address their students' needs. Readers also benefit from many opportunities to discuss students' writing, as well as from the chance to read alongside the more experienced teachers among the ECB's faculty. All the stakeholders, then, can trace some benefit from the portfolio.[4]

However, not all the stakeholders were happy about the idea of establishing a portfolio-based assessment. Instituting an entry-level portfolio-based writing assessment immediately brings the writing program into contact with the business of the admissions office (if the portfolio is too difficult, fewer students will accept the offer of admission), the state departments of education and higher education (the requirements of the state's most influential university impact other universities, as well as secondary education), the dean's office (whose financial and political support was crucial), the provost's office (where concerns about *any* change must be allayed), the president's office (where a major change in requirements might affect major agendas), and others. Reaching beyond the boundary of the writing program involves crossing into other people's and agencies' turf—into what can sometimes seem like enemy territory. This is a daunting prospect.

Additionally, because the act of assembling an entry portfolio requires a not insignificant effort on the student's part, admissions officers and vice provosts in charge of tuition revenues tend to worry about the effects of a portfolio requirement on enrollments: given a portfolio requirement at School A but not at School B, students may tend to choose School B because it does not require a portfolio. The consequences—in the eyes of admissions and the provost—include altering the quality of the student body or adversely affecting the numbers of students who enroll, and hence the budget, at School A. In the event, as director of admissions Ted Spencer reported, students did just the opposite. Attracted to Michigan by the upfront demonstration of individual attention, students accepted at a higher rate than before. The portfolio was one factor among several (e.g., the establishment of first-year seminars) that actually *attracted* students to Michigan, even as they seemed to add to a student's workload.

Such concerns about negative consequences in the larger context mean that arguments for a portfolio-based entry assessment need to be compelling. The greater face validity of a portfolio is a strong argument in their favor within the writing program context, but is not sufficient beyond its boundaries—neither should it be a sufficient argument *within* the writing program. Within the writing program the argument that carries most weight is essentially one of construct validity: Portfolios capture more of what people *actually do* when they write, and so portfolios used as

---

[4]Despite the successes described above, Michigan is discontinuing its entry-level assessment as of Fall 1999. This act is part of the Department of English Language and Literatures' determination to abolish the ECB.

assessment instruments enable readers to see more of what writers have done, and therefore of what they can do. As explained in chapter 1, at the present time the view in educational measurement is changing from an emphasis on classical measures of reliability to a view in which reliability is a factor within an overarching definition of construct validity. Thus, we argue, we have the right construct: Now the ways must be created to measure the construct appropriately and accurately. The arguments for using portfolios must go farther than face or traditional construct validity; they must encompass the principles of consequential validity identified by Messick (1989) and elaborated by himself ("Standards in Validity") and other educational researchers such as Moss (1994), Jaeger (1995), and Guion (1995), and these values must be realized in practices that will enable us to show the powers and special interests outside the writing program that we know what we're doing; the principles and practices must be persuasive on both political and educational grounds.

One principle that is easily argued concerns the role of portfolios in retention. If the university is to be considered a "good citizen"—thus partially justifying its state appropriations—then it should be doing something to develop or support improvements in education in primary and secondary schools. Requiring a portfolio, as just noted, makes transparent the expectation that students will have done a certain amount of writing of certain kinds, in turn influencing teaching at the lower levels. Moreover, it can be argued that introducing portfolio-based writing assessment at entry, with its impact on high school curriculum, will improve students' readiness for college and thus make them less likely to drop out on academic grounds. Universities that use standardized test scores or timed essays for entry placement into writing courses implicitly invite secondary-level teachers to teach to those tests. As a result, students often arrive well prepared to take multiple-choice exams or to write short-answer essays, but they struggle when asked to produce a longer, denser, more considered piece of writing. However, when universities use an entry portfolio, they are inviting teachers, explicitly or implicitly, to teach to the university's portfolio requirement. We would expect that students will arrive more broadly prepared in one of the college level's most fundamental intellectual tools—writing—and better prepared to succeed in college (and beyond). This too is a question to be investigated—and it will take some years, and a longitudinal study, to reach solid empirical conclusions.

The proof for these arguments must, of course, be established by research and experience. One area where there is currently too little evidence is the reliability of portfolios—in any context, but particularly in the entry context. Giving readers more to read—particularly at the entry level because the readers know nothing beyond what the portfolio tells them about the writers or the writers' instructional contexts—makes their decisions about placement more difficult. More evidence, in other words, unless each piece is absolutely consistent with the others, raises more questions about what course or courses would be appropriate for a given writer, or about how to describe a given writer's competencies, or how to rank one writer in relation to all the others, and so forth (Hamp-Lyons & Condon, 1993). The difficulties involved in making these judgments means that, oddly, greater construct validity can potentially result in lower reliability. In the past, when portfolios were employed by individual teachers in order to evaluate their own classes, reliability was not an issue. Now, however, as program after program adopts portfolios as a way to establish collaborative grading, reliability becomes important. If one reader would give a portfolio a "pass" and another would not, that disagreement is not a "mere statistic": It is important because it bears significant consequences for the students involved. It signals that the portfolio assessment program has not yet arrived at a consensus about the kinds of writing it will value, which might mean the writing program itself has not reached consensus about the kinds of writing it teaches and expects across classes at the same level. The reliability obstacle, in some local contexts, has been overcome. Miami University's reliability statistics, like Michigan's, are within the .8 range of holistic essay assessments, for example, and as each institution refines its procedures, reliability should also increase, as a function of the fact that readers share a high level of local context. Readers know the courses into which they are placing students, so their rate of agreement, especially as criteria become more solid, should also increase.

To date, experience with large-scale portfolio assessment is so limited that no research yet exists to support the notion that local successes can be translated into other contexts. This question, as well as others that are addressed in chapter 5, needs to be part of a research agenda for portfolios. However, we do believe that in the stories of success and struggle within specific programs there is much that can be learned by programs newly considering similar kinds of portfolios. We do not say, "Do what we do"; but we do say, "Here is what we do, and here is how it works, or doesn't."

Nevertheless, we can see that the potential benefits from using portfolios as a tool for entry-level college writing assessment are great. In a well-designed portfolio-based writing assessment, the greater face validity (compared to either timed impromptu essay tests or standardized tests) means not only that students can present a more representative sample of their writing, but also that colleges are perceived as giving credit for that writing. Greater construct validity means that writers truly are rewarded for what they can do in writing, and that the writing to be rewarded is appropriate for the context in which the students will write in the immediate future. Portfolio assessment gives students at once a greater investment in their writing and an empowering sense that the university values students as individuals—that students' experiences *count* for something in this new and often overwhelming institutional setting. This is a different kind of face validity—it gives face validity to the institution.

In another vein, when the portfolio assessment program has achieved good reliability, the placements that result mean that colleges can address students' needs more effectively from the beginning. This ability may mean that the college saves money by offering fewer writing courses, which is the case at Miami University (Daiker et al., 1990). At Michigan, greater reliability has meant that students, placed more consistently and at appropriate levels, feel better about their placements and do better work in their first-year writing courses; that is, because fewer students are required to start in a course that is too advanced for them or not sufficiently advanced, students exhibit less resistance to their course assignments.

In summary, the benefits of entry-level portfolio assessment can be immense—far outweighing the costs. At Michigan, the portfolio assessment annual budget is approximately $90,000 to $100,000; by contrast, the old essay test cost about $65,000. Thus, increasing the budget by 50% brought all the tangible and intangible benefits described earlier. And because the dust from such an entry assessment has not yet fully *risen,* much less settled, more benefits will likely become apparent over the long term, when the effects on secondary curricula, on the quality of entering students, and on the first-year composition curriculum can be revealed.

Portfolios Across the Curriculum

A common complaint in the latter part of the millennium as we labor under the information explosion and the globalization of information access and exchange is the fragmentation that is occurring in knowledge and understanding. Education has for the last century and a half tended to be seen as the piecemeal acquisition of the bits and pieces needed for a particular career or job. This attitude of expediency, desirable or not, worked well enough until the amount of detail that existed overwhelmed us. Now in colleges and universities we are beginning to recognize that this kind of learning serves the interests of neither individuals nor nation well. Across the United States there are attempts to bridge the gaps in academic curricula and to address learners' inherent needs to find the coherence in their courses of study. Interdisciplinary programs are burgeoning as part of this attempt, but the longest-standing and most extensive effort to create this needed continuity and coherence is probably WAC. If we look at the underlying assumptions of WAC, we can see its potential for allowing both learners and teachers to see some of the common elements in what they do from class to class, semester to semester. WAC assumes that we cannot separate writing from thinking, reading, investigating, or oral communication. These competencies—what we might call the infrastructure of higher education, perhaps of education in general—are so closely allied that treating them as if we could teach them separately is simply wrong.

WAC also recognizes that one important way people discover what they think is by writing about it, that thinking and writing are recursive and complementary processes. Next WAC assumes that writing and speaking about a topic is a powerful tool for learning about it, and that writing ability develops over time and across opportunities to write. It does not develop all at once, in only one class. Moreover, because each discipline has its own ways to pose questions, seek answers, and communicate results (in other words, to make knowledge), learners need help as they develop into members of a particular discipline's discourse community. Finally, we teachers serve as the mentors for students seeking entry into those discourse communities, so our oral and written interactions with the learners in our charge are crucial to the learning process (Walvoord & McCarthy, 1990). WAC helps bridge the gaps in our academic community because its assumptions transcend our most common institutional structures—programs, departments, schools, and colleges—thus undercutting the assumptions on which those structures are founded. WAC begins to disassemble the academic assembly line because WAC operates on the assumption that the stations on that line really cannot be separate and distinct from one another.

Portfolio-based writing assessment extends WAC's assumptions, even, one might say, allows them to be realized in concrete form. If we consider what WAC's assumptions mean in terms of how we teach, and then compare that with what happens when teachers use portfolios, we can see that WAC and portfolio-based assessment are natural partners. For example, as Walvoord and McCarthy pointed out, WAC demands a shift from content-centered to assignment-centered instruction. Rather than focusing on what a course will cover, teachers focus on what learners can do, on how and to what extent learners demonstrate what they know at a given point in time. Because, in part, a portfolio is a collection of the products of learning, portfolio-based assessment reinforces this aspect of WAC, making the conversion easier by giving the teacher the means to accomplish two significant ends: first, to keep track, as the items for the portfolio evolve, of the students' learning in process and second, by manipulating the portfolio's contents, to maintain an accurate yet flexible outline of the learning opportunities the course presents. In addition, the focus of the WAC course on writing and on creating a way for learners to join the teacher's discourse community demands that learners be given frequent opportunities to receive feedback on and to revise their written work. In this way, learners move from outsiders to insiders, from observers of a discipline to participants in it. Finally, WAC assumes that active learning is better than passive learning, that students will learn more and faster if they are actively engaged in the knowledge-producing methodologies of a discipline. One of the most powerful benefits of portfolio-based writing assessment is that delayed grading creates more time for active learning to occur and for students to become successful in their learning. Thus, portfolio-based assessment reinforces the major components in writing across the curriculum courses.

In order to bring this potential for portfolio-based writing assessment across the curriculum into reality writing faculty have to go out and work with the members of the other disciplines. We have to sit with them and listen as they read and respond to their students' work; we have to talk with them and try to understand the values of writing and doing the discipline that they bring to their task of reading and judging their students' work. We have to insert ourselves into the interdisciplinary conversations that are beginning on most campuses, reminding our colleagues that we are there, and in a position to offer them our expertise. We have to find ways of investing disciplinary faculty in using writing to help them assess the learning of the students in their discipline. And we have to make certain that faculty in those other disciplines have and maintain a strong voice and active participation in portfolio evaluation. We can do this, first, by establishing an atmosphere of mutual respect, of two sets of experts contributing what they know.

The first part of this can be done by asking questions and by listening carefully. In any interdisciplinary enterprise, each group must acknowledge the special knowledge the other brings to the task—faculty in other disciplines may not have the vocabulary to speak about writing, but we do not have the vocabulary of their fields, or their understanding of how knowledge is constructed in their fields. Working together, we can reach a shared view of what is important in the writing of that field and how to talk about it. But we have to beware of our own tendency toward simplistic responses, the search for a simple position or view that will "capture" that discipline for us, because even within a discipline there is disagreement about what constitutes evidence, or how knowledge is constructed, or who is allowed to speak, to whom, and for what purposes.

We also have to overcome a fair amount of distrust from some faculty. We have all been in situations where faculty in other disciplines claim that they have had to "undo" what was done to them in the English or

Writing department! We like to think that we offer great flexibility and variety of writing assignments and discourse structures or modes in our advanced composition or WAC writing classes, but we will never be able to cover the great variety that is actually out there in disciplinary writing and in the expectations of faculty across the disciplines. We often expect science and social science faculty to prefer papers with a deductive structure that places an introduction and a thesis up front. However, the reality is much less straightforward: Shown such a format, one criminal law professor said, "not that one. I want them to discuss as many of the variables as they can before they offer a conclusion." One very common text structure is the situation-problem-solution-evaluation structure described in detail by Hoey (1979). This works well in many disciplinary areas, where papers are commonly expected to begin by describing the background to a (disciplinary) problem, analyzing the issues that surround it, and then proposing several plausible solutions to it. But even within those same areas, a professor might want papers with define-analyze-prescribe formats. In humanities and arts fields, similar variations exist: Art historians look for extended definitions, detailed descriptions, and personal response; for many literature professors structure or "format" per se is not an issue, but the ability to do textual analysis and to quote appropriately and in approved format is. At least in format, the Aristotelian rhetorical form we know best, with clear beginning, middle and end may not be what our students will be asked to do in their disciplinary writing, or it may be only a minor part, perhaps a background assumption, of what is expected of them. Even a factor as basic as verb tense can matter. The historical present, preferred by English teachers in literary analysis ("Shakespeare says . . .") is inappropriate in a history paper, where the fact that a person is dead matters ("Shakespeare said . . ."). We will not be able to work productively with our cross-disciplinary colleagues unless we discover the ways they make and report knowledge in their disciplines. Until then, we will not be valuable as consultants in setting up a portfolio assessment in the local WAC context.

The second way we can invest faculty in using writing in their courses is by demonstrating tools that they can use within their current teaching methodologies. Compositionists can suggest a whole host of tools and techniques for integrating writing into disciplinary classrooms, and helping faculty understand how to use portfolio evaluation is one important step, not only for the assessment's immediate benefits but because it brings with it ease of access to many of the other benefits, that is, it makes them possible.

The type of portfolio that is most likely to appeal to faculty in other disciplines is fairly formal, with a number of papers written in response to formal assignments gathered together. Good assignments are no less important in the portfolio classroom than in the traditional disciplinary classroom, and there is a good deal we can do to help faculty deconstruct their assignments and discover what their own expectations are. As faculty collect writing from their students, we can work to help our colleagues not only grade the writing, but find ways of looking at it that reveal strengths and weaknesses in the assignments, and strengths and weaknesses in the learners. As the assignments come in through the semester, we can help faculty see how to put this evidence together to form a longitudinal picture of each student, revealing what they have done, how well they have done it, and what remains to be known about them that is important to the professor. As our experience using portfolios grows, we see for ourselves the range of possibilities and the space for imaginative use the portfolio offers, and we can offer this experience in our work with faculty who are beginning to think about setting up a portfolio assessment for their courses. From these activities grows a perspective on the value of longitudinal evidence that convinces many faculty of the value of portfolios. This special perspective is the third way we can get faculty to invest in writing portfolios as assessments in their courses: by showing them that using portfolios, both in teaching and in assessment, gives them information and a view on their students' learning that isn't available to them in other ways. To reach that far requires an act of faith on the faculty member's part; but that act of faith made, the reading of portfolios at the end of the semester is both an uplifting and a humbling experience for many faculty. We learn so much from it, as individuals and together.

Helping in this endeavor is the fact that many kinds of portfolios exist, that no "portfolio police" wait out there ready to legislate the rights or wrongs of a particular kind, and that each faculty member can develop a portfolio assessment that fits his own needs, limiting its role in the course assessment to whatever he feels comfortable with. Table 3.2 is a heuristic for helping writing faculty work with faculty in other departments or programs to help them look inside their course sequence, their major, or whatever, and discover for themselves the questions to ask and some of the answers. It contains questions that have proven useful as Hamp-Lyons has worked with faculty in the disciplines who are interested in developing portfolio assessments for their classes.

Each part of the heuristic represents what may be an extensive discussion, even a need to re-evaluate program purposes and processes. This is because at most schools the curriculum is built up in a fairly haphazard way, and what we dignify with the names of "programs" are often only the result of faculty interests and personal values about their discipline, rather than a system of knowledge represented by a parceling out into courses. The self-reflection required to develop a portfolio plan for a program, as in a graduation portfolio for instance, can be a frustrating and invigorating process for faculty.

Table 3.2. Template for Thinking About Portfolios With Faculty Across the Disciplines.

I. What do you want to know and why?

- About mastery of content
- About thinking skills/processes
- About the ability to convey concepts, ideas, relationships, significances, etc.
- About the ability to create an acceptable text (acceptable to whom?)
- About the program
- About the class
- About individual students' progress in the discipline
- ?

II. What will achieve that information?

- Text types/artifacts/work samples
- Formal written papers
- In-class writing
- Specialized text types (e.g., lab reports)
- Group projects
- Forms of evidence other than writing (e.g., diagrams, sketches, objects, audio/videotapes)
- Time period/knowledge range
- Sampling a single class/course sequence/multiyear program, etc.
- How important is evidence of growth? What kind of evidence will show growth/progress?
- How important is it to see a range of knowledge/skills from each student?
- What is that range?
- Are the skills expected the same at all stages across time? If not, should sampling be different for different phases in a program? How?
- ?

III. How is the portfolio to be evaluated? Why?

- Prescriptively or descriptively
- If descriptively, where does the language for evaluation come from?
- If prescriptively, where do the criteria and standards come from?
- Should papers be (or have been) judged individually?
- Who makes the judgments or writes the descriptions? How? (See I and II)
- Do students' self-judgments play a part? Where?
- ?

As faculty in other disciplines become more convinced of the value of portfolio assessment for their own courses, major, or department, we can work with them to help them set up their own portfolio program. Here again the processes of asking questions and listening carefully are vital. Also absolutely central is the meeting over artifacts, the same kind of conversation that we have described as vital in exploring and setting up a portfolio assessment within the writing program. In a single course, for example, we can sit down with the professor and a copy of all the assignments for the course, with the grading criteria, copies of papers—whatever artifacts exist. We can then talk through with the faculty member what course objective or larger goals of disciplinary membership each assignment fulfills. We should stress that although each of these objectives can presumably be assessed separately, placing them together in a portfolio gives both student and teacher a different perspective on the course as a learning progression. In most classes, faculty have complex and multiple objectives for what students will learn or accomplish. Each assignment may be a representation of one of those goals. Thus, reviewing each student's performance on an assignment as the work comes in will be useful for evaluating assignments and student learning needs for the next phase of the course. In addition, seeing work collected into portfolios at the end of the semester creates a valuable opportunity for the faculty member to see each class member as a whole person, as a learner who succeeds in some ways and (perhaps) is less successful in others. A portfolio also presents a helpful way for the faculty member to assess the degree to which the course was successful, to identify some points where perhaps there was less success, and begin to see why. The portfolio becomes an important course development and improvement tool.

The template in Table 3.2 contains questions because the process begins in questions, as we have already noted. Composition faculty must begin by listening, by finding colleagues' needs and matching those needs against what the portfolio (as tool) can deliver. Enlightened self-interest is a powerful motivator. If we can promote in our colleagues the discovery that the portfolio is just what they need in order to reform their courses positively or assure that their majors perform acceptably, or provide their graduates with an effective set of materials that credential the graduates as they move into careers or graduate or professional schools, then we will find the conversion to the WAC portfolio to be simple.

The story of the WAC portfolio at Eckerd College in St. Petersburg, Florida, is instructive in this regard. Eckerd students had been required to fulfill a graduation requirement by taking an essay test. Eckerd faculty expressed wide and growing dissatisfaction over such a hurdle, especially because it required such a simple task from students who, preparing for graduation from college, should have been capable of much more complex tasks than a simple essay test and much more complex thinking and knowing than such a test requires. So, as Harrison (1995) wrote, after much discussion, Eckerd switched to "a portfolio-based writing competency graduation requirement" (p. 39). This change grew out of an emerging consensus that all faculty share the responsibility to help students develop as writers. In effect, the portfolio requirement acted to make that growing consensus into a self-fulfilling prophecy because the project that not only "engage[d] faculty in a collaborative development of an assessment tool" but also involved them in frank discussions of common and disparate theories of learning and pedagogies. And the longer the WAC portfolio is in place, the more faculty take part in these discussions as faculty cycle through the role of portfolio evaluator. Gradually, as faculty discussed writing among themselves, they acquired a vocabulary for evaluation, and they saw examples of students' writing, examples that often led faculty to form higher expectations for their own students. By becoming aware of the kinds of thinking and writing that were occurring across Eckerd's curriculum, faculty were more secure in defining, assigning, and evaluating the kinds of thinking and writing students were doing in disparate courses.

Harrison also reported positive results for students. The portfolio helps students see themselves as writers with real audiences, rather than simply as writers trying to give a professor what she wants. Students have focused on writing as a transaction with the reader, and they realize that writing improves gradually, across courses, rather than simply as the result of taking a writing course. The portfolio prompts students to see beyond a single grade on a single paper, to look past an individual assignment so that they can track their own development as writers.

Eckerd's experience suggests that a carefully instituted portfolio-based cross-curricular assessment of writing does extend the benefits of a WAC program or WAC requirement. This magic works because the portfolio creates an occasion to bring faculty from different departments together in service of a common purpose and to provide students with an opportunity to attend to their progress as writers across assignments, courses, and terms. In short, Eckerd's cross-curricular portfolio prompts learners to make connections among the seemingly discrete, disparate learning experiences that the typical college curriculum presents.

Eckerd College provides an encouraging, even inspiring success story, a case in which the needs and goals of faculty, administrators, students, and curriculum converged neatly on the portfolio. Clearly, establishing the requirement, designing the portfolio, deciding on criteria for ratings, all these decisions and more involved faculty in an arduous process. Just as clearly, the outcome has both benefited and satisfied all the constituencies involved in it. Lovett and Young (1994) provided a more cautionary example, one that we find useful in contrast with the Eckerd story. Lovett and Young, writing in *New Directions in Portfolio Assessment*, reported on the experience of being invited to develop an assessment tool for the Finance Department in Clemson University's School of Business. Lovett and Young proposed a well-designed, innovative portfolio-based system that would have evaluated students' writing across several courses—a WAC portfolio requirement similar in spirit to the Eckerd model. The finance faculty, objecting on the grounds of academic freedom, flatly refused the proposal. Perhaps lulled by the invitation to design an assessment tool, Lovett and Young admitted that they assumed too much, that, relying on the department's apparent willingness to adopt a new measure, the developers jumped too far ahead of their audience. As a result, the portfolio system conflicted with what the finance faculty felt were their own institutionally valid needs. In effect, as Lovett and Young described it, they located another example of what Pratt (1991) described as a "contact zone": a place "where cultures meet, clash, and grapple with each other, often in contexts of highly asymmetrical relations of power" (p. 34).

Working with faculty to move portfolio assessment into the disciplines is not easy, as Lovett and Young's story demonstrates. Crossing boundaries is always risky, and doing so in such an open environment as the one necessitated by portfolio assessment is riskier still. But once the door is open, faculty can be tempted within, because the portfolio assessment can offer them much. Using WAC portfolios as an assessment allows the faculty member to change the emphasis from what the course covers to what the students can do in order to demonstrate that they have acquired a specific body of knowledge. Portfolio-based assessment, with its combination of performance assessment and delayed evaluation, gives learners the means of assuming responsibility for their learning, lets teachers become genuine mentors for learners, and creates a time period, a space, within which learning can progress. These changes can alter the way a course is conducted, changing the whole dynamic of teaching and learning, offering more opportunities to learn, and thus potentially furnishing each learner with the means to succeed, both in the sense that she achieves the goals and objectives of the course and in the sense that she earns a favorable grade. Combining WAC and portfolio-based assessment, even within the confines of a single course, provides a bridge from one learning experience to another, a means both for tying the experiences together and for creating a document that encourages learners to reflect on the ways those experiences reinforce or build on each other.

Portfolios at Graduation

Another expression of this sort of learning mechanism is the graduation, or end-of-program portfolio, a portfolio that comprises the work a student has produced in a variety of courses, over an extended period of time. The graduation portfolio provides an unprecedented record of learning, of course, and as such is an extremely useful tool for assessing both the student's skills and the ability of the curriculum to accomplish the goals it was designed to meet. More importantly, however, the act of assembling a graduation portfolio, reflecting on it, and discussing it with fellow students and with a teacher provides a rich capstone experience for any college student. When the portfolio is based in, or strongly related to, the structure of the student's major, it becomes an important mechanism faculty might use to ensure that graduates leave with both a firm knowledge of their strengths and needs as writers and a means of demonstrating their abilities to prospective employers and any graduate and professional programs they might seek to enter. Looked at as a longitudinal record of a student's growth and exploration within a discipline or through the student's college years, the portfolio is a powerful window into the student: not only as a writer; not only as a novice member of a disciplinary community; but also as a person. Furthermore, extending portfolio-based assessment beyond the context of a single course means providing learners with the occasion to discover some of WAC's most important lessons: (a) learning is continuous, (b) writing is itself a learning process, (c) communications abilities improve over time and with practice, and (d) no one act of learning is ever fully isolated from any other act of learning. As long as such an assessment does not become a mechanical, reductive barrier assessment, it promises a rich set of diagnostic and learning experiences for students and faculty alike.

Portfolios for "Articulation" Between College Settings

Higher education, as all education—and some might say, all of society—has become fragmented. We have preschool, elementary school, middle school, high school, each of which typically occupies a different building. In an extension of this physical separation, faculty are often divided into specializations that emphasize the differences between levels and locations. Educators with degrees in elementary education do not teach in high school, nor do teachers certified in physics teach second graders. As young people leave high school and enter college, admissions processes encourage teachers and students alike to focus on the ways these two stages differ more widely than any of the earlier stages. Assessment helps the admissions process accomplish this end. Tests, scores, transcripts are all used to validate students as worthy (or not) of entry. And, often, at an orientation session several weeks before enrollment, students take even more tests in order to qualify for levels in the college's curriculum. Once in college, students choose a concentration that determines which building or perhaps which campus will house their classes, which library will serve their research needs, and often which dormitory will be open to them. The very fact that we test students again once they enter our doors suggests that we view them as blank slates to be written on; that they leave their past contexts behind when they go to college. This view is not peculiar to composition programs, but it is damaging to students' sense of themselves as real people of value in college, and requires them to take on the identities given to them by the outcomes of the measures applied to them, or to invent new identities for themselves.

An entry portfolio assessment, such as the one we described at Michigan, calls that fragmentation into question, forcing participants on both sides of the boundary to learn about each other, about each other's practices, values, and expectations, in order to help learners make the transition. This first step toward learning about each other, toward easing the passage from one educational level to another, is part of *articulation*. Entry portfolios articulate the transition from high school to college; at most universities they also articulate the transition from junior college to 4-year university for all transfer students. The work involved in describing both contexts, defining their boundaries, and building the bridge from one context to the other seems a complex and formidable one. How can writing teachers presume to take on such a daunting task?

We can presume to do this because we are in fact already doing it. Even if we are only using a portfolio-based writing assessment for exit from a writing course, we are by implication defining one half of the equation in an articulation relationship. When portfolios are used as an exit assessment method in writing programs, they operationally define the required standards for exit from that program level, but they also implicitly define the entry standard for the next level. Equally, every time we state our expectations for entry into a class within a teaching sequence, we consciously or unconsciously also state our expectations for exit from the level prior to it in the teaching sequence. Our decisions, our judgments, rarely stand alone, although we often practice as though we believe they do. When we make unilateral pass/fail decisions (or grades that have pass/fail consequences) we implicitly state what we expect the teachers at the next higher level to teach in their course; we act as though we know what the standard for the next course is. When we set entry standards for a course, even the first, most "basic," writing course in our own college, it might be argued that at the same time we state what we expect teachers in the prior level—even in another context entirely—to teach. Thus, we potentially impact teaching in other programs. The articulation aspect of assessments has been mostly ignored, but the greater clarity and transparency that portfolios demand is bringing this issue to the fore.

The use of portfolio-based assessment for making decisions about exit from freshman writing seems simple, but of course it is not. To use portfolios well for this purpose (i.e., to design assessment procedures that produce acceptable reliability and that do not limit the various kinds of validity we have attached to portfolios and portfolio assessment) it is necessary to develop and implement portfolio *standards* that encapsulate the shared expectations of the community of writing teachers at that level; and these shared expectations, thus encapsulated, must in their turn depict a version of writing realities that will be acceptable to the local (departmental) administration of the writing program, and to the larger bureaucracy of the college.

Let us take as an example the case of CU-Denver, where the lowest level of the composition sequence, 1010, is not a required course, but some students are placed into it as the result of an assessment at the start of the semester. Students who are placed into 1010 must pass it with a D+ or better (the same standard as all noncore courses) before they can take 1020, the standard "freshman comp" course. It follows that the expectations for a D+ in 1010 define the minimum expected entry standard for entry to 1020 (in other words, anyone whose writing at entry already fits the description of the D+ level in 1010, or better, would not have been placed in 1010 at entry; anyone whose writing fits or exceeds that description at exit would be passed to the next level). This is a fully articulated program. What, then are these expectations or standards?

Exit from 1010 is determined by a portfolio assessment, which was described earlier in this chapter, and that is common to it and 1020. Through the papers in the portfolio, a student must both demonstrate a certain level of achievement, and show signs of growth beyond that level. Table 3.3 shows the description used in evaluating portfolios for exit from this level, which has been developed over a period of 4 years. This exit standard is at the same time the standard required (of students who took 1010) for entry to 1020: Students whose writing meets or exceeds this description go on to 1020. Therefore, students who have placed at 1020 level directly, on the entry placement test, or students transferring in to CU-Denver with credit for 1010, should be writing at least at this standard.

When courses occur within a single department or program, the fact that they act as a sequence is obvious from the course schedule and the department's rules of placement. Surprisingly, however, it is not always obvious from the design of or statements about the standards of the courses. Once we had arrived at a stable and satisfactory set of expectations for exit from 1010 at CU-Denver, which was in 1994, we began to ask, in the context of reading portfolios: "But wait a minute . . . if we are expecting this much from a student leaving 1010, shouldn't we expect at least that much from a student who we're going to place into

Table 3.3. Criteria for Exit from Lowest Level.

Proficiency Goals

- Fulfills the assignment/task
- Contains a worthwhile central idea
- Maintains paragraph unity
- Shows a clear sense of direction/purpose in all revised papers
- Audience awareness, even if audience accommodation is uncertain
- Has appropriate diction (word choice) in all revised papers
- Has confident, consistent control of simple sentence structures
- Has no fragments, run-ons, comma splices in revised texts
- Has no editing/proofreading problems in revised texts

Developmental Goals

In reading texts across the length of the semester, or reading successive drafts of the paper that has its "life history" included, the following elements of growth should be visible:

- Expanding base of ideas/material for writing
- Increasing development
- Improving organization
- Expanding vocabulary
- Greater ability to recognize and correct own errors
- Increasing length

1020?" The answer was "yes"—we should, we can, and to some extent we are. When we read placement essays at the beginning of the semester (the traditional timed impromptu is still used for placement) we do not read against criteria but in a model much like that described by W. Smith (1994) at Pittsburgh, where teachers judge essays on whether the student would be appropriately placed in their own class, or not. In making this decision, teachers keep in front of them the statement of expectations for portfolio placement out of 1010 and into 1020; they use this as the operational definition of the boundary between the two levels.

When we began to compare the 1010 exit-1020 entry criteria to the criteria for exit from 1020, developed a year or two earlier, we ran into a problem. Table 3.4 shows the expectations in 1994 for successful exit (passing) from 1020: We can see immediately that the first expectation for 1010, fulfilling the assignment/task, is nowhere to be seen. What other differences are there?

Table 3.4. 1994 Criteria for Exit from Second Level.

- Papers in which purpose can be seen
- Clarity is within reach although perhaps not fully present; papers may wander toward it, with draftlike gaps, irrelevance, under- or overstatement
- Stretches of text may be writer-based, but other stretches are reader-based, showing audience awareness if not confident audience accommodation
- An emerging voice, although an overriding impression may be of a writer whose voice is stilted by the struggle to write for unfamiliar, "academic," audiences
- Development at the paragraph level can be seen in stronger and revised pieces, although other pieces may show less development
- Reasonable organization is present even if weaknesses of paragraph and sentence transitions do not always make this easy to see
- Revised papers free of typos, spelling errors, and global errors

The expectation of purpose seems to be about the same in both, although the more general nature of "purpose" in the 1020 description suggests that it is expected in all writing, and is therefore a more stringent expectation. The audience awareness expectation, although stated differently, does not seem more demanding at 1020 than 1010.

We can make these comparisons throughout the two documents and see the breakdown of a sense of articulation across the two levels, from the point of view of their exit expectations. This is a common occurrence in multilevel writing programs that do their own program design and development; those of us who look closely will find it also in many large-scale testing programs run by testing agencies. These articulation problems were resolved in the next year by revising the 1020 criteria and standards to be congruent with those for 1010, as shown in Table 3.5.

Clearly, care in monitoring one level of the portfolio program must be matched by care at the other levels, and by attention to the overall scheme. Furthermore, when articulation across levels is not carefully monitored, the effects of mismatch can lead to cumulative disjunction between entry and exit expectations at yet higher levels in a multilevel program. Table 3.6 shows the 1994 stated expectations for entry to 2024, the research paper course at CU-Denver (now renumbered 2030).

Despite the emphasis on clarity, purpose, audience, and voice from the 1010, prefreshman writing level (as shown in Table 3.2), the

Table 3.5. 1995 Revised Criteria for Exit from 1020.

On Any Single (Formal) Paper:

- The writing fulfills the assignment/task, whether set by instructor or student-nominated
- A clear sense of direction/purpose
- Deals with worthwhile ideas and uses meaningful material
- Audience awareness, and generally competent audience accommodation
- Beginning control of register; texts are written with appropriate language choices for the subject matter and the audience
- Beginning control of voice; the identity of the writer is felt in the text
- Paragraph unity
- Consistently accurate control of sentence structures except for the most ambitious forms; no fragments, run-ons, comma splices
- Editing/proofreading problems have been fully corrected on final versions

Over the Student's Semester-Body of Work:

- Evidence of a range of writing, the least successful of which meets the minimum requirement above; some texts will be stronger than others
- Evidence of development in most of the areas above
- Evidence of engagement with significant ideas and issues; the writer should be using writing as discovery, about self and the world
- While informal and way-stage writing may show need for improvement in many areas, final versions of texts should meet expectations for published excellence: no typos, clear, accurate sentence and phrase structure, and documents that are carefully presented

expectations for these elements of writing ability at the highest (core) level are still very modest here. The process of examining our own program's portfolios, and making explicit what we expected in them, showed us that there was very little movement of expectations from the lowest level to the research paper course. These criteria too have been revised, and are now more demanding, as shown in Table 3.7.

The problems of inconsistency of expectations across the elements of a supposedly articulated program occur not only at CU-Denver but in

Table 3.6. 1994 Criteria for Exit from 2024 (2030).

Since C is the passing grade for 1020, students who have performed at the C level in 1020 will be in the 2024 classes. By looking at the report of the latest standards-setting exercise carried out in the 1020 portfolio readings, we can see that we should expect minimum entering performance of those who have passed through our own sequence to be as follows:

- Writing free of typos, spelling errors, and global errors but possibility of needing to deal with local errors by using handbook exercises, guided self-correction, conferences, or in writing center
- Material will be organized into rational paragraphs; but transitions may be muddy, and ideas may need major work on development
- Many writers will need to work further with developing a personal voice; most will need to learn to blend their personal voices with acceptable voices within the academy
- Allied with uncertain voice is the uncertain audience awareness some students will bring; many will need more practice with writing to audiences other than the archetypal "English teacher"
- Clarity cannot uniformly be assumed, and many students will need to be taught to close the gaps, eliminate digressions and irrelevancies, stop wandering and head straight for the point
- Attention will need to be paid to teaching students to discover and define their purpose for a piece of writing
- Ability to work with textual support or with documentation cannot be assumed
- A predominance of the above characteristics indicate a C paper according to the standards set by the 1020 portfolio readers.

---

many other contexts and are usually unexamined (we note that because of the fragmented departmental status of composition at Michigan a similar exercise has not been carried out there). They occur not because we are bad people, or lousy at our jobs. They occur because we are always focused on the task at hand, on making better that which we must do, right now. We rarely have time to step back and look at the big picture. But the problems occur too because of political pressures, because absolute standards are untenable in the "real world" of educational politics. A particular pressure point between the search for a clear and fully accountable model of writing assessment across all program levels and the college or university's need for flexibility occurs in the transfer program.

Figure 3.7. 1996 Criteria for Exit From 2030.

On Any Single (Formal) Paper:

- Content is significant
- There is evidence of critical thinking
- There is evidence of locating and understanding the problem
- Readers are convinced of the significance of the topic for the writer
- All material is closely attached to a clear and worthwhile thesis
- Supporting material in the form of data, descriptive examples, or whatever specifics are appropriate to the content and purpose of the writing are provided, so that facts or arguments are adequately developed
- Organization is effective and unintrusive
- Others' words and ideas are used both appropriately and effectively
- Overall impression of the writer's style or voice is one of competence if not of excellence

Over the Student's Semester-Body of Work:

- Evidence of learning about ideas and about building texts out of the raw material of ideas—as opposed to technical reporting of facts and the ideas of others
- Evidence that the student can do this successful text-making for a range of audiences and on a range of subjects; flexibility as a writer is important.

Students at CU-Denver are most likely to be "nontraditional": only about 500 freshmen begin college each year from an undergraduate population of some 6,000. Many transfer from one of the five area community colleges with which CU-Denver has an "articulation agreement." Although many of them will transfer in full completion of the required writing courses, many others transfer only partial completion. Thus, in CU-Denver's "freshman comp" class—the "1020"—students are likely to be a mix of "our own" writing students and those who have placed into the level as a result of passing the equivalent of the prior level course elsewhere.

Looking back to the statement of the minimum level for passing 1010, we might expect that every student who has taken a semester-long writing class will meet those very modest expectations. Such is not the case, however. A proportion (large enough to give teachers some serious problems) of transfer students arrive with writing skills well below the minimum expectation as we have stated it. Because of the credit toward the composition sequence that they transfer, they can appear in classes at any level; teachers at every level face a real mix of stronger and weaker writers, and are faced with making sense of passing expectations for them all. And for students entering without transfer credit, with the use of a timed writing as a placement assessment a situation develops in which teachers, generally unfavorably inclined toward the timed writing context, give writers the benefit of the doubt; or see insufficient evidence one way or the other in the short, unplanned, unrevised text written under these conditions to make a negative judgment. We also have a few of our own 1010 graduates whose writing at the course's end does not in truth match up to the expectations for 1020. Teachers, especially writing teachers, are people of good will and kind hearts, and in their classrooms they place value on aspects other than absolute writing quality: effort, attendance, amount of progress, and so on. Not surprisingly some students do not meet the standards and are still moved on.

These problems of discontinuity are by no means unique (if they were there would be no point in revealing them!): many writing programs would discover similar problems for similar reasons were they to look within. In most programs, however, there is no mechanism for taking that look. But a portfolio-based writing assessment by its nature—of collaboration, of conversation, of community, and of care—opens up every aspect of the program to its own gaze, so that problems can be seen that may never have been noticed before. But more than that, with a portfolio-based writing assessment at every level in the articulation context it becomes possible to find ways to overcome the problems. Teachers see enough evidence about an individual's writing to make better decisions; writers have time and opportunity to work on their writing and ensure that it meets the expectations. When teachers across levels of the program start to read students' portfolios together and talk about students' writing, these disjunctions become visible, and the talk can begin to focus on what should be done. Teachers at different levels can compare their expectations in concrete terms, looking at what students in their classes have actually done and how it has been valued. Faculty from one college can meet with faculty from another higher or lower in the articulation sequence, they can read portfolios together, and begin to work out in concrete terms their understandings of what each expects, because they can look at what students in each of their classes have actually done, and how it is valued both inside and at the other levels. Working through the territorial defenses of all of our programs to develop a clear articulation agreement that will be acceptable to all colleges involved, and that teachers in classrooms can believe in for their own students, is not easy and takes a great deal of time. But if all programs involved start with portfolios of actual student work from their classes, and meet together over these texts in a spirit of goodwill, then the cooperation and consistent accountability that eventually results becomes another benefit that emerges from a portfolio-based writing assessment.

Portfolios and the Assessment of Nonnative and Minority Writing

One of the concerns regularly raised by Black, Hispanic, and other minority educators is that minority students are disadvantaged in testing situations. Such disadvantage is known as *test bias*. In its psychometric sense, test bias refers to situations where groups identifiable by race, class, gender, language background, or other variables that are not the ability being tested can be seen to receive systematically lower scores on a test. When systematic test bias is observed, it becomes necessary to discover whether the test instrument is discriminating against specific groups of students, or whether there are factors in the educational or broader contexts of those groups that might explain their disappointing performance as a group. When we realize that more than 17% of the population of the United States comes from homes where a language other than English is used, and then add in all the other minority groups whose rights to education and language use can be endangered by inappropriate and unfair testing practices, we see that this is a significant problem.

The impact of essay tests is different on different racial and language groups, as has been shown repeatedly by large-scale studies carried out on its own tests by ETS (the issues of the FairTest Examiner regularly attest to this). In a study of nonnative writers' strategies and performances on timed essay tests Hamp-Lyons found that of the four students she focused on, three seemed to rely on formulaic approaches of one sort or another, and two of those seemed to be hampered by lack of experience or knowledge to inform their writing. One seemed to be impeded by conflicting cultural expectations about what types of ideas, material, arguments and text structures might be unacceptable in the U.S. formal academic context, while the genuine "international student" (international in the sense of being a recent and temporary visitor for study purposes only) appeared to share the same kinds of expectations about what is legitimate in formal college writing as majority American students. Of course, Hamp-Lyons could not draw conclusions about whether essay tests disadvantage culturally and linguistically diverse college students on the basis of a sample of four students (even though these were extracted from a larger sample). Rose's (1989) *Lives on the Boundary* and work by others, such as Ritchie (1989) and Fox (1990), suggests that problems such as those Hamp-Lyons found with three of these minority students are not unique to linguistically and culturally diverse students. But she did expect to find indications that ESL writers of English would be at more of a disadvantage than bilingual writers, who would in turn generally—but not universally, of course[5]—be more disadvantaged than African-American writers: The finding that the most obvious outsider (the international student) in the U.S. college context was the only one to attain a traditional standard definition of excellence in either written product or writing process was a surprise.

As Farr (1993) showed, the "standard definition of excellence" implied by essay test criteria is itself problematic: an individual's "ways of speaking," by which she means verbal performances, whether oral or written, may be seen by others as inappropriate for what she called "essayist literacy" (p. 32). Bartholomae (1985) argued that college students are often expected to "invent the university" for themselves, and the genre of the gate-keeping essay test is clearly one in which essayist literacy is expected, and where students are certainly expected to perform to the norms of this kind of literacy, even though they may not yet have had opportunities to learn what these norms are.

As a classroom tool portfolios open up the potential for the teacher to understand the learner-writer and his or her needs much better; portfolios as an assessment offer the potential for teachers to decide to value a wider range of writing styles and voices than are privileged in an essay test. Thus, as assessments they potentially offer a great opportunity to nonnative writers and members of minority groups, to show what they can truly do in writing.

One question raised by examination of portfolio scoring criteria, and one of particular interest when considering issues of fairness and opportunity for nonnative and other nonmainstream writers, is whether they simply replicate the same "standard definition of excellence" or are more flexible and expansive in accepting different kinds of excellence in what writers can do. Yet accepting that the answer to that important question remains uncertain, even the simple change from evaluating a single piece of writing to looking at multiple texts promises to benefit ESL and minority writers in a number of ways. The structure and ethos of a well-designed portfolio evaluation offer richer options for feedback to the learner in both responses and in evaluations. The opportunities for students to work on pieces of writing, revise them, receive peer evaluation, decide

---

[5]The progression is based on the extent of second-language/dialect interference one expects to find in language users who often struggle to write in standard written English. It is of course true that many fully bilingual speakers of English are at an advantage, rather than a disadvantage, because of their additional language knowledge.

to make them into portfolio pieces and shape them further to reflect what they are learning and to provide an example of some of the things they can do in writing, all this time and attention, benefits all students but especially nonnative writers and other writers grappling with unfamiliar genres and tasks, and working to meet standards of excellence in grammatical and mechanical accuracy that they cannot reach on first drafts. But it also offers them, as it does every student, the opportunity to stand back and view their writing at a greater distance and therefore more "whole-istically." They may see strengths in their writing they hadn't noticed up close: a consistent personal voice, perhaps, or an ability to use convincing and detailed examples from a wide experience to support arguments. As they review their portfolios around the mid-point in a semester, students may discover gaps—nothing in a personal voice, perhaps, or maybe nothing using formal academic style. Through the process of talk and negotiation over portfolios, minority writers discover writing goals for themselves for the remainder of the course and approach their following interactions with peers, teacher and texts more purposefully. For ESL students, many of whom are first- or second-generation immigrants in a family where the previous generation has not gone to college in the United States and does not use English at home, it is a way into the complex and often unstated expectations of writing in academic communities which are otherwise very difficult for "outsiders" to enter.

Although there are benefits for ESL students of using portfolios as an instructional tool, there are evaluation benefits, too. First, unlike essay tests, portfolios are good at exhibiting growth in writing. Second-language writers who are literate in their first language are often in a more critical growth phase and on a faster growth curve in their language development than are first-language writers, who at the college level are often taking an English class with required writing for the fifth or sixth time. Thus, the second-language writers' growth is more easily observed in the portfolio over the course of a semester. But we must note that while this is particularly likely to be true for international students and recent immigrants, it is not necessarily true of college or high school *bilingual* learners, who may have struggled through a full school education without seeing significant growth in their writing skills—only through excellence and sensitivity in teaching can we start that growth at this stage. Portfolios may nourish such excellence and sensitivity, but they do not create it. Second, the writing skills, needs, strengths, or problems of second-language writers are complex. The multiple texts contained in a portfolio reveal this complexity. Traditional single-sample timed writing tests can result in simplistic judgments of second-language writing. As we suggest when discussing the criteria for scoring portfolios in chapter 4, such complexity in texts needs to be scored with a suitably complex instrument.

Relatedly, portfolios are particularly good for allowing teachers to identify cases of uneven writing skills development, and these cases are especially common in ESL learners. Noticing these complexities and unevennesses does not make our job easier, but we do not move into portfolio-based writing assessment to make our job easier—we do so to make sure we do it as well as possible.

Perhaps the advantage of portfolio assessment most commonly seen for ESL writers is that although "speeded" tests (i.e., tests that are administered within a specific, limited time period) are generally acknowledged to disadvantage ESL learners, the longer timeline that writers have as they work through a course and build up material for a portfolio allows them to overcome that disadvantage to some extent. Conscientious ESL writers prosper in the process classroom because of the repeated opportunities for revision, visits to the writing center for tutoring and editing help, and usually too the use of the word processor. A portfolio evaluation that shares the values of the process classroom (and not all of them do) will reflect those opportunities.

PORTFOLIO-BASED WRITING ASSESSMENTS: THE GREAT DIVERSITY

The collection by Belanoff and Dickson allowed us to see inside a range of portfolio programs. Elbow and Belanoff opened that book by describing the program that started it all in college composition in this country: that at SUNY-Stony Brook. In their follow-up chapter in the same book they stress collaboration and community as key in their processes of moving toward better portfolio evaluation. In an addendum to that chapter, Belanoff confessed her doubts about the progress of the Stony Brook portfolio program compared to those at some other schools, and her envies of some of those schools who, starting later, have been able to progress further, while reaffirming her commitment to the endeavor. Belanoff's addendum reminds us all that we can only do what the context permits us to do; but also, that we won't know what is possible in our context until we try. There are boundaries; but they are rarely fixed at the point we see them on first glance. Moving the boundaries, although it may not feel like enough, means that in all that comes after the boundaries, the point of negotiation is somewhere farther along.

Although we have offered examples of the portfolio assessment programs best known to us personally, there are many, many portfolio assessment programs across the country, and the number grows greatly every year. These programs vary a great deal too, and the variation is due to a variety of factors, all of which we can lump together under the rubric of *context.* In chapter 4, we develop a theory of portfolio-based writing assessment as far as we feel it is possible to do so with the state of knowledge in the field at present, and we show how the theory grows from context-based experiences and problem solving that we ourselves, and those who have spoken and written publicly about college-level portfolio assessment programs, have acquired. The theory is incomplete, and the contributions of many others will be needed before it satisfies us, but a beginning must be made for the reasons explained at the beginning of the chapter. Also in chapter 4, we work through a heuristic intended to help those new to portfolio-based writing assessment, or those dissatisfied with what is happening in their own situation at present, to think through the important constraints and potentials on decisions and action.

Chapter 4

DEVELOPING A THEORY FOR
PORTFOLIO-BASED WRITING ASSESSMENT

Chapter Outline

A THEORY OF PORTFOLIO ASSESSMENT

As the portfolio assessment movement in composition enters its second decade, portfolio-based writing assessment remains an experimental process. In part, continuing experimentation is a welcome state because the nature of a constructivist paradigm is to remain open, to stay in motion, responsive to local contexts and the exigencies of educational and political forces operating on the system. But it is also a matter of some concern because one of the major fronts on which portfolios have been assailed is their ambiguity and evasiveness. One of the things known about portfolios by comparison with other assessments is that they are more expensive—even when they are not more expensive in financial terms, they still require more teacher, more student, and more managerial time. Those who pay the bills feel they have the right to be informed of what they are getting for their money, and more specifically, what they are getting for their additional money that they were not getting, and could not have gotten by other means. A portfolio assessment, then, must be accountable, not only in the sense that all participants in the process conduct themselves with clear consciences and the best welfare of students in mind, but in the more mundane and yet vital sense of being answerable for the use of resources—increasingly scarce in the current era—and for the quality of decisions about individuals, programs, and policies that are based on them. To date, portfolio assessment, at least as it is manifested in college writing programs, has been on weak ground in this regard because it has lacked a credible, well-articulated theoretical base. It will be necessary, indeed is already proving necessary, for credible and accessible theory to be available in order to protect the emergent alternative assessments, portfolio-based writing assessment specifically, from the forces of economic imperative that will come to threaten them— that, as seen in chapter 1, are already threatening them.

Theory allows us to apply reality checks or tests to phenomena to discover whether they meet the criteria, established by the theory, for entry to the category in question, in our case, the category "portfolio." A theory of portfolio assessment should reveal, at least, what a portfolio is— not in the usual, essentialist terms that we see in the portfolio literature to date, but in a more conceptual sense. What we need to know is not whether Person A calls what he or she uses a portfolio, but whether Person A ought to call it that. In an interpretive sense, as defined by Moss (1996), what different people may call "portfolio" is less important than whether the lived experiences of those same people are actually similar.

To adopt an analogy from chemistry, "life as we know it" is carbon-based. Chemical theory tells us that. However, life as we know it comes in many variations: plant, animal, vertebrate, invertebrate, single-celled, multicelled, simple, complex. All these forms, no matter how dissimilar, are still carbon-based. But if there is no carbon, then whatever is there is not "life as we know it." For portfolios, what is the carbon? What combination of the characteristics allows us to say, "We have a portfolio here" with the same certainty that we can say, of a carbon-based living thing, this is "life as we know it?" What "lived experiences" are acceptable as—can pass the tests for—portfolio-based assessment experiences? When, for example, does a collection of pieces of writing stop being a *portfolio* and become just a collection of pieces of writing? (Or, to ask the question the other way round, as most teachers will consider it: "When does a collection of pieces of writing earn the name *a portfolio?*") In order to develop this interpretive sense of the term *portfolio,* the first thing a theory of portfolio assessment must do is to define the thing itself. We have been moving toward that definition throughout this book, and go further in this chapter.

The second thing theory must do is provide an understanding of how something works. To take another example from the physical world: It is not enough to know that the sun and the moon and the earth exist in shared space; the next step is to learn what they do in that space, how they move in relation to each other, how they affect each other. Like children everywhere, we want to reach and touch the stars, to experience them. In the same way, we want to know how portfolios work, what happens when they work well, what happens when they don't, and how we can tell the difference. There is a sense in which this kind of "process description" can be argued to be embedded within the definition of the phenomenon *a portfolio,* but we prefer to complicate our theoretical framework a little and look formally at how it works as well as what it is.

But it is easy to see that this is just a very small step from the big question: why? A theory will not be complete until it can provide an adequate explanation of the phenomenon: witness the increasing dissatisfaction with earlier, simpler theories of physical behaviors that have led to the development of chaos theory, and the fact that the incompleteness of chaos theory lures so many researchers into it as a field of study. We do not claim to have a fully adequate explanatory theory of portfolio-based writing assessment, but we believe we have begun to uncover enough patterns and relations among elements in the framework of portfolio-based writing assessments that we can start to ask good questions around the central question: "Why do portfolios work?" Why does it matter that, for example, students should select the writing to go into the portfolio, or that teachers and not "objective raters" should read students' portfolios, or, that . . . The questions that have been asked and are still to be asked about portfolios, as represented by the discussions in this book, are many, and yet they are by no means all the questions that can be asked, and that must be asked before we can say we have developed a theory of *the portfolio-based assessment of writing.*

Nevertheless, and in the spirit more of opening the theoretical discussion that is long overdue than of claiming to be providing definitive answers, in this chapter we gather together and formalize the elements of the book that we believe can contribute to developing theory, and suggest a framework within which theory might develop further.

Defining *the Portfolio*

Most studies to date—our own early work included—define the *portfolio* in an essentialist manner; that is, they describe the actual portfolio in use in a particular place and at a particular time (see, e.g., Condon & Hamp-Lyons, 1991; Elbow & Belanoff, 1991; Roemer et al., 1991; Weiser, 1992). As useful as these examples are, an attempt to describe the portfolio in less site-specific ways provides an account of characteristics common to all or most portfolios, characteristics that were introduced in chapter 2. In chapter 2 we described nine characteristics of portfolios, all of which are important; but it is necessary to consider which of these are essential: Which are the characteristics without which we cannot claim to have a *portfolio*?

We believe that the other characteristics can logically be subordinated to three main ones: *collection, reflection,* and *selection.*

Before everything else, a portfolio is a collection. Whatever the items collected, the fact that items is plural matters a great deal. The simplest portfolios collect products—finished responses to more than one writing assignment. Other portfolios collect not only the finished products, but also preliminary drafts. Still others specify that the portfolio include more than one genre of writing, writing produced under varying circumstances (e.g., some revised and perfected, some produced as timed, in-class writing, some individually produced and some collaboratively produced, etc.), writing addressed to different audiences or written for a variety of purposes, and so forth. Most portfolios include at least one piece that provides the student with an opportunity to reflect on his or her own writing process. But at its most basic level, *a portfolio* must consist of a collection of writing that contains a multiplicity of texts and that incorporates information about the writing context, not merely the writing itself. The theory of portfolio-based writing assessment grows from this primary building block. Recall that the reason portfolios emerged is that they supply a need for more information, for writing assessment that is connected with the instructional context in which the writing was produced. If we don't care about that connection, we can use direct tests of writing because they typically operate outside the instructional context.

But if we decide that assessment should support instruction, or that we need to know more about a writer's development, strategies, processes, and so on, or that we want, in the interest of fairness, to be able to evaluate a student's performance in light of that student's opportunities to learn, then we need more than the direct test will provide. We need a context-rich form of assessment—portfolios, appropriately constructed, can do that. When we have a context-rich collection of multiple texts, we have the RNA, the basic set of components, from which all portfolios are built.

But to continue the analogy, RNA is not enough; it must be combined in special ways to create recognizable life—"life as we know it." For the portfolio, the process of combination to create recognizable portfolio-life forms occurs through two further processes: reflection and selection. Everything that we have read about how and why portfolios work successfully, as pedagogical tools, teacher development tools, and as assessment tools, teaches that without reflection all we have is simply a pile, or a large folder (and this exists not uncommonly in primary schooling, where the collections are often known as "writing folders")—a collection of texts. Reflection starts the deliberative process, recognizes strength and need, places pieces together mentally, relates them to each other, engages in a host of mental processes: This can happen with just a collection, but a collection is not a portfolio until the reflection is there (i.e., physically included in the portfolio or self-evident in the result of the process of assembling the portfolio) because it is not accessible to the reader otherwise. Reflection is an ordering mechanism that turns our RNA into strands of DNA. But also, reflection is like a biological engine, an imperative: Once it is turned on it naturally wants to keep going and move into selection, into discrimination and thus to discarding some elements and making others more prominent. Through this process is shaped the recognizable life form that is each person's unique portfolio. For a writer to learn from the work she or he has produced and collected, reflection is necessary. For a reader to learn from reading the student's work, the student must reflect on that work. For a teacher or reader to learn with the student about strengths, pleasures, weaknesses, dispreferred topics, she or he must engage in reflective conversation with the student. For the student to interpret her or his work for a reader, reflection about the work is necessary. Inherent in this kind of reflection about one's own work and its effect on a reader is self-assessment. In our theoretical model, the role of the portfolio in developing self-assessment through reflection is a key difference between the consequences of portfolio-based assessment and other forms of assessment. The reflection that brings self-assessment is, we would say, the "DNA threshold," the point at which a collection of texts begins to take on life and shape.

What shape the collection takes, whether it becomes a minimal, highly disorganized life form, or a more complex and sophisticated life form, depends on the quality of reflection the writer engages in, and on the selection of texts that follow logically from reflection. Without a process of selection, the work of reflection would have no substantive purpose; the teacher would end the teaching cycle by seeing an undiscriminated collection of everything the student produced; he or she would be unable to see into the student's reflective processes, would be unable to judge how much the student understands about his or her own strengths and needs as a writer, about his or her own writing pleasures, about those aspects of writing he or she does because he or she has to, but does them well enough, and so on. Without selection, the writer would be unable to present the work of which he or she is most proud, would be unable to shape the portfolio as a conscious exhibit of what has been done, what has been learned, what is there to be understood about the individual as a writer. Without selection, portfolio readers would face a thankless task of wading through "stuff" from which they would have to create a coherence, and from which they would need to find a writer. Selection, then, is the final component that, when present, creates from the RNA—>DNA proteins a form that is not merely "[portfolio] life as we know it," but a differentiated form that demonstrates planning, judgment, reason, personal style—the characteristics, in fact, that make the fully realized portfolio a *higher life form.*

These three—collection, reflection, selection—are then, the basic components, the essential proteins, from which we believe all portfolios must be built. The other characteristics referred to in chapter 2 can be logically inferred from them, but we have seen portfolios and portfolio systems that do not demonstrate them, and to the extent that the other characteristics are not present the portfolio model that is used in that situation will be less than it could be; will be a lower form of life. It may walk like a portfolio, it may talk like a portfolio, but it doesn't *think* like a portfolio.

For instance, in our own early work with portfolios, on the University of Michigan's exit portfolio from practicum, the basic writing course, the range of texts students could include was not very wide because the course aims were not very wide, and because in those early anxious days we were careful to restrict student control rather narrowly, in order to answer our critics' predicted concerns about poor reliability. Students could only include argumentative writing, timed impromptu writing, and one "other" text, which for many students was also argumentative writing, because that was all they had produced in the course. In that early program, we also did not ask for the "paper trail" or "process history" of papers, and as a result we had no ability to see development over time within a single paper. Since then, we have come to see great value in the view into single papers that a "process history" allows. At that time also, we did not have formal evaluation criteria for portfolios: None existed in any other program (or at least, none were publicly available), and so there was no formal mechanism for judging growth along parameters, such as in grammatical control, lexical range, handling of coherence, paragraphing, topic continuity, or anything else. We now understand that, not only is it extremely difficult for portfolio readers to make judgments of portfolios without clear criteria and guidelines, but it is also difficult for students to know what is expected of them without access to the bases on which readers' judgments will be made.

Figure 4.1 models the most basic characteristics of a portfolio. It is the first step toward our emerging theory of portfolio-based writing assessment. The Figure shows the significance of the "loop" between reflection and selection, the intellectual and writerly work that must go on before a student, given control over the contents of the portfolio, can make good selections. It is in this loop that the other portfolio characteristics introduced in chapter 2 play their important parts: self-assessment, growth along specific parameters, development over time and, closely related to them, range.

The writer's conscious selection of texts, and text histories, to show these processes breathes life into the heretofore undifferentiated collection of texts. But the writer may have other reasons for including or excluding certain texts, that reflection on his or her writing experiences and life experiences leads him or her to select, or to reject, for the portfolio. Some such selected texts may not be the strongest pieces, and the writer's reflective letter, written reflection on the portfolio, or whatever it is to be called in any specific program, must let the reader see into the decision processes that the writer engaged in, so that the chosen pieces may be valued for the valid grounds individual writers put forward. Reflection and selection are iterative processes that the writer goes through in turning the collection of writing into a public document, an artist's portfolio, which can be shown to the teacher and to other readers with pride.

The loop in Figure 4.1 shows in diagrammatic form the theorized relationship between reflection and selection; interrupting the flow of the arrow through the various parameters of choice that are available in making selections based on reflection is the term *student-centered control.* As college-level portfolio-based writing assessments enter their second decade, the trend in education as a whole is toward allowing learners to assume a greater measure of control over their learning. This is reflected in most portfolio-based writing assessments, which place the responsibility on students to make reflective choices for their portfolios. In our diagram, the arrow is shown as interrupting the flow because if control is denied to students, we theorize that much less reflection will take place, and the role of selection as a positive learning experience will be undermined.

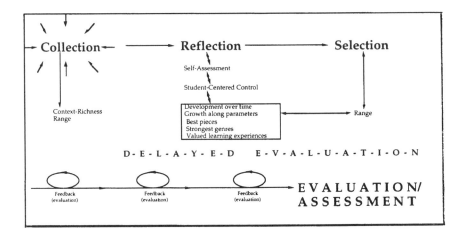

Figure 4.1. Basic portfolio characteristics

Finally in Figure 4.1, the bottom line leads to evaluation, but the line represents feedback, which plays different roles in different kinds of writing classrooms, as described in chapter 2, but that can be one of the most powerful underpinnings of a portfolio assessment-based writing course. (Some roles for feedback of different kinds and from different participants are described in chapter 3.) In good writing courses, feedback is frequent and rich; students always know "how they are doing," although they may not be receiving grades on each piece of work. But even if they do receive grades on papers once they are completed, as long as the portfolio at the end of the course itself receives a significant component of the course grade, the door is left open, work can still be done, the portfolio can still be crafted as an entity in its own right, revealing the full spectrum of what the writer has done, what he or she has learned, how far he or she has come. Our theory of portfolio assessment holds that there must be some element of delayed evaluation, because enough time must pass, at least, for the writer to amass a collection to reflect about and to select from. More significantly, however, without delayed evaluation there is no role of significance in the student's bounded classroom world for the making and presenting of the portfolio: It becomes a pointless exercise, possibly satisfying the teacher's ego and some arcane demand of "Them"—the ones who make the decisions about schooling—but satisfying no need of the writer's own. In effect, the absence of some sort of meaningful assessment of the portfolio, the stakes, for the student, simply do not justify the effort to reflect or to shape the collection. Delayed evaluation is a consequence of collection—and therefore not on our list of primary characteristics; nevertheless, it is the characteristic that makes portfolio assessment worthwhile for the person being assessed.

Developing From the Theoretical Foundation

Growing out of the theoretical model for a portfolio is a theoretical basis for making decisions about the structure of a portfolio program. From the description of the model in Figure 4.1, we clearly see that every portfolio will be different, reflecting each individual learner or writer. It is, we think, becoming clear that every portfolio program context is different too: Portfolio programs grow out of local contexts, out of classrooms, and out of programs, but also out of local educational needs and tensions, out of the educational theories that teachers bring to their teaching, out of local political and economic conditions, and consciously or unconsciously they are shaped by local conditions. This is true even when they are designed to address public policy needs. It follows that every portfolio-based writing assessment program will be different.

It follows from this that a book about portfolio-based writing assessment that hopes to be useful to a wide audience has a problem. It is impossible to outline a single approach to or exemplar of portfolio-based writing assessment that would be applicable to every possible context. Neither is it possible to provide enough guidelines for all conceivable local contexts to cover all eventualities: The latter would be impracticable and impossibly long, but both would violate almost everything we have said so far about portfolio assessment. Built into the theory, into the model, is the requirement that program planning decisions must be made in individual contexts. All good assessment is local. However, even though every portfolio assessment will be different, there are some common considerations, some common questions, that those wishing to implement a portfolio assessment need to consider. We provide as complete a set of those questions as possible, but these lists are intended to be generative, rather than definitive, descriptive rather than prescriptive. As issues within a particular context arise, these questions may need to be asked in new ways, and new questions will inevitably arise.

What emerges as this chapter progresses is a series of heuristics that represent as complete a set of considerations—of questions to consider—as we have found. In our view, the organization of the questions and considerations into these heuristics, into a scheme of decision points, contributes to the further development of sound theory for college-level portfolio-based writing assessment; but we are not ready to claim that we have uncovered all such questions, that we have understood all the decision points that may be faced by program administrators and teachers in such contexts. We hope that by bringing all our work together in this book, by collating all the thinking we have done, and much that we have learned from the work of others, in the form of these heuristics, we not only offer something others will find helpful, but stimulate others to question the heuristics themselves.

As teachers or program administrators design requirements for the portfolios, derive criteria for judging them, and in particular decide what sorts of feedback to provide to the learners, the contexts and needs of learners, assessors, teachers, and other stakeholders need to be considered. Each portfolio-based assessment program is the outcome of the difficult balancing act between the often conflicting demands of these groups. Each of the heuristics that follow can be applied to thinking about issues relating to each of these groups: How decisions are made from the mixture of all these elements depends on the participants.

Focus on the Learner

Portfolio-based assessments of all kinds share a pretheoretical assumption, a fundamental belief that all learners are different and deserve the opportunity to show their differences. But portfolio-based assessments are also performance assessments: They make judgments about students' knowledge, ability, or learning by referring to actual samples of the student's performance. We, therefore, should expect to learn, from a portfolio-based assessment, how well a learner can perform various relevant tasks or skills. As teachers or program administrators consider the development of any portfolio-based writing assessment program, therefore, they keep in mind the need to look at actual performances; and the need for the performances to reflect the writer whose work is being assessed.

Portfolios: Learner Context Heuristic

1. How many of the multiple contexts for the texts can the assessment acknowledge? How many of those contexts can it accommodate?

2. How extensively can the texts in the portfolio represent the learner? Is there enough text for the learner's identity to be revealed? What do the texts themselves indicate about the learner as a writer? What do the learner's choices about what to include and how to arrange the texts indicate about the learner's values, sense of self, ability to address an audience, academic acculturation, and so on?

3. What evidence do the texts and supporting materials present about the extent to which teachers have influenced the learner's texts or choices? How will that evidence affect judgments about the portfolio? About the writer?

4. To what extent has the assessment itself affected the texts in the portfolio? How have instructions about preparation, communications with teachers, public representations of the assessment, or information that is distributed "on the grapevine" shaped the ways the learner uses the portfolio to address its audience?

5. To what extent is the portfolio a product of the student's learning environment, and to what extent is it the learner's production? Does the richness and variety in the portfolio seem to come from the writer's choices of tasks, or from the richness and variety of the curriculum? Similarly, does the thinness or sameness in the portfolio reflect most on the learner or on the schools through which the learner has progressed?

6. What evidence of the student's home environment does the portfolio present? To what extent does the learner's worldview seem congruent with that of his or her home and family? To what extent is it incongruent? How does the learner position him or herself as an individual? As a writer?

7. What evidence does the portfolio present about the learner's preparation for life after schooling? How have the learner's conceptions about the short- or long-term utility of writing affected the texts in the portfolio?

8. What do the texts in the portfolio reveal about the learner's discourse communities? Do the texts seem to address identifiable communities? Do the texts address more than one community? Do the texts indicate the learner's ability to address different audiences, for different purposes, in different texts?

9. What revelations does the portfolio invite learners to make about socioeconomic class, race or ethnicity, gender, political leanings, and so on? How will readers react to such revelations?

10. To what extent does the portfolio invite and present evidence of the learner's worldview? Does the evidence in the portfolio

indicate that the student has his or her own worldview, or is the student expressing a set of received ideas and values?

Although we are not ready to claim that this list is comprehensive, it does indicate the range of factors that the portfolio incorporates. It is worth emphasizing that in any authentic assessment, the instrument always elicits more than the assessors need in order to make judgments of a limited scope. Portfolios naturally incorporate, to different extents and degrees, far more information about the learner than the readers can use in order to judge competencies in writing. Often, this information will help in making those judgments: Information about rich or limited curriculum may help readers discover how to regard the richness or thinness of the texts. Sometimes, however, the "extra" information may interfere: Readers' preconceptions about members of certain racial or ethnic groups may interfere with their judgments, or learners may present values or beliefs that are abhorrent to readers or attractive to readers, thus potentially sabotaging effective judgments. Thus, thinking about the whole range of what a writer might present in a portfolio helps anticipate potential problems in the situations that portfolios, in fact, do present.

Focus on the Teacher

A key aspect of portfolios when used for assessment (although not necessarily so for portfolios used as purely instructional tools) is that these texts, these collections will eventually be read for the very special purpose of making judgments of writing skill. We have found the act of reading the collection of texts from different times as a complex and multifaceted yet single text to be in many ways the most interesting, if not the most important aspect of portfolio-based writing assessment (Hamp-Lyons & Condon, 1993). In a traditional writing assessment, a timed essay test, the moment of assessment exists outside the confines of a course, and even within a single college writing program essays are read anonymously, with names removed, replaced with numbers, or covered. In other words, the act of assessing writing and the process of teaching or learning writing are seen to be separate and distinct from one another. A portfolio assessment of writing is very different.

Portfolios by their nature reveal a great deal about the writer—particularly when the portfolio contains reflective writing—and so concealing the writer's identity not only makes little sense, it runs counter to the whole ethos of context richness we have stressed throughout this book. Portfolios allow readers to see more of what the writer can do and therefore make a sounder judgment about a writer's needs, level of accomplishment, rate of progress, and so forth. And so, in the environment of portfolio-based writing assessment, involving teachers in assessing their own students' writing—in contrast to the usual dictum against that in holistic assessments—not only enriches the context but connects the processes of teaching and assessing writing in ways that benefit students, teachers, and writing programs alike. In a portfolio assessment program such as described here, portfolio readers are not only reading the portfolio; they are also "reading the writer." Only now, this is not an unsought incursion of interpretive, subjective reading practice—it is a natural part of a holistic process, in which teacher and outside reader(s) share their understanding of their program and its goals and standards; of their own classes and the ways they teach and their students are led to learn; and of the individual learners whose writing is to be weighed and valued in this portfolio reading process: It is a practice for which there are guidelines and expectations of ethical practice, and whose subjectivity and interpretiveness are embraced as essential and valuable elements in good reading and therefore in good judgments.

There are direct and practical benefits, too, of including the student's teacher as a reader. First, students retain the comfort level of knowing at least one of those who will be judging their writing. They can get to know that person. They develop trust in the requirements the teacher lays on them, knowing that at least one reader will fully value the work assigned in the class. The students' motivation for working to improve their writing comes not only from the level of control they have over the writing in the portfolio but from the personal relationship with the teacher as well. Second, the teacher need not fear that the assessment process will undercut his or her classroom efforts. Because the teacher is also a reader and can interact with other teachers or readers, these colleagues can define the assessment process in such a way that it directly supports what they do in their classes. Teachers are directly invested. Thus, they can have more confidence in the assessment and more confidence in the fact that the writing they assign and the processes they teach really do have an impact on a student's outcome. Finally, as we keep stressing, writing programs benefit from constantly involving teachers in conversations about curriculum, assignments, course design, standards, and so on. Providing occasions for these conversations to occur as a natural part of the process of teaching a course means that the program can constantly respond to the needs of the students it serves, of the faculty who teach in it, and of the university at large. And the fact that the authority for passing students through the program or assigning course grades is shared lends greater credence to and creates more confidence in those decisions in the larger university community.

Even in traditional, graded courses in which the classroom teacher is solely responsible for evaluation and grading, the act of reading the students' work as collections instead of as single texts, and right at the point in the term when grades are assigned is significant. The teacher finds him or herself bound up in more than the process of assigning grades; this act of reading and its timing lead to reflection on assignments, sequencing, curriculum, methods, and every element of the context. We have found portfolio assessment of writing particularly beneficial in situations where writing courses are ungraded (pass/fail) or where the portfolio forms the whole basis for the grade: In graded writing courses the scoring or grading of portfolios and the interrelation between portfolio grades and course grades is more problematic and takes a different kind of management and program development, as described in chapter 3. But even in the most constrained of circumstances, one of the great benefits—and challenges— of a portfolio-based assessment is that its outcomes go beyond judgments about individual students' competence to include judgments about the effectiveness of the course in the classroom and in the program as a whole.

Focus on the Assessor

In this chapter so far, the learner context heuristic has focused on the learner's contexts, and led to considerations of the multiple influences that affect and shape the texts the learner places in a portfolio. The assessor context heuristic which follows, based around the seven Cs already introduced, focuses on the other important actors in the dynamic of a portfolio assessment. Without a strong and wholly appropriate form of assessing them, portfolios are nothing more than folders of writing that hold great meaning (we hope) for their authors, but have nothing to say about individual learning, the values of a program, or about what the writer should be told about his or her writing—what course he or she should take next, or what areas he or she should work on independently while moving on to other courses. In classroom-based portfolio assessment, the teacher is the assessor; in college writing programs that use portfolio-based assessments, the assessors again are the teachers themselves. The importance of a reflective and participatory system for working with teachers in the program to ensure they are able to assess portfolios fairly and meaningfully, and for teachers to work together to agree on the structure of the portfolio, the criteria for assessment, and the value to be given to the readings of all concerned, cannot be overstated.

Portfolios: Assessor Context Heuristic

1. *Community.* In what ways does the assessment affect the teaching community in which the assessment occurs? How does

it affect teaching communities outside the context in which the assessment occurs? What role(s) do members of those teaching communities play in the assessment? How do those roles help members of the communities feel invested in the assessment? How does participation in the assessment affect teachers professionally? How does the assessment accommodate teachers' time, energy, remuneration, status?

2. *Criteria.* Are the criteria explicit (written down) or implicit (stemming from readers' knowledge about curriculum and course requirements)? If explicit, are they shared widely among members of the teaching community? Among learners? How are readers using their knowledge about criteria in order to make consistent decisions? Are all criteria weighed equally, or are some more significant than others? Is that difference consistent with the objectives of the assessment? To what degree are the criteria congruent with the goals of the teaching community? Are the criteria fair to the learners? Do they demand performances of a kind or at a level that learners can reasonably be expected to attain?

3. *Control.* In what ways is control shared among teachers, students, administrators? Who controls what aspects of the assessment? Of the portfolios? Of the reading process? Of the outcomes? Is control over the different aspects distributed logically? Are the different constituencies satisfied with the level of control they have? Is control distributed in such a way that the objectives of the assessment are achieved more clearly and easily, or is the specific distribution of control hindering the assessment in any way?

4. *Context.*

   - Needs and goals of all the parties involved in the context. Who are all the parties involved in the context for the assessment? What are their needs? What are their goals? How do their needs and goals differ? How can the assessment address as many of those needs and goals as possible? What other contexts—and what other parties—does the assessment affect? How will they express their needs and goals? To what extent can the assessment accommodate their needs and goals?

   - Restrictions on the context. In what ways is the assessment constrained? What administrative, financial, logistical, or pedagogical limitations exist? How will the assessment respond to those limitations? Do any of the limitations act as a bar to the assessment? How do the constraints limit the possibilities for the assessment? How do the restrictions impinge on the ability to obtain the necessary judgments? What can or will be done about the constraints?

5. *Consensus.* Who needs to play a part in the consensus process? Who will lead it? How extensive will it be? What specific aspects or characteristics of the assessment will it address? In what order? Which consensuses must occur before the assessment begins (e.g., contents of the portfolio, goals and objectives of the assessment)? Which consensuses are ongoing, as part of the assessment process (e.g., criteria, timing, reading process)? How satisfied are the different parties with the level of input they have into the necessary consensuses? How responsive are the consensuses and the consensus-building process to the teaching communities, the learners, and the multiple contexts which the assessment affects?

6. *Care.* What steps are being taken to assure that judgments are sound? Who will assure reliability and validity, and how will he or she do it? What data are available to indicate whether the assessment outcomes are valid—whether, in effect, the assessment has predictive validity? What steps are being taken to maintain the community and its level of consensus(es)? What steps are in place to assure that the reading process itself is reliable, fair, and thorough? What measures will assure that readers actually use the agreed-on criteria? That they read the whole portfolio? That they define the criteria in similar ways? That they apply the criteria in similar ways?

7. *Conversation.* What provisions are in place to foster conversations about portfolios among the readers? Among the teachers? Among learners? Between or among those groups? What are the goals of those conversations? Are those goals consistent with the goals for the assessment? What conversations take place before the portfolios are assembled? What conversations take place after the portfolios are read? What forms will these conversations take? Who will be party to the conversations?

We place great importance on recognizing and valuing the roles of learners and teachers or assessors in portfolio-based writing assessment. This is not only a values-based position, it is also a pragmatic one because we and many others have discovered that portfolio assessments are not very effective when they are built from the top and imposed downward. The impetus may come from above (as when a new writing program director joins a program) but the enthusiasm must come from below, and that happens only when teachers are invested and engaged.

Focus on the Program

Although it may be possible to generate a set of heuristics that would cover the whole expanse of information a program might collect in a portfolio assessment, it is essential that choices made are based on the specific needs of your own program; if they are not, the portfolio assessment will not in the long run be successful. This means that out of the universe of information that one could gather, the person or people planning an assessment must select that information they actually want to gather about the writers they are assessing. This information, then, translates into how many texts of what kinds the portfolio will collect, and it bears on how the portfolio will be judged. Knowing what one wants allows one to decide what to collect, and those two together enable one to think about how to produce the necessary outcomes—placements, scores, rankings, grades, and so on. So the first question is, "What do you want to know?"

- About the learner's writing ability (multiple competencies)?
- About the learner's thinking skills and processes?
- About the learner's text creation processes?
- About the instructional setting(s) in which the texts were produced?
- About the writing program from which or into which the learner is passing?
- About the learner's broader educational history (e.g., courses taken, grade point average, number of credits at time of assessment, native language, etc.)?

As the questions show, program decisions are made not only based on what we want to know about writers, but also on what kinds of information will further our broader literacy and educational goals—and some of the answers will depend on the political and economic imperatives under which we are running our programs. Answering those questions—and other, similar ones that may emerge in the process of designing the assessment—provides the basis for deciding what to collect and what degree of control to maintain over the portfolio's contents. In other words, once one has decided what information to seek, one asks, "What kind of portfolio will provide that information?"

- How many texts will you need in order to learn what you want to learn? What kinds of texts will they be? How long will the individual texts be? How long should the overall portfolio be?
- Should some or all of the writing tasks be specified? How specific should the requirements be with regard to genre? Length? Content?

- How fully do you want or need to sample work done in class, as opposed to work done under the writer's usual constraints of setting, time, and so on?
- What kinds of writing should be required? Who will be allowed to make those decisions?
- Will portfolios contain process work or only product work? How important is evidence of process (e.g., drafts)? Of growth? What kinds of evidence will you need in order to learn about progress and growth?
- What role will reflection and self-assessment play? And which will you elicit: reflection or self-assessment? Both? How?

As already seen, making decisions about portfolio characteristics such as how many texts to collect or whether or how long to delay grading will have repercussions in the design and redesign of other components of the portfolio system. It must be clear by now that no element of the portfolio process or context can stand alone or be decided alone: It is a highly iterative and interactive process. Basically, this iterative, interactive process revolves around a recurring set of questions:

- What tools do you want students to acquire?
- What opportunities can you present that help students acquire those tools?
- How will you know whether students have acquired those tools?

Once the developers have answered the questions about what they want to know and what evidence will provide them with what they want to know, the design elements of the program should be clearer to them. It would be tempting to think that at this stage we have a portfolio-based assessment program—but this is not yet true.

Reflection on the third and final question will reveal the complexities within it. So far the heuristics have enabled us to design the collection of valuable, meaningful portfolios from learners and classes. They have not, however, shown us how to turn those documents, those texts, into meaningful statements about what learners can do and how well, and in what circumstances, they can do it. We have built the front end of our model, but we do not yet have a back end.

In order to build the back end, we need to design a method of actually assessing the portfolios so laboriously and lovingly created through an instructional program, and the method of assessment must be congruent with the values we have designed into the model so far.

READING PORTFOLIOS IN AN ASSESSMENT FRAMEWORK

For composition teachers, the processes of reading portfolios become intermingled with practices of scoring portfolios in particularly interesting and problematic ways. As literacy advocates and scholars we value the texts and the processes of text-making through which our students have gone, and thus we value the evidence of their literate practices highly even when the texts lack some of the polish of "conventional" skilled prose. But as teachers whose art comprises in part the knowledge of the end purpose of instruction in our specialist area, and the ability to help learners understand how far they have come and how far they have to go; and as members of a community of whom accountability is expected, we must put a term on that value. We must find ways to reconcile our selves as readers with our selves as evaluators. We must score or grade the portfolios. When our minds turn to scoring, they turn to what we know about writing assessment practices in nonportfolio circumstances, and thus we think first of holistic scoring and of achieving reliability.

Simply put, there are two ways to achieve reliability in readings of portfolios, and these methods echo the two principal movements in writing instruction: product and process. First, a program may focus on scores—the product of the reading. This kind of program typically uses holistic reading and uses "anchor" samples of previously scored portfolios that have been carefully chosen to represent certain score levels, training readers to read by matching live papers to those samples. If a reader cannot understand why the anchor illustrates a certain level, or if he or she cannot consistently match other samples to the anchors, then he or she is not considered to be a "good" reader and may well be removed—dismissed, or given some other task that does not involve scoring samples. But another approach works in almost the opposite way. Instead of focusing on scores, readers spend time bringing their reading processes into line with each other. They read and discuss samples with an eye toward developing and refining a shared sense of values and criteria for scoring. In other words, this method fosters a reading community in which reliability grows out of the readers' ability to communicate with each other, to grow closer in terms of the ways they approach samples (see Decker, Cooper, & Harrington, 1992; Hamp-Lyons & Reed, 1988).

Which approach is better? It is immediately evident that in the context of single classrooms the issue does not arise—the teacher is all there is. In the context of the writing program, where all the available portfolio readers or judges are class teachers in the program itself, it makes little sense to say to any one teacher: "You are not a 'good' reader of portfolios" and send the teacher to do something else while another teacher scores the portfolios. Furthermore, this would be a breaking of the trust, the implicit contract, that the teacher who has invested so much time with these learners will also be given a voice in the judgments to be made. Thus, in the writing program, too, the "process" approach is the one that has been implicit throughout our description of the characteristics and benefits of portfolio-based writing assessment. Although as we move to wider and wider contexts for portfolio assessment, the questions and processes become more complex and some elements of the seven Cs may be left aside because of some exigencies of the situation, they are always our guide and our goal.

Scoring Portfolios

Because portfolios are complex and varied, both internally and among samples, we can expect them to be more difficult to score. For one thing, "anchor" portfolios less effectively illustrate a particular score level. If the sample is short and rigidly controlled, as it is under strict time limits for the writing, then the anchor method is likely to work because the range of possibilities for what writers can include is limited. However, the longer and more open the sample, the less likely that anchors exist that adequately illustrate each score level. Readers cannot simply look to the major characteristics of anchors; the elements in portfolios vary too much from one to the next. There has so far been little research into the consistency of portfolio scoring using any method, but the reports of the Vermont K-12 portfolio project (Koretz, Stecher-Klein, & McCaffrey, 1994) have suggested that portfolio scoring, as conducted and reported in the traditional psychometric ways accepted for essay tests, is not very reliable, and measures taken to improve reliability not only started to chip away at the edges of the validity of the portfolios as visualized by the teachers who participated in the project, but also failed to improve reliability more than marginally. Koretz et al. described some of the "problems" in the Vermont program: "unconventional and ambiguous delineation of genres . . . the raters were not employees of a testing firm (but) volunteer teachers . . . lack of standardization of tasks" (p. 12). Traditional holistic methods as used by large agencies such as ETS, ACT, and the Rand Corporation (for whom Koretz and his team work), it appears, do not work very well in the portfolio context. At the University of Michigan, the ECB has done much better in achieving formal reliability in its scoring of portfolios, both at entry to the university and at exit from the ECB Writing Practicum. On exit portfolios, using the process described in Condon and Hamp-Lyons (1994), The ECB has achieved reliability—judged as readers' agreement on scores—exceeding .8; thus, the readings can be characterized as consistent and efficient. After 4 years of reading—two pilot studies and 2 years of running a full-scale entry-level portfolio assessment on more than

5,000 students a year, ECB methods have resulted in an overall interrater reliability of .85. Both these results place the reliability of portfolio readings at or above the .8 benchmark for holistic ratings of timed writings. Similarly, in reading exit portfolios at CU-Denver we found that readers almost never disagree about pass/fail decisions (perhaps 1 in 100), and disagreements about grades are rarely more than a single grade point. It is possible, then, to achieve levels of reliability in portfolio scoring that indicate that portfolio-based writing assessment can be at least as fair as, to use White's (1994) equation of reliability with fairness, and, of course, far more valid than now-traditional direct tests of writing that are based on timed writings scored holistically.

Even though we can establish portfolio-based writing assessment as effective and reliable and valid according to commonly used positivist methods, that does not mean that those methods are the best to use in validating these assessments. Moss et al. (1992) suggested an approach to portfolio-based assessment that turns away from formal, traditional methods and instead draws from the emerging tradition of naturalistic inquiry (e.g., Lincoln & Guba, 1985), based especially in the work of Erickson (1986). Their approach involved teacher research to develop "an interpretive framework—a coding scheme" (p. 15) against which to analyze the data, that is, the work in the portfolios. This approach and its goals has much in common with the strategies we discussed for reaching consensus, and it makes explicit, as we have also stressed, the need for accountability, for leaving what is called an "audit trail" (Lincoln & Guba, 1985) so that methods and conclusions can be reviewed by others. Moss et al. developed a framework that is used by the teacher to record the student's work, the role of teacher, student, and others in the making of the piece, the degree to which various features are present or absent; and whether revision increased or diminished the evidence of a feature. Developed for use with eighth grade children, the framework contains such features as vision (something to say), voice (conceptual framework, etc.), development (elaboration, focus, structuring, multiple perspectives, etc.), reader's response (compelling/interesting, accessible, etc.), and sense of the writer (comfort, general self-evaluation, audience awareness, revising, etc.). The teacher uses these frameworks as the raw material for writing of a narrative profile describing the student's achievements and growth as a writer. This methodology is a more developed form of the "portfolio check list" used at CUNY-Hunter (August, Jones, Markstein, Parry, & Smith, 1994) and at CU-Denver.

The process, as Moss et al. (1992) described it, was used by a single teacher in a single classroom, and was integrated into the teacher's usual work cycle; although it did involve additional teacher time, this was not very heavy, and even the final writing of the narrative profiles, informed by so much data, took only about 30 minutes each. The added benefit to learner, parents, teacher, and program are quite significant for a modest commitment of additional effort. Such a program offers considerable promise to a portfolio-based assessment program already taking itself seriously. The development of the components for the framework fits well with the seven Cs: Community, consensus, and conversation are all necessary if a group, such as the teachers in a single writing program, are to create a mutually meaningful framework. Equally, we have stressed shared criteria and standards; and the explicit nature of the framework, once created, and if used in a collaborative structure, should lead to shared understanding of criteria and standards. The shared control we have stressed becomes inevitable when a program agrees to work with such a framework. We have stressed care in all aspects and phases of the development, application, maintenance and validation of the assessment, and the example Moss et al. put forward of the framework shows all these characteristics.

Whether adopting a framework approach such as Moss et al.'s, or the less fully documented (and probably more achievable for most teachers and most programs) approach we describe later, we believe that portfolio assessment, like all performance assessments, must find new ways of satisfying accountability and excellence expectations than the traditional crude measures of interrater reliability and criterion validity.[1] We must learn to understand what we do when we make judgments of writing so that we can document what we have done, how, and why. Thus, we turn away from "objectivity" (if such a thing ever existed) and toward interpretation, toward understanding writers and writing, teachers and teaching, and the processes of coming to share insights about what is to be valued.

To our knowledge, there is no empirical research into the efficacy of the kind of process-oriented, community-oriented approach to portfolio scoring we have both described and advocated. Our own experiences and the reports of colleagues have formed our belief in it, but moving toward a better understanding of what we do, whether it works, and if so why, is high on our research agenda. And this research agenda is not simply a theoretical pursuit of academics: As we discuss in chapter 5, it is imperative that we provide empirical data of kinds that bureaucrats find credible if portfolio-based assessments are to grow and to replace less satisfactory ones. Although face validity should not be discounted, and construct validity is vital at all stages in the portfolio process including the reading process, the assessment must also be, and be shown to be, reliable

---

[1]Criterion validity is the expectation that a test will measure people in the same order or at the same level as other, older tests claimed to be measuring "the same thing."

in ways we can make credible to external agencies. We are not persuaded by Elbow's (1991) argument that validity should be enough. The problem with that argument, it seems to us, is that validity and reliability should not be either-or choices, as Messick (1994) has clearly and powerfully argued. Indeed, they need not be; we can have both, as Michigan's and Miami's assessments have established. Here, then, are some questions to consider in planning the scoring process so that the assessment can both take advantage of the portfolio's greater validity and achieve high reliability as well.

1. Who will score? From what contexts will the readers come? How widely can scoring decisions be shared among stakeholders and still produce reliable judgments? Can scoring include stakeholders from source and destination contexts? Can learners have a voice in scoring? How?

2. What experiences should scorers bring to the work? Should they be teachers? Should they be writing teachers? Should they have taught the courses into which students are being placed? Should they be drawn from a cross section of faculty in the destination context?

3. What sort of training will readers receive? How will reading portfolios differ from their usual reading or grading practices? How will they respond or adapt to the criteria? How will they become invested in the portfolio as an instrument for assessment? How will they respond to each other as their discussions help them create a reading community?

4. How will the reading day proceed? What kind of standardizing session is best? How long should or can it last? How often will it be held? In what spirit will it be conducted? Where will authority be located (i.e., whose judgments about sample portfolios are given greater weight)? Who has control over how readers interpret and apply the criteria, and so on? How many portfolios can readers be expected to score in a day? How long will the day be? How will readers deal with fatigue?

5. Should readings take place in a common location? At a common time? Does controlling the setting for the reading increase or decrease the reliability of readers' decisions?

6. How many readers will read a single portfolio? Why that many? Will some portfolios receive more attention than others? Why?

7. What sort of data will be produced each day? How and how quickly will disagreements surface? How will they be resolved (e.g., by a third reading, a consultation, or some other method)? Will readers be asked to collect data as they read (e.g., about the

contents of the portfolio, the length of the pieces or the portfolio as a whole, the usefulness of a portfolio for standardizing, the idiosyncratic features of a particular portfolio, etc.)?

8. What sorts of data will be produced for each scoring occasion? How will the results from one scoring occasion help increase the efficacy of the next one? How will readers' reactions to criteria, workload, standardizing practices, and reading sessions be collected? How will it be used? To what extent can readers feel that they have input into the scoring process?

Again, these questions cannot be exhaustive because no single set of issues can accommodate the needs of every setting in which portfolios are scored. But they represent a core set of questions, ones that any assessment should deal with in planning the process of scoring portfolios. As a result of thinking through these common concerns, planners in differing contexts will most likely generate questions and answers that speak to their local contexts.

It should be clear that our own response to the questions in Item 1 fits our belief that teachers who are familiar with the students and the program should score the portfolios. If scoring is to have validity, readers need to come from the same context as the portfolios themselves, or at least, a very similar context. The further from the contexts the readers are drawn, the more difficult it will be for them to picture the portfolio program within its instructional setting and to grasp the values the teachers have worked to embody in the display of students' work through the portfolios. This will also have implications for reliability. Although scoring can include stakeholders from source and destination contexts, as more kinds of stakeholders are involved in scoring, in making decisions about the value of portfolios, it becomes harder to produce reliable judgments because there is so much distance for readers to travel in understanding each other, and probably, less time in which the necessary acculturation to the program can be done.

As for the last part of Item 1, although we are not aware of any published work reporting contexts where students have a say in the scoring of their portfolios, we have spoken to individuals who have experimented in that direction, and have done so ourselves in our own classrooms. Most teachers with whom we have talked seem to feel that students who have been well taught in writing courses that value peer critique and workshopping of papers can, in that process, learn to judge their own and their classmates' portfolios rather well. We have found this ourselves, and believe that allowing students' self-assessments of their portfolios to be weighted into their scores, within an ambitious portfolio assessment, is worth seriously considering.

In response to the questions in Item 2, although it is generally agreed that those who read and score portfolios should be teachers, there seems to be little evidence that teachers, even writing teachers, make better judgments than other properly prepared adults. We are accustomed in traditional writing assessment to the view that judgments, especially holistic judgments, are made better by people who are similar to others in their experiences, especially in experiences in the kind of program learners are being assessed from (see, e.g., W. Smith, 1994). But the evidence is quite tentative on this, and we would encourage experimentation with other significant groups of stakeholders as portfolio readers. For instance, Washington State University's Junior Portfolio assessment successfully uses faculty from disciplines across the university as judges of the portfolios. In doing so, the writing program forges stronger links with other departments and with the faculty at large; and writing teachers who interact with these faculty readers are better able to understand the expectations in courses in other disciplines.

We deal extensively with questions of portfolio reading within the assessment context discussed here, with questions of criteria and approaches to scoring, suggesting—if not answers—indicators that help answer the questions just raised. These questions (like all questions about the use of portfolios) are complex and resist simple answers; but the general principle is that all decisions we make about these things are significant.

Disagreements about the worth of specific portfolios will either emerge through data-analysis processes, if the program uses traditional forms of holistic or multiple-trait scoring with multiple readers; or through the conversation between teacher-readers if the program uses a more collegial and collaborative form in which agreement and understanding are reached discursively. Whether the program uses third readings, consultations, or some other method to decide on the small number of cases where differences between readers have a pass/fail effect depends on the basis of the program as a whole. As portfolio programs get larger, it becomes inevitable that more formal processes of reading portfolios and noting scores are put into place, and together with those formal processes a formal decision process for portfolios about which there is substantial disagreement will arise. We have found an "appeals committee" of three to four most experienced teacher-readers to be a good group to make such decisions.

When a portfolio-based assessment program is new, readers are likely to be asked to collect data about things like the contents of the portfolio, the length of the pieces or the portfolio as a whole, in order to help build up the understanding in the members of the team about the significant elements in a portfolio and in a decision about the "worth" of a portfolio. As the program and its members mature, such data gathering becomes less essential, and may be done occasionally in order to, for example, find new portfolios that could be useful for training sessions for those new to the system, and for refresher training for experienced readers, in which it is useful to have some more idiosyncratic portfolios that will generate discussion of newly emerging issues.

Answers to questions of what sorts of data should be produced for each scoring occasion will depend on the oversight and accountability processes that are in place in a particular context. But whatever approach is used, clearly a complete record of what scores were given to each portfolio, and the bases for those scores, must be made. This is the data base from which all accountability-driven reporting will be derived. Furthermore, the results from one scoring occasion cannot help increase the efficacy of future readings unless they are fully documented and carefully considered after portfolio readings have taken place. The team, or certain senior team members, need to make the time to look back over the processes used, the decisions, made, and consider what has been learned from it. What unusual portfolios were seen? What problems did they lead to? How were these problems resolved, and were the resolutions satisfactory to portfolio readers, the class teacher, and the student concerned? If not, why not? Reflection on issues like these, on the portfolio assessment experience in all its aspects, will lead to better understanding all-round and to thoughtful improvements for next time.

Developing Criteria: Some Guidelines For Judging Portfolios As "Texts"

Portfolios, at base, are collections of texts selected from the writer's corpus for a particular purpose. If the writer understands the principles of selection, then the portfolio itself will emerge as a text, as a whole greater than the sum of its parts. In addition, the writer who understands the reasons behind the selection is more likely to achieve his goal—a high placement, acceptance into a particular course or program, a job, and so on. If the writer has no access to the principles of selection, or if they are not presented clearly, then the portfolio is less likely to create a whole, to become, in effect, a single text. In this event, the writer is less likely to achieve his or her goal. The process a writer uses for a particular selection begins to take shape as he or she studies the criteria for judging the portfolio. Once a writer has enough information about the criteria for judgment and some idea of the person or people making the judgments a portfolio can be assembled that is more likely to meet the writer's own and the assessors' needs. Thus, developing criteria is a significant part of implementing an assessment, and sharing the criteria with the writers is vital if the portfolio is to be an occasion for learning.

Some of the decisions in developing criteria can be made by whoever is in charge of the assessment; some will come from the institutional setting; most will come as the result of negotiated consensuses among the teacher or reader community carrying out the assessment. The major questions to be considered in designing criteria are as follows:

1. To what results will the evaluation of writing lead? Why are those results appropriate to the assessment? To the learners? To the teachers? For the course, program, or institution? The main kinds of results and ways of reporting them are:

   - pass/fail
   - credit/no credit
   - acceptance/rejection
   - grade on a scale
   - rating on a scale
   - direct placement into a course.

2. Where do the criteria and standards come from? Which participants have input into developing criteria? Are the criteria open to revision? How often, and through what process(es)? Expectations as represented by criteria and standards may be imposed by the context (e.g., through an elaboration of a common grading scheme, a set of program-wide requirements, or institutional decisions about WAC competency, etc.); they may be derived from a careful consideration of the dimensions of the texts in the portfolios being assessed.

3. Who makes the judgments? What qualifications and experiences will the readers need? How inclusive of the community can the reader group be? What will readers learn by assessing portfolios?

4. Should readers judge individual texts within the portfolios? If so, how will the separate judgments be combined into a judgment of the portfolio as a whole? If readers are encouraged to read holistically, how will they avoid comparing or contrasting individual texts?

5. What part do students' reflections and self-assessments that appear in the portfolio play formally in decisions about the 'worth' of the portfolio? How heavily will readers rely on those statements? Can or should learners have a significant voice in their own assessments?

As the discussion of the CU-Denver portfolio criteria (in chapter 3) revealed, we believe that complex instruments such as portfolios need to be judged in ways that acknowledge the presence within them of more than one dimension of writing, perhaps even of more than one quality of writing;

also, they need to be judged in ways that enable readers (and external agencies later) to see them as narrative macrostructures, as stories about the writer's progress and not a snapshot. Criteria for valuing portfolios will include not only text features; they will expand to include not only awareness of processes (invention, revision, etc.) but also dimensions of thinking, of working with others, of self-reflection, and perhaps others. When judgments of portfolios are based in such complex criteria, we should not expect that those judgments can be faithfully reported as a single number; even when our more complex criteria and scores must be reduced to the simplistic level of a single score for some purpose (e.g., for purposes of assigning a grade or making a graduation decision), we must always remember, and assert to those others who demand the reduction, that in such a reduction most of the valuable data is lost.

In portfolio-based assessment there are many advantages to a multiple-trait system where traits would be tied to text types, stages of the draft, purposes for writing, and so on (Hamp-Lyons, 1991-1992, 1991). Although there are advantages, too, for such a scoring instrument for timed essay tests, this more complex approach comes into its own when scoring more complex products, such as portfolios. The process of uncovering the criteria that exist within a program helps the program understand itself; the process of constructing criteria in a program that has never had a shared set of values is even more important; the building of a set of criteria that every teacher in the program can become invested in is a lengthy but rewarding process, feeding not only into the assessment but into the whole educational community. This process, following the seven Cs, can play the central role in helping faculty or TAs to identify the key concerns about student writing, to appreciate the stumbling blocks to making encompassing judgments of all the writing that the tremendous diversity of writers will bring (e.g., in noting the grammatical weaknesses of some ESL writers but noting too the strength in ideas and critical thinking their writing reveals); and it will also lead naturally into the even more difficult process of arriving at shared standards for judging writing. In what follows we provide two heuristics for generating criteria. The first was developed at CU-Denver as a heuristic for first-year composition teachers to use as they met during the term to develop the criteria they would use to grade students' portfolios and to provide feedback at the end of the term (see Table 4.1). The second, developed at the University of Michigan for the first pilot year of its entry-level portfolio assessment, emerged from a 2-day intensive workshop involving teachers of first-year composition from several programs (Figure 4.2).

In this first heuristic, Hamp-Lyons provided the teachers in her program with a set of questions intended to guide their collaborative development of criteria for grading. In CU-Denver's exit assessment program, the outside readers actually grade the portfolios, and they

Table 4.1. CU-Denver Heuristic for Developing Criteria.

1. Range of writing

   Is there evidence of a range of writing—genres, audiences, purposes? Students may be better at some kinds of writing than others, but there should be signs that they are willing to engage multiple genres and tasks of different levels of difficulty. How adaptable are they?

2. Development of writer's abilities

   Is there evidence in the portfolio, through early and late papers, and through drafts of the same paper, that the writer has been developing? Can you determine in what areas the writer has developed? What areas are as problematic now as in the beginning? Is revision substantive or on the surface?

3. Engagement with ideas and issues

   Is the writer tackling "important" material (whether in her or his personal life or in the public forum)? Can you see signs of writing as discovery—about self and the world? Or, is the writer choosing subjects that are well rehearsed by others, dealing with them in a tired way? What are the signs of the writer's excitement, about writing and about thinking?

4. Textual excellence

   Is the writer presenting final versions that meet your expectations for published excellence—no typos, good grammar, etc., and documents that look good collected together into an attractive portfolio binder?

5. Self-reflection

   How insightful can the writer be about her or his own writing products and processes? Has the writer set worthwhile and realistic goals, both for this course and for the future? In discussing the texts in the portfolio, are there signs that the writer has been able to self-evaluate her or his own writing? Is the context for each text clear? Is the portfolio as a whole embedded within a self-presentation of the writer that is conveyed so the reader can respond with that skilled subjectivity of a composition teacher-scholar that is what we can best offer to every writer?

---

provide written feedback to the students. In that context, teachers have a high investment in developing criteria that work and that are fair to each others' students. Thus, the list of questions is only the beginning of the process.

Figure 4.2. Dimensions for assessing portfolios

The second heuristic, developed at Michigan, was aiso a collaborative document. A group of 11 composition teachers from several departments and programs met to read a number of portfolios and find a way to describe the writing in them. What emerged by the second day was a set of dimensions of writing that readers could use in thinking about the degree of accomplishment a portfolio demonstrated. Participants were asked to read a set of portfolios and to record the factors they noticed as they read, without worrying too much about whether the factor was positive or negative, whether it presented evidence of high achievement or profound need. The outcome was a set of dimensions, neutral descriptive words and phrases that readers could use as they thought about the degree of accomplishment a particular writer had achieved. These dimensions provided a framework that allowed readers freedom to weigh their decisions in the light of their own experience as writing teachers, and it assured that we would meet our goals for high reliability. Using these dimensions, readers were able to achieve reliability at least as great as that in the better instantiations of holistic scoring. In later years, the dimensions have evolved into more context-specific scoring guides, so the dimensions have allowed the Michigan program to develop even more precise criteria, on which readers experience even greater reliability. These dimensions have also proven useful in working with faculty and teaching assistants in Michigan's WAC program as they develop criteria for judging the texts learners produce in those classes. All in all, then, this chart of dimensions of writing in portfolios has proven sufficiently versatile to be offered here as a useful starting point for developing criteria for a variety of local contexts. Figure 4.2 can best be used as a starting point, as a heuristic that ensures coverage of the various factors teachers or assessors weigh in their readings. Local readers will need to negotiate which dimensions they will attend to, as well as the definitions of each dimension, and they will need to decide how heavily to weigh each one.

Although these two heuristics grew out of different programs, for different assessments that answered differing needs, they represent the kinds of thinking that goes into developing criteria, and we believe they are readily adaptable for use in a wide variety of programs and contexts. Their value for planning lies in their thoroughness within their own contexts, rather than in their applicability to all contexts. We offer them here as examples of how two different programs developed criteria for the most frequent applications—exit assessment and entry assessment.

The process of developing criteria is inextricably bound up with the process of scoring portfolios. We approach portfolios with some expectations in mind, so with some criteria already partially developed, but we continue to develop our criteria as the scoring process happens and, in particular, between scoring cycles. What we learn from one scoring session of necessity feeds into the next session, whether consciously or deliberately, or not. Even in the most informal and disorganized of assessments, someone involved in the first session learned something that is carried over into the second session. The better systems, of course, count on this process, create opportunities for the accumulation of knowledge and experience to occur and ways of incorporating that knowledge into the scoring criteria and into the reading and scoring process. Performance assessments by their nature lead to a bottom-up approach to the development of criteria and the setting of standards, as opposed to a top-down model, because the obvious place for criteria and standards to be derived is from performances themselves. As more performances are seen, and as the range of performances and readers' responses to them are better understood, criteria become clearer and a sense of required standards grows. Actual performances on tasks such as creating a text from idea to draft to formal structure to polished result differ to a greater extent than answers on a multiple-choice test or time-limited responses to a rigidly controlled topic can. This means that in performance assessment the criteria and scoring processes must remain flexible, must preserve the ability to respond to the work learners have done. Thus, although the criteria and scoring practices inculcate as well as represent the values of the reading-scoring community—which we call the *destination context*—they must remain open to input from the community of learners too, as well as from the goals and objectives in the source context—the learning site where the texts originated—as expressed in the texts collected in portfolios. This responsiveness ensures that the portfolio assessment retains construct validity, and it preserves the portfolio's greatest real-world advantage: very high face validity.

Setting Standards For Portfolio Scores

In the end, it will always come down to standards. And here is where many composition teachers feel most uncomfortable: Teaching composition is a complex activity, and judgment or grading involves the clear articulation of the elements to be factored into those grades or those judgments. Every composition teacher has to decide what is to be weighed, and what weighs most heavily. We have to think about effort, progress, "distance" between entry point and exit point. We have to think about absolute writing quality (i.e., on a fixed yardstick called "ability in writing," which is general and not context-dependent, where is an individual placed?). In large-scale portfolio assessment the problems are fewer, because individual writers are not known to portfolio judges or scorers, and there are no obstacles to the application of a fixed yardstick, an absolute measure of writing quality. But this simplicity does not necessarily lead to the most appropriate judgments for individual writers. When teachers are directly involved with making judgments about their own students' writing, things are not so simple. Teachers know things about the writers in their classes that prevent "objective" judgment. They know to what extent a portfolio is the result of "assisted performance" (Poole & Patthey-Chavez, 1994); they know how much the student labored over a modest text; they know how much of the student's "growth" is truly visible in the portfolio collection. It might seem necessary to tell portfolio raters that scores should be assigned purely on the basis of what is visible in the portfolio. But we know that human judgments do not work that way. Our problem-solving capacities work to pull in all data seen as relevant, and for teachers that means a great deal of other "stuff" about the learner and the context. A portfolio-based assessment program that has followed principles such as those we have suggested throughout this book consists of a complex mix of available evidence and of criteria to apply to that evidence, and has the advantage that it becomes unnecessary to apply one single, absolute standard. Multiple evidence, multiple criteria, these produce multiple judgments, and so each teacher or reader can look carefully at any portfolio for the strength or weakness of the evidence on one particular criterion and make a judgment (or a statement, if that is the preferred approach) without prejudice to any other evidence or any other judgment. Readers can build up a portrait of the writer from the portfolio, which can play its part in bureaucratic decisions (such as pass/fail or placement in a particular program or level), but need never make a direct pass/fail or "gatekeeping" decision. Such decisions emerge from the interplay of strength and weakness in the multiple aspects of the portfolio, and they allow the complex mix of elements that work in the rater's mind full play. Among those elements, however, we insist that "absolute writing quality" in its various manifestations must play a significant part. Perhaps the most important reason for this is one we return to in chapter 5: the role played in decisions about persons and programs by higher authorities, and the need to be fully accountable to those authorities for the decisions we make.

The Standards for ESL Writers

In portfolio writing assessments at any college where there is a mixed student population (the norm these days), issues of how to judge ESL writing will come up and must be centrally addressed. In discussing portfolio criteria and standards, many teachers have problems understanding what an ESL student needs to be able to do to pass a level, versus how much the student can be expected to do in a single semester, and whether the expectations should be different for ESL students. The general consensus among teachers, who are sensitized to issues of ESL and other minority writing, is that the expectations should be the same, but that certain perceptions among portfolio readers need to be revised. For example, teachers may respond negatively to fossilized linguistic errors in portfolios just as they do in timed essays. In discussing the ESL writers in our own classes in the general portfolio meetings and in the meetings of portfolio teams, we must take opportunities to talk about how significant those problems are in comparison to the level of ideas, of ability to provide appropriate support for ideas, of macrostructural control, and so on. Because useful discussion about portfolios necessitates sharing a good deal of contextual information such as the kinds of assignments given, the writing skills taught and practiced, the role of reading in the course, the challenges posed as stimuli to writing, and so on, in the context of portfolio-based writing assessment within a writing program teachers have a lot of opportunities to think about the special needs and problems of ESL students. Every question teachers raise about how to respond to an ESL portfolio strengthens their own and each other's skills in looking at ESL writing. In most composition programs, where there are only a small number of ESL students and only maybe 3 or 4 ESL trained teachers out of 30, that sharing of skills and knowledge is very important.

Administering Portfolio Assessment: Some Concerns

A final set of context-specific concerns relate to how the portfolio assessment fits into its local context, and, in turn, what standing the writing program that houses the assessment enjoys within the institution. The overall status of the writing program, including the status of its faculty and its budgetary independence, determines, to a great extent, how venturesome the assessment can be, and how large a role it can play within its institutional context. Where a composition program exists within a multifaceted English Department, as is the case at CU-Denver, then the assessment is likely to find itself limited to the context of the first-year composition requirement, as the assessment at CU-Denver did until a larger "core competencies" assessment was mandated. But when assessment is the responsibility of an independent unit, one that reports to a dean, rather than to a department chair, as was the case at Michigan from 1977 until 1996, when the English Department absorbed the ECB, and at Washington State University, then the assessment can have an impact that spans departments and programs and speaks to the curriculum of an entire college or university. These administrative concerns are hardly academic: They have very real consequences. So asking questions about the status of the enterprise within its home institution is a practical necessity.

In order to look at the status of portfolios within the political climate of a particular campus, we might begin with a consideration of who teaches writing. We see the key elements of a professional writing program as:

- A professional faculty—the existence of a strong core of trained and well-qualified composition specialists, either on tenure lines or holding secure contracts with a fair salary and full benefits.
- A strong support program for teaching assistants—including courses in composition theory and pedagogy free of tuition charges; paid apprenticeship in classrooms before being asked to teach and thorough mentoring once they begin teaching a section of their own; an adequate stipend and benefits while teaching.
- A professional, tenured or tenure-line writing program administrator (or several such who divide the duties among them) who receives appropriate release time, salary comparable to other faculty of the same rank, and whose research is expected to be in areas relevant

to her or his practical and scholarly interest in composition pedagogy and theory.

Where these characteristics exist, the writing program is more likely to enjoy respect within its institution, more likely to enjoy a certain amount of room for the kind of academic entrepreneurship that makes for an effective, long-term portfolio assessment. Or, if the program does not enjoy that kind of respect, at least it enjoys the kind of permanence that will allow a complex endeavor such as portfolio-based writing assessment to evolve and to demonstrate its effects on students, teachers, and the writing program.

What if these qualities do not exist? In that case, whoever is in charge of developing the assessment needs to make certain that institutional support exists for the program and for the teachers who work within it. A few questions are crucial:

- Who pays for portfolios to be administered? Is that budget secure? Have provisions been made for that budget to grow with the assessment?
- Is it reasonable to ask composition instructors to spend the extra time portfolio assessment requires without paying them extra? If not, then how will they be compensated for the extra work?
- If composition instructors will have to spend extra time without extra compensation, then will the same conditions apply for tenure line faculty, full time instructors, part time instructors, teaching assistants? If not, then how will the work be distributed in an equitable manner?

Basically, some administrative arrangements have to be in place to account for the differences portfolios make in workload and in the timing of the workload. In some instances—program portfolios at exit from first-year composition, for example—the portfolio may not create extra work, but it may relocate that work so that grading is concentrated at the end of the term. In that case, the institution may not have to provide extra compensation, but the writing program administrator may need to coordinate the reallocation of time. If, for example, these courses are staffed primarily by graduate students, then moving all grading to the end of the term, when their own major papers are likely to be due, may require coordinating the timing of the assessment with the timing of requirements in courses the graduate students are taking. Whatever the context, if the assessment is to have a significant impact—make a significant difference in students' learning, contribute to the professional development of its faculty, provide information for improving curriculum, and so forth—then the assessment has to have a stable institutional space, and that space must be secure over time.

CONTEXT-SPECIFIC DESIGN FACTORS THAT OVERLAY GENERAL HEURISTICS

So far, this chapter has focused on the general issues that affect the success of a portfolio-based writing assessment. From here, we develop a model for thinking about specific contexts. Here, too, we cannot expect to provide a description for every situation; instead, we think we can provide a model that individuals can use in planning their own assessments, whether for individual courses, for writing programs, for writing across the curriculum, or for cross-institutional contexts. In developing such a model, we have identified four dimensions for teachers or assessors that we believe account for most, if not all portfolio assessment contexts. In developing these dimensions, we proceed on the assumption that the teachers or the assessors (and in many contexts the two categories describe the same set of people) determine who controls the various dimensions of the assessment. These teachers or assessors determine who can assemble a portfolio, for example, and decide how much control students will have over it, how much input learners and others outside the assessment program itself can have. Each decision represents a point along a dimension, and those points, taken together, account for the various elements of the assessment in a given context. Of course, these dimensions exist in tandem with the decisions implied in the heuristics developed earlier in this chapter. The dimensions simply provide a framework within which we can see the relationships among those other decisions. Each dimension, then, represents a range.

Context-Specific Dimensions

The dimensions are as follows:

- *Access:* Who can submit a sample for judgment? The assessment, on one end, could be open for anyone, as in a portfolio-based writing contest or an optional certification in writing. Learners would not be required to enter the contest or seek the certification, but choosing to do so means that they submit a portfolio for judgment. At the other end of this range, the submission of a portfolio would be limited to a certain set of students, all of whom would have to prepare a portfolio for judgment: Students in a class that required a portfolio, for example.

- *Assessing:* Who actually makes the assessment of portfolios? At one end of the scale, the only assessment would be a self-assessment. At the other end, the assessment would be made by people whose relationship to the students and their texts is solely one of authority.
- *Control Over Portfolios' Contents:* At one end of the scale, students might have absolute control over what texts go into their portfolios. At the other end, teachers or assessors would lay down rigid, specific requirements for a portfolio's contents.
- *Control Over Context in Which Portfolios Are Prepared:* At one end of the scale, the teachers or assessors have absolute control over the context in which students prepare their portfolios. A classroom portfolio that could only contain writings from that class, for example, allows the teachers or assessor total control over the context. The writing contest or the optional certification present situations in which the assessors have little or no control over the context within which the texts were developed.

Taken all together, we might represent these dimensions as a chart, similar to that shown in Figure 4.3.

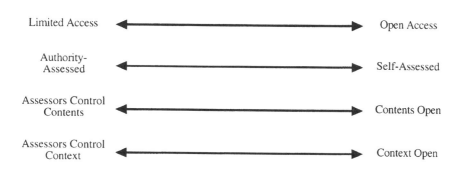

Figure 4.3. Dimensions for teachers or assessors

We can use this figure to develop models of various possibilities. Each context for portfolio assessment, with all its variations, can appear on the chart as a graph of points along the dimensions.

Classroom Portfolios

The first context, the classroom portfolio, presents a number of possible variations, as we can see if we represent, on the graph in Figure 4.4, the characteristics of three different classroom portfolios, A, B, and C.

Teachers who ask themselves how their portfolio assessment will proceed might first ask themselves how their classes would look on the chart. In all three classrooms—and for all classroom portfolios, probably—the ability to assemble a portfolio and have it assessed is predicated on membership in the class—limited access.

In Classroom A—unfortunately, typical of many classroom portfolio assessments—the teacher or assessor controls all other dimensions as well, performing all the assessment, specifying which texts can go into the portfolio, and limiting the contents to texts produced in that class. This level of control diminishes most of the characteristics of the portfolio. Collection is present only to the extent that the teacher specifies multiple texts. Range is limited, too, by the teacher's specifications, as well as by the simple fact that all the texts must come from the one class because the teachers' control over the context from which the texts are drawn is complete. Perhaps most significant, however, is the severe

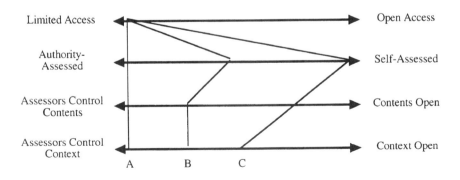

**Figure 4.4. Dimensions for teachers or assessors
of classroom portfolios**

limitations on selection—a limitation that takes away student-centered control to a large extent and that limits the usefulness of reflection or self-assessment by placing close constraints on the texts on which the student can reflect and that he or she might self-assess. A class that operates under the teacher's total control markedly diminishes all the characteristics of the portfolio, but portfolio assessment may still benefit the class more than other forms of evaluation can. Again, seen in the examination of portfolio theory and writing theory in chapter 2, portfolio assessment will support this kind of class, and this kind of class portfolio may actually serve the teacher well by providing students with at least some sense of control over their own fates, some ability to take responsibility for their own learning. Classes B and C open the process by allowing learners to self-assess to varying degrees and by opening the portfolio to texts from other classes. Giving up absolute control over the context, in these cases, also increases range, and that, in turn, places the broader context in which students learn about writing before the teacher or assessor. Increasing range in this way also implicitly teaches that writing is not learned in only one class: Writers learn to write by writing for a variety of purposes, for a variety of audiences, on a variety of occasions. That lesson alone justifies opening the portfolio to texts from places other than the single class being assessed. The graph, then, allows teachers to plot the various kinds of class they might have—at least in terms of sharing authority—and plotting the kind of class helps think about how the portfolio's characteristics will apply in a given instance.

Program Portfolios

The same dynamic applies to the program portfolio—portfolios collected in multiple sections of a single class and assessed collaboratively by the faculty teaching those classes. Again, Figure 4.5 examines the possibilities for portfolio assessment within a given program.

Here, as in the classroom portfolio, we see that the degree of control a program asserts over the learner—the degree to which authority remains vested in teachers and administrators—affects the way the portfolio assessment works. Again, we begin with the most constrained portfolio—Program A. In program portfolios, as in classroom portfolios, the set of learners being assessed is closed, since only students enrolled in the course can submit a portfolio. In Program A, teachers share no authority with students, but they cannot absolutely control the contents of the portfolios they will read, nor can they fully control the contexts under which the portfolios will be prepared. Because teachers will read portfolios prepared in their colleagues' classes, they will need to accommodate differences, to recognize that a variety of tasks may fulfill

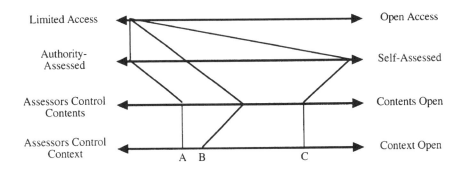

Figure 4.5. Dimensions for teachers or assessors of program portfolios

the common objectives shared by all the sections. Those in charge of Program A can use the graph to discover the areas in which they need to focus efforts to develop shared consensuses. If a teacher from one class holds all the portfolios he or she reads to a single standard (his or her own), then the teacher will automatically favor one group of students (his or her own) over other groups (his or her colleagues'). The teacher's readings are also likely to be divergent from those of his or her colleagues, if they are allowing for differences among texts and contexts, a divergence that will harm the assessment as a whole by making it less reliable. This model is likely to arise when relatively inexperienced instructors are used, because less experienced and less knowledgeable teachers are less able to understand the variety of valid perspectives that exist, and more likely to want to hold tight to their own sense of their knowledge, power, and status of being "right" in the classroom. Because of its context (in using master's-level graduate students) CU-Denver is always struggling to escape from this model.

Portfolio B in Figure 4.5 approximates the configuration of the exit assessment from Writing Practicum at the University of Michigan's ECB, before fall 1997. Here, readers credited learners' reflective self-assessments, and most sections moved students through a process of whole-portfolio peer review and self-assessment, so students had some impact on the actual assessment. In addition, for a variety of pedagogically sound reasons, teachers allowed students to bring into the Writing Practicum texts prepared for other classes, so the portfolios incorporated writing assigned by a teacher outside the program. Thus, the teacher had less control over the context in which that paper was prepared (these papers also went through a revision process within the practicum, however, so that surrender of contextual control was not absolute). This arrangement of teacher or assessor dimensions allowed the writing course to affect more of the scope of a student's writing than it could have if all the texts in the portfolio came strictly from the assignments made in the practicum. The measure of control the practicum instructor surrendered to the student, then, resulted in heightened attention to more writing because the students completed all practicum assignments, as well as having the option to bring into that context a piece of writing in which they were also highly invested.

The weighing process implicit in this distribution of control along the dimensions is the key to understanding not only how the dimensions work as a descriptive tool, but also how the distribution of control affects the exit assessment. Sharing authority with students invests them more highly in their own learning, and it increases their confidence in the fairness and openness of the class. Giving students permission to include writing from other courses also helps them assume responsibility for their own learning. In effect, this provision gives the students a measure of control over their own curriculum, and it allows them to direct their energies toward their own priorities, which include performing well in classes other than the writing class. Finally, the ability to include writing from other classes broadens the focus of the endeavor of learning to write. This shared control encourages students to think of writing as a cross-curricular tool, as an intellectual activity that they practice—and learn about—as a result of opportunities to write, instead of only in writing classes.

Describing a class along these dimensions of teacher or assessor control speaks to portfolio characteristics as well because it affects the range of texts available for the portfolio, and it increases student-centered control over selection. It also broadens the scope of the students' reflection and self-assessment so that they think about writing more as a cross-curricular learning activity, rather than merely as the work they are doing for a single class. Including texts from other classes probably also extends the parameters along which the writing teachers can assess students' progress. As can be seen by comparing Class A with Class B, even a simple action such as opening the portfolio to texts from other classes alters the portfolio, the scoring dynamics, and the locus of authority for the entire assessment. Thus, thinking carefully about the structure of the class or program helps plan more thoroughly and usefully for the assessment.

Program C presents another possibility, a hypothetical writing program in which self-assessment dominates and in which students import all their texts from other classes. Such classes would have no assignments of their own; instead, teachers would assist students in preparing texts for other classes, and a selection of those texts would make up the portfolio. Although few programs would be this open, the configuration is possible, and we know teachers who incorporate one or more of these dimensions, for sound pedagogical reasons and with good results. We present the hypothetical example because discussing such an avant garde program helps demonstrate the fact that portfolios accommodate any context, any pedagogy, any theory—and that thinking about context, pedagogy, and theory beforehand helps make both the program and the assessment more effective.

In Program C, range would be a primary characteristic because students would bring into their classes—and their portfolios—texts from a wide variety of settings. The advantages are clear: In reading each others' texts and portfolios, students gain exposure to a much wider range of assignments and responses than they can glean from their individual experiences; and students are more likely to see their writing as "real" than they will if they work solely on the assignments a writing teacher sets for them. In addition, the Program C portfolio would be context rich, in the sense that it would bring together the student's experiences of an entire semester. Selection and reflection and self-assessment would, of course, be heightened because transferring control entirely to the student creates a situation in which those characteristics are as central and meaningful as possible.

Reviewing these three program situations reveals how the dynamics of portfolio assessment, as well as the portfolios themselves, differ from one context to another, and helps show how extensively a portfolio assessment can affect its entire context. Planning for the assessment involves reconceiving the class itself, or the program's goals and objectives, in order to decide what to include in the portfolio, how closely to specify the texts, how heavily to control the context, or to what extent teachers will exercise their authority over judgments. If portfolio assessment is to be effective at all, those who practice it cannot merely stick one into a convenient spot; instead, they must take account of learners' experiences before and after that spot, and they must exercise whatever control they have in order to make the experience leading up to the portfolio, as well as the experience of compiling the portfolio, as educational as possible.

WAC Portfolios

Thinking about the WAC portfolio in terms of where the texts will come from and who will assess them links the political considerations embedded in an institution's WAC program with the practical and logistical considerations underlying the portfolio assessment. Although any performance assessment should emerge from the learning needs of the population being evaluated, the planning process nevertheless must consider political and practical constraints. WAC portfolio assessors, for example, necessarily preside over a system that has more open access than the classroom or program portfolio. Although they can limit access to those students who have satisfied certain preliminary requirements—first-year composition, junior standing, completion of a writing-intensive course, and so on—these requirements will necessarily be few because the greater the number of requirements, the more difficult it will be for students to complete the requirements in a timely manner. Portfolios A, B, and C, in Figure 4.6, demonstrate the difference in access that, for example, requiring that some texts be produced in a certain class or set of classes (A) and simply allowing the texts to come from any class in which the student may have been assigned writing. The difference may be slight, but it affects range and collection because limiting the sources for texts limits range, and specifying some of the items in the portfolio constrains some of the advantages that accompany collection. Similarly, the decision in Portfolio A to open access means that control over the context in which texts are produced is also shared, even in a case like Portfolio A, where portfolios are judged solely by authorities and where the assessing authorities completely specify the texts that will go into the portfolios.

In Figure 4.6, WAC Portfolio A focuses control in the hands of a central assessing authority—perhaps a campuswide writing program, perhaps a campuswide testing office. The model is one in which writing produced in a variety of settings is gathered for and assessed by some agency that can be invested with the expertise for making the necessary judgments. That agency, then, can do more or less as it pleases, as long as its actions are endorsed by the central administration or the faculty at large, depending on the institution.

Given such a setting, Portfolio B—which resembles the Junior Portfolio in effect at Washington State University—actually seems the more likely scenario. Texts can come from anywhere within a student's college experience; students have some input into the assessment (i.e., their self-assessments figure) into the decision directly or indirectly; some of the portfolio's contents are specified, in the interests of comparison, whereas the rest are left open for students to select; and control over the contexts within which texts are prepared is limited only by the range of

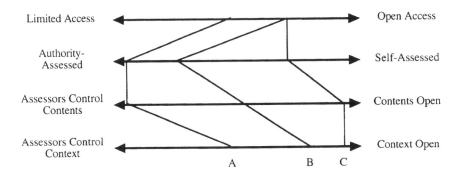

**Figure 4.6. Dimensions for teachers or assessors of
WAC portfolios**

contexts in the institution's classes. This portfolio offers enough range and collection for selection, reflection and self-assessment, and student-centered control to be meaningful, and it allows sufficient specificity for assessors to focus on what they want to learn, while providing enough flexibility for students to be able to show developments that are important to them. On balance, Portfolio B places the characteristics of the portfolio in action in ways that provide a tool for assessment that students can invest in as well; thus, it serves both the institution's and the learners' needs.

Portfolio C represents an even more wide open assessment that is, nevertheless, potentially powerful in its promotion of learning. Students submit portfolios that are assessed by themselves and their peers, rather than by teachers or other assessors, and students themselves determine what texts to include in the portfolio. In certain special circumstances, this combination would so invest learners in the characteristics of selection, self-assessment, and student-centered control that the system would be worthwhile because of the way it would encourage students to take charge of their own learning and to become invested in themselves as writers. Again, Portfolio C is a kind of avant garde example, provided to show that portfolio assessment can support even the most experimental of goals, just as, in Portfolio A, it supports fairly standard objectives. Thinking at once about the context and about the goals and objectives of the assessment provides the opportunity to create an assessment that serves multiple needs, and it increases the likelihood of tapping into the ancillary benefits described in chapter 3.

Cross-Institutional Portfolios

Portfolio assessments that cross or span institutional boundaries are sufficiently rare that it is perhaps wise to focus on actual examples, rather than hypothetical cases, as we think about how the teachers or assessors' dimensions allow the assessment to achieve its goals, while positively affecting the stakeholders in the assessment. Figure 4.7, then, presents our view of some existing programs and some programs that are (or have been) in the planning or piloting stages.

Michigan's entry-level portfolio assessment was limited to students accepted to the university who had already paid their enrollment deposits. Assessment was performed by trained readers from the destination context, although students' reflective pieces were given strong consideration, so students had some input on their placements. In talking with secondary-level teachers across the state, Michigan found that it could not realistically dictate the contents of the portfolio, so it set some broad parameters, thus sharing control over the contents with the source context. Finally, those at the college level can have little control over the context within which the texts are prepared, but over time, the fact of the portfolio's existence should exert some influence on the kinds of writing taught in the source context, and perhaps even on the ways in which writing is taught. Certainly, it is hoped that the portfolio will help secondary teachers as they try to make writing more central to curriculum in their schools.

Miami University—the pioneer in entry-level portfolio assessment—assesses a small portion (approximately 20%) of its entering students in order to determine whether they might be exempt from all or some portion of the sequence of required composition courses for first-year students. Thus, access is restricted to a very small group—a subset of students entering Miami each year. The portfolios are authority-assessed. In addition, Miami enforces specific requirements for the portfolio's contents, so that assessors can take advantage of a high degree of comparability, making discriminations easier. Miami also carries on an active program of communication with teachers across Ohio, hoping to have some impact on how writing is taught in Ohio schools. This kind of contact does not amount to actual control over the context, but it does create a situation in which we can say that exerting influence provides a measure of control over the context in which the samples for the portfolio are prepared.

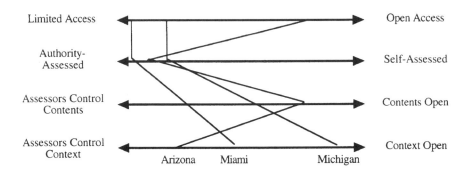

Figure 4.7. Dimensions for teachers or assessors

During 1994, in response to a now defunct state mandate, a consortium of teachers from high schools, community colleges, and universities began to devise an "articulation" portfolio assessment, under the leadership of John Ramage of Arizona State University. Because the state repealed its mandate, the assessment proceeded no farther than the early planning stages; still, the Arizona plan supplies a useful model to contrast with Miami's and Michigan's assessments. Under this system, students would have prepared a portfolio as a record of their learning in one context, so that when they changed institutions—moving from high school into community college or university, or from community college to university or university to community college, or transferring laterally from one institution to another of the same kind—the portfolio could have acted as a robust representation of their strengths and needs. Here, access would be wide open, because students enter community college from a range of educational and life experiences, and although the portfolios would probably have been authority assessed, the fact that the authority would have been shared among a wide range of teachers at three levels in the educational process would have created unique opportunities for collaboration, for common goal setting, and for exchanging information about each others' contexts. The Arizona collaboration would have alleviated a need to exert strong control over the portfolio's contents because the planning process incorporated a study of the kinds of writing produced in each kind of institution. Thus, the portfolio would have built on writing students were already doing, obviating the need to specify contents beyond existing categories. Finally, because the planners were building into the system realistic views of the contexts within which the texts were prepared, they would, unlike the other cross-institutional assessments, have had a fair measure of control over that context. Shared information from these three levels, incorporated into planning the portfolio, thus could have become a valuable force for setting common goals and moving in common directions, strengthening education by making it more consistent and potentially more responsive to students' actual needs.

All three of these assessments (two actual, one projected) confront practical, financial, and philosophical constraints in order to create a portfolio that preserves and employs most or all the portfolio's characteristics. All three, for example, strive to collect work students already have on hand (collection), so that students will be able to practice selection and the portfolios will be context rich. All three, too, include or planned to include a substantial reflection or self-assessment in the portfolio, giving students a chance to demonstrate metacognition about writing and creating an opportunity for them to turn the act of assembling the portfolio into a powerful learning experience. Logistical constraints on reading time eliminate the possibility that any of these assessments takes overt or uniform account of progress along defined parameters or development over time, although all are open to evidence of such progress or growth (Miami's portfolio does include drafts for one piece, but the drafts go unread).

SUMMARY AND OVERVIEW:
DEVELOPING A PORTFOLIO ASSESSMENT

Although this chapter has focused on the notion of heuristics in order to create a set of resources, rather than specific advice, for anyone planning a portfolio assessment, we conclude with what we feel we can point to as good advice. Although portfolio assessment remains in its infancy, collective experience so far has led to a few principles which one ignores at one's peril. Here, in summary form, are those principles as we see them.

1. Teachers must be committed to the concept of portfolio assessment, and they must be involved in the assessment itself. Involving teachers is crucial for many reasons, but primarily, if the program is to reap as many of portfolio assessment's ancillary

benefits as possible, then teachers, who are the key stakeholders, have to be involved in as many stages of the assessment as possible. Teachers are the agents for melding the assessment with instruction and with curriculum, for example, and the teachers will also be the agents for programmatic change, as they work to make the assessment meld with their own goals and values, as well as with the goals and values embodied in the curriculum. Only if teachers are involved will they see the effort portfolios require and the information portfolios produce as useful.

2. Students must be able to "own" the portfolio, to see it as their own. Students who see that they have control over their portfolios will also perceive that they can to some degree control their own fates—grades, placements, and so on. That kind of ownership leads to greater investment in learning, which in turn leads students to spend more time and effort and heap more care on their writing. If the portfolio is sufficiently student-centered, students will take the opportunities to examine their writing as a whole, rather than as a series of attempts, and they will begin to focus more on how to improve their writing than on how to produce passable writing more quickly and efficiently. In other words, students will become more aware of their own writing processes, and they will use that awareness to improve both their processes and their products. The portfolio's invitation for reflection and self-assessment reinforces this kind of progress by providing the opportunity to "discover what I've learned." Portfolios must promote self-assessment, and in order to do that, they must include texts that involve students in some kind of reflection and self-assessment.

3. Portfolios must respond to their local contexts. Portfolios exist within institutional contexts: classrooms, writing programs, colleges and universities, schools and school districts, national testing efforts, and the like. Each of these contexts must recognize and take advantage of the portfolio's ability to serve a number of goals and objectives at once. Out of consideration for students' and teachers' workloads, portfolios should collect no more writing than will fulfill the purposes for the assessment—but they must remain open to all the writing that will fulfill the purpose. Selection is no more important than collection, in other words, and these two characteristics complement each other in an effective assessment. The system designed to evaluate portfolios must also reflect the needs and values of the local context.

4. The roles of other "stakeholders" must be taken into account. The parameters set in the criteria and the methods by which those

criteria are enacted in the readings must maintain contact with the needs, goals, and objectives of the stakeholders—students, teachers, administrators, even external agencies and institutions. Above all, this system must be responsive to change—especially to the change it instigates. As long as the portfolio assessment can produce information valuable to students, teachers or readers, and administrators, and as long as the assessment is open to change as a result of input from students, teachers or readers, and administrators, then all these stakeholders will see the portfolio as meaningful, and they will continue to value it. As soon as the portfolio system becomes closed to this kind of change, it will require more effort than it is worth, from the standpoint of one or more of these stakeholders. But it is not enough to have buy-in from teachers and administrators within the writing program if academics and administrators across the college as a whole are opposed, or skeptical. A portfolio program needs to gain credibility with the academic community overall, so that results based on portfolios are accepted and valued, and so that portfolios as artifacts revealing an individual's learning in meaningful ways become in themselves objects for discussion as questions about standards are raised, as happens often these days across campuses.

5. Despite all the hype and the newness, portfolios are still tests. They escape only some of the constraints of other kinds of test. First, portfolio assessments do not happen as if by magic; they require full and careful development, and the effort of maintaining an ongoing assessment is at least equal to the effort of maintaining any other form of test. Second, portfolio reading requires the same attention and devotion to training and standards as any other form of direct test of writing. The temptation to rely on readers' inherent standards, on their experiences as graders or evaluators of writing, may be strong, but it leads to low reliability. No matter how close and congenial a program's faculty may be, no matter how long their work together has lasted, portfolios will reveal their disagreements over genres, definitions of terms, goals, objectives, and standards. Training has to provide time for the participants to achieve consensus on these aspects, or the reading will suffer. Third, the parameters should take into account traditional psychometric considerations. Practices should be tested to ensure they are fair, that judgments are consistent within an acceptable range, and that results are properly stored and reported. The best evaluation is useless without adequate feedback to those being evaluated.

Portfolios open a whole range of possibilities for feedback, but they by no means obviate the necessity to provide feedback.

6. Any portfolio assessment must have clear direction. Portfolio assessment can appear relatively amorphous, and it is by nature a highly collaborative activity. The best assessments generate, refine, or reinforce communities of readers, readers who in turn help maintain the assessment at a high level of effectiveness. Still, someone has to be in charge; someone must be delegated to oversee the assessment, to ask the appropriate questions. Without a clear locus of responsibility, the assessment may well drift off course, lose its contact with the interests of stakeholders. The community that evolves around portfolio assessment can only remain healthy if it has a system of governance that the stakeholders have installed and that they recognize. Finally, a system of internal and, ideally, external evaluation must be established and maintained. Without regular evaluation—from routine daily measures that ensure reliable readings to elaborate outside scrutiny—the assessment is in the same danger of drifting off course as it is from a lack of proper governance. No assessment can be installed and left alone; no matter what form of assessment one uses, one must continually re-examine that assessment in order to be sure that it is accomplishing its goals— and even that its goals are still legitimate.

7. Portfolios are still an experimental method. Each new instantiation of portfolio assessment creates new knowledge about this form of assessment. Each new attempt—successful or not—adds important data to understanding where, how, and with whom portfolios succeed. Assessments need to be designed with an eye toward their own self-assessment, or this new knowledge will be lost. Portfolios have come a long way in the decade since this new explosion of the form began, but there is still a great deal to learn, a great deal to teach each other.

Chapter 5

TOWARDS A RESEARCH AGENDA FOR PORTFOLIO-BASED WRITING ASSESSMENT

Chapter Outline

As we conclude this attempt to provide a comprehensive look at the state of the art in portfolio-based writing assessment, our attention necessarily turns to perhaps the most pressing need in this still young field: the need for research that validates the claims various practitioners—including us—make. Like so many other proponents of portfolios, we believe that portfolios constitute a "better mousetrap," that they provide—or can provide—a better method for collecting data about teaching and learning and, that, by involving instruction with assessment, they concurrently provide a powerful mechanism for promoting learning for student writers, for teachers, and for the people who bear responsibility for curriculum at any level. The previous sentence contains perhaps the broadest claim anyone in the brief history of portfolio assessment has dared make—and yet note the verb: *believe*. So far, this book has been partially about what we know—what we have learned from experience and from the research that has only just begun to generate the questions that future research will need to answer—partially about the theory we can deduce from portfolio assessment practice to date, and partially about what we believe. For the most part, however, it has been about what we believe we know. So in the broadest sense, the central question researchers confront, to paraphrase a political cliché, is, "What do we believe we know, and why do we believe we know it?"

Even in beginning to address such a question, we confront the fact that research that justifies any kind of assessment has to satisfy different audiences, which means that it must address different kinds of knowing, different ways of knowing. Often, portfolio proponents' claims (and here we implicate ourselves as well) are based in practitioners' knowledge, on what we in our roles as teachers see happening in our classrooms, on "what works for me and my students." Such evidence—and such a way of knowing—is powerful and shareable within the community of teachers. Outside that community, however, audiences are likely to demand evidence that fits a different epistemology. If portfolios are to become broadly favored—or even accepted—as assessment tools, then we have to translate the "teacher sense" that we rely on into the kinds of evidence that other audiences—specialists in testing and measurement, college administrators, government officials, even the public at large—will accept as convincing.

THE CONTEXTS FOR PORTFOLIO ASSESSMENT

As we suggested throughout this book, the portfolio is a context-rich kind of evaluation. Figure 5.1 provides some idea of the contexts that are encompassed by the portfolio assessment and of the range of possible

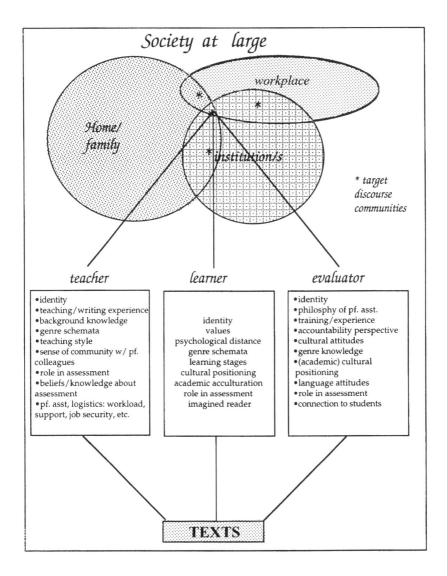

Figure 5.1. The contexts for portfolio assessment

stakeholders. It attempts to open up for us to see and become conscious of the interactions that exist between the three "major players" or stakeholders in portfolio-based assessment and the other, less evident stakeholders. Figure 5.1 begins to sketch out the facets of each of these groups of stakeholders that are brought into the mutually shared (yet not accessible, or even visible, to all stakeholders equally or in its entirety) context where the portfolio is written, the portfolio assessment is designed, and portfolios are evaluated.

Figure 5.1 shows that writing portfolios occur within a particular and limited context, at the intersection of home, workplace and institution, in a region we can think of as "target discourse communities" (i.e., the ways of talking and writing that are valued by the community where these people come together to share work, learning, or living). Within that region we are specifically concerned with schooling, and even more specifically with college education. The straight lines lift the "actors" out of the background of the target discourse community, revealing them as teachers, learners, and evaluators, and the boxes show some of the roles each of these kinds of actors plays and the influences they bring from, and into, the context as they participate in portfolio making and evaluating.

The nature of the portfolio program as a *living* system, as a vital, reactive force, ensures that the system remains responsive to and reflective of local needs, especially as these needs change as a result of the influence of the portfolio assessment itself. In chapters 2 and 3 we discussed at length some of the practical concerns that arise as a portfolio-based writing assessment comes into being, grows, matures and, perhaps, declines; and we described some ways that writing program administrators and teachers can respond to these concerns as they move beyond traditional forms of assessment to create more valid, more flexible, and more responsive and responsible forms. However, Figure 5.1 makes clear the fact that the full context within which portfolio assessment evolves extends beyond its immediate and most prominent stakeholders. Learners, teachers, administrators, assessors, the workplace, school or institution, agencies that fund institutions, society at large, all have at least some stake in portfolio assessment, and all have needs that must be addressed as portfolio assessment—and, more generally, performance assessment—replaces older, more traditional methods of assessing the performances of learners, teachers, programs, and schools.

This chapter, then, develops along sound rhetorical lines, focusing on audience and purpose, in order to generate a research agenda that can begin to cross the lines that too often separate one audience community from another. In proceeding audience by audience, we hope to identify and explore the interests these communities share with each other and the differences in the kinds of evidence each accepts as valid, as constituting *knowing,* rather than believing. We are working with a kind of matrix, one that maps audiences onto dimensions in order to generate the central questions that each audience for portfolio assessment would ask and to account for the kinds of evidence each audience will accept as convincing, as *knowing.*

THE AUDIENCES FOR PORTFOLIO RESEARCH

The audiences we identified as concerned with portfolio-based writing assessment are represented in Figure 5.2.

At the center of all our concerns—and equally central to the concerns of every other audience—are the students whose needs as learners properly lie at the center of the whole educational enterprise, from any vantage point. As we move into wider circles, the needs of each audience community are constructed on top of the kinds of proof that satisfy the "interior" community or communities. Thus, teachers begin to examine any new method or device by asking questions about how it will affect their students and then themselves. Teachers may be willing to invest in a new strategy solely because it helps students learn more or more quickly or more happily. If the new strategy also creates clear, provable benefits for teachers, then they are even more likely to adopt it. Writing program administrators, too, begin with questions about what a new strategy does for learners, but then the WPA wants to know how the innovation will affect the teachers whom the WPA supervises. Finally, the WPA wants to know about effects on him or herself, about how the change will affect the program as a whole. Thus, for WPAs, if a change improves learning, if it creates benefits for those teaching in the program, and if it makes the WPA's job easier, more productive, or more pleasant, then it is likely to be adopted. These three audiences are, in effect, closest to the learner and the classroom, so their questions, their ways of knowing, center perhaps most intimately and most directly on what happens to learners in classes and on how the teaching and learning environment changes in response to introducing portfolio assessment.

The next wider circle in Figure 5.2 represents the testing and measurement community, which we argue is the key audience, the key set of needs—and this position in itself represents a change, represents progress. We discussed some of the different needs and emphases of this community in chapter 1, but in order to better understand the concerns of this group, it is helpful to recall their history. Springing from the development, during and after World War I, of "new type" tests (G. Miller, 1926), and in keeping with the movement at that time to view education on a "factory model" (Stephens & van Til, 1972; Williamson, 1994),

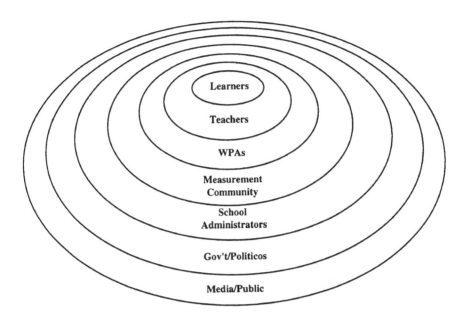

Learners

Teachers

WPAs

Measurement
Community

School
Administrators

Gov't/Politicos

Media/Public

Figure 5.2. Audiences for portfolio research

conceptualizations of "literacy" as a liberal education were subordinated to pragmatic motivations. The new type test methods were amenable to scoring automatically and easily subjected to statistical analyses, fueling an industry of statistical methodology development for educational agencies—the armed forces, states, federal government agencies, and large testing agencies such as the college board.

The measurement community focused almost solely on the test and the results it generated, not even on their uses. The experts working in providing the methodology and delivering results were answerable for the accuracy of the data they provided, and if sometimes decisions themselves proved inaccurate (e.g., aptitude tests have traditionally had only about 25% success rate in decision making), at least the methods used to reach them could be proved to have been statistically unassailable. The shift in recent years to a broader focus for testing and measurement represents a major change in beliefs and values for many in educational measurement: a paradigm shift.

Until quite recently (the 1985 revision of the *Standards for Educational and Psychological Testing,* heavily influenced by the work of Messick and Cronbach, may mark the beginning of this change) their studies barely acknowledged the test-takers because test-takers were almost wholly invisible in the assessors' thinking and planning, except as sets of responses to be elicited or behaviors to be measured. The tests were responsive to no curriculum in particular, to no learners in particular, to no context in particular. They were responsive only to the demand for reliability, for scores that could be perfectly replicated in parallel forms of tests, or with the same learner on different occasions. However, as indirect tests have given way to direct tests and as these in turn have given way to performance assessments of one kind and another, the testing and measurement community has, first grudgingly but now with increasing commitment, undergone a kind of sea change as well. It has begun to understand better some of its own premises: that depending on statistical prerequisites for "a good test" is not only educationally but even theoretically unsound. For example, internal consistency—a characteristic without which it was long claimed a measure could not be considered a test in the sense that it could be submitted to the statistical formulae needed to derive reliability quotients—has finally been understood to be not only difficult to obtain for direct assessments like essay tests and portfolio assessments, but—and this is the breakthrough—undesirable of real performance.

To say a test is internally consistent means that all its parts (items, questions, pieces of writing, whatever) are measuring the same thing. The message seems to be finally getting home to the majority of educational measurement experts that in assessing real performances we in fact do not want to repeatedly measure the same thing! We value authentic assessments, performance assessments, specifically portfolio assessments, because they do not measure one narrow ability, but a range of skills, of strengths and weaknesses. We do not find it surprising that a learner's performance is not "internally consistent": We find that information reflective of the realities we encounter in classrooms. The advocacy by such long-term leading figures of the educational measurement community as Messick (most particularly in his seminal reconceptualization of validity in his 1988 and 1989 papers) of the need to look beyond test and human-as-test-taker to consider how tests impact the test-takers' contexts is a courageous move onto ground where statisticians have traditionally been most vulnerable. Educational assessment researchers are broadening their definition of what their jobs must encompass, moving gradually but noticeably closer to the view of multiple contexts as suggested by Figure 5.1. For example, Messick (1989) was an early voice arguing to expand validation into the teaching and learning contexts encompassing the perspectives of both test developers and teachers. And newer voices, such as that of Moss et al. (1992), extend the call to find new bases for understanding such testing precepts as reliability and validity, so that the tests created out of that new understanding can function generatively—can help promote learning even as they assess progress. Even the harder of the hard-line psychometricians are beginning to see that as new kinds of assessments produce positive outcomes, those successes demand that the measurement community, in turn, ask itself some hard questions (Resnick & Resnick, 1991). If the old, mathematical ways of determining a test's effectiveness cannot accommodate the new kinds of test, then, some influential psychometricians are asking, "What does that say about psychometrics?" (LeMahieu et al., 1995).

The fact that the testing and measurement community has begun to ask those kinds of questions, after decades of simply discounting any new tool that could not be validated by the old measures, means that this influential community has become of necessity more allied with learners, teachers, and program administrators. This alliance in turn forces psychometricians to think more broadly about the effects of assessment, about the impact that a particular assessment has on all its contexts—on the learner or test-taker, on the curriculum, on teaching (and therefore on teachers), on the programs the tests evaluate, or within which the test is administered, on schools generally, and so forth. This recent change of emphasis has opened doors, within the measurement community, to performance assessments, to authentic assessments, to portfolios.

The change has occurred for a number of reasons, though two stand out, to us, as primary. First, as noted in chapter 1, the results of indirect tests are often used in ways they were never intended to be—despite the warnings of the test makers that such uses were spurious (e.g., using SAT scores to rate the effectiveness of school districts, or even the progress of national education). Thus, the test-makers have become increasingly uncomfortable with the uses to which their neatly "valid" (in the traditional sense of internal and criterion validities) and reliable tests were being put. Second, as performance assessments in general have become much more widespread, it has become clear that they are not simply going to fade away because the psychometricians would not treat them seriously. As a result, the psychometricians have turned their attention to these newer tools, and the evidence they are gathering has already contributed a great deal to a broader acceptance of the new kinds of assessment. All this activity means that the tests being devised today are more likely to attend to context(s) in ways that provide useful information to the agents acting within that context, as well as to the agencies outside the context—government agencies, actors in the political arena, the media, and the public at large.

These latter audiences are critical to the broad acceptance of any assessment measure because, ultimately, what happens inside the writing program has to be acceptable within the academy generally, and what happens within the academy has to be acceptable to all the academy's constituencies. Even as the testing and measurement community is developing the means to provide learners, teachers, and program administrators with useful information that can guide us to construct more effective learning environments, it can also, as it always has, provide evidence of our programs' effectiveness to college administrators, to government agencies and elected officials, to the media and the public at large. The measurement community has always provided the statistics and other data by which our effectiveness is judged by those outside our classrooms and our programs. As they develop evidence for the effectiveness of portfolio assessment, that information, too, will be passed on to the people who, in one way or another, control the flow of resources to or away from our classrooms and our programs. Thus, we teachers and WPAs cannot pass up the opportunity to form a productive partnership with the educational measurement community, and we should be eager to help that community develop the kinds of measures that will validate these new tools, tools that we have found so beneficial in the classroom. The measurement community, in effect, can help us turn outward, from our larger community of learners, teachers, and WPAs, to the even larger, more public constituencies that our programs serve.

Moving outward to the next audience circle in Figure 5.2, we encounter college administrators, whose concerns often seem inexplicably and unfortunately removed from the classroom. Their questions relate to educational effectiveness, on some level, but this audience also focuses on budgets and on public relations. Administrators want to know whether a program works, but they also want to know what it costs and why the program is worth the encumberment of funds. They want to know whether the program, as showpiece, can generate funds, either in the form of grants or donations. Finally, they want to know how any change will affect funding from students, in the form of enrollments that generate tuition dollars; and how it will affect funding from the legislature, in the form of higher budget allocations resulting from the perception that the institution is meeting its obligations to the public. Administrators can require quite a lot of convincing, and they are never persuaded solely on the basis of "what works in the classroom." The research we develop must provide evidence of effectiveness, of excellence. The research has to show that the benefits equal or outweigh the costs.

State boards of higher education, legislators, accrediting agencies, all these constituencies and more are also interested in cost-effectiveness. And they are even less willing than college administrators to take the teacher's word that a new method works. Satisfying these audiences requires us to design studies that extend beyond a single classroom, probably beyond a single program. This research must demonstrate the efficacy of the method as method, as well as the positive impact on individual learners. This task requires that portfolios meet the standards being developed by psychometricians, and clearly, to date, portfolios have not achieved this level of endorsement, as the reports from the National Assessment of College Student Learning demonstrate (1993, 1994, 1995). Legislatures and bureaucracies operate on facts and figures; in the halls of government, there is a high level of distrust for "warm fuzzy" evidence. At the same time, we need to produce the kinds of anecdotal evidence of progress, of effectiveness, of learning, that can grab the attention of the politico or the bureaucrat. Once we have their ears, we have to be able to tell them about the more positivist warrants that justify our new courses of action.

Finally, the broadest audience, and perhaps the trickiest to satisfy, is the public in general, as "informed" by the media. Without the kinds of evidence that the media can grasp and interpret for the public, new methods of teaching and testing can never achieve the kind of public acceptance that will ease the way with legislatures and government agencies. In this arena, we need to be able to justify new tools with clear evidence of effectiveness, because we can be sure that constituencies who oppose change generally will be ready to exploit any weakness in the case for change. Think, for example, of the "new math" fiasco of the 1960s or today's controversy over the whole language method. In both cases, a new method that was never intended to be the answer to all learners' needs was torpedoed, despite quite a bit of evidence in favor of its effectiveness, by those who twisted and exaggerated the claims of the method's more responsible proponents. To gain a fair hearing in the public arena, evidence that favors portfolio assessment has to address the media's and the public's skepticism about academe, about throwing good money after bad, about change for change's sake.

These different audiences demand different kinds of evidence because they participate in different ways of knowing. The warrants, in effect, that convert *believe* into *know* differ in kind and quantity for each audience. Research projects to examine the effectiveness of portfolio assessments must be designed to address as many of these audiences as possible. The key audience, as indicated previously, is the testing and measurement community, for in our discussion, we have framed this audience both as the outer ring of the "inner circle" (comprising learners, teachers, WPAs, and measurement community) and as the inner ring of the outer circle (measurement community, college administrators, politicos, public). Janus like, the measurement community faces in both directions, addressing the needs and concerns of both outer and inner circles. These researchers are accustomed to providing the kinds of public forum evidence required to validate innovation, and their recent attention to the full educational context for testing creates an opportunity for teachers to become partners in this research.

DIMENSIONS FOR DESIGNING PORTFOLIO RESEARCH

Although portfolio-based writing assessment is too young to have generated definitive research, it is old enough that researchers have begun to identify the dimensions along which fruitful research can be designed. Eight useful dimensions for thinking about the kinds of evidence and the kinds of research we can use in order to address each of the audiences described earlier (and explored further later) are provided in a perceptive article by Linn et al. (1991). Briefly, here are their dimensions, along with our summaries of each:

> *Consequences*: The reactions of the participants (students, teachers, administrators, score users) to the test and the impact of the testing program on participants (Messick, 1989); the portfolio assessment movement, as exemplified by our own text, argues strongly for the beneficial consequences of portfolio assessment.
>
> *Fairness*: In the educational measurement community, fairness means freedom from racial or ethnic and gender bias (Mehrens, 1992; M. Miller & Legg, 1993). A common argument is that portfolios benefit nonmainstream learners particularly (Hamp-Lyons, 1997; and throughout this book).
>
> *Meaningfulness*: Evidence of whether portfolio assessment is more meaningful to students than the more traditional and administratively easier forms of writing assessment has yet to be collected.
>
> *Transfer and generalizability*: Outcomes of the assessment must be meaningful to those in other contexts (Linn et al., 1991; Moss et al., 1992); these outcomes must be stable enough for interpretations of outcomes to be relied on (M. Miller & Legg, 1993).
>
> *Cognitive complexity*: New forms of assessment should better capture a student's mastery of complex cognitive tasks than traditional assessments could (Linn et al., 1991); we have claimed in this book that portfolios, especially writing portfolios, enable the assessment of complex thinking.
>
> *Content quality*: Linn et al. (1991) suggested that the quality of test content may be compromised in portfolio assessments; the question of how to define "(test) content" in the portfolio

assessment context appears to have been little addressed by the assessment community, but we have tried to address it throughout this book.

Content coverage: Portfolios allow a much wider coverage of content than traditional writing tests, but with selection as well as curriculum restrictions taken into account their coverage may be less than that of a multiple-choice test with many items.

Cost and efficiency: There is as yet no clear proof that will satisfy bureaucrats that portfolio assessment gives us any advantages that we cannot obtain in cheaper and more efficient ways. The problems that the portfolio assessment movement will face over justifying their greater cost and lower efficiency have yet to be addressed by its advocates.

As we proceed, we provide a basic research agenda for portfolio assessment. The agenda is just that: a plan. We could hardly, at this point in time, arrive at a definitive plan. Indeed, portfolios have come only so far as to allow an agenda that we intend as generative; as provocative of further questions, further issues; and as public and continually negotiable. In other words, this is not a plan for our research, although we hope to be involved as research in the field progresses, but it provides an outline, a set of priorities by which the field, all of us together, might provide the kinds of evidence we need to provide. By mapping the audiences for research onto the dimensions that affect portfolio assessments (see Fig. 5.3), we have created a mechanism that will allow us to see as far down the road as possible, given our current vantage point; and that will allow others, coming into the field later on, to see farther than we have.

MAPPING THE DIMENSIONS ONTO THE AUDIENCES

Learners

The first concern for most learners about portfolios is likely to center on the consequences of their assessment. Their most likely questions are as follows:

- Will this be more work for me?
- Will it be "a harder test"?
- Who will read my portfolio?
- How will it be graded/scored/judged?
- Will it allow me to do better?

	Learners	Teachers	WPAS	Measurement Community	School Administrators	Government/ Politicians	Media/ Public
Consequences	1	1	2	1	2	4	1
Fairness	1	1	1	1	2	4	3
Meaningfulness	2	2	2	1	1	2	1
Transfer and Generalizability	5	4	1	1	1	1	3
Cognitive Complexity	4	1	3	2	3	5	5
Content Quality	2	2	1	1	3	5	3
Content Coverage	2	1	1	1	4	5	2
Cost and Efficiency	3	3	2	3	1	2	1

1 = Of Primary Importance; 2 = Very Important; 3 = Somewhat Important; 4 = Not Very Important; 5 = Not Important

Figure 5.3. Audience/dimension matrix

From a learner's point of view, the portfolio may appear to be a more valid measure of his or her writing abilities. This is primarily *face validity*; that is, the assessment looks more valid to the student. The learner would probably describe that kind of validity as fairness. Portfolios look like a fairer way to find out what and how well someone can write. This judgment is probably based on learners' perceptions about the meaningfulness of the task of preparing a portfolio, because of what they see about the content quality and coverage enabled by a portfolio assessment, and the fairness of having their portfolios evaluated by their own and other teachers. Learners' perception of the portfolio as a meaningful assessment is probably heightened by the availability of good information about what readers will look for in their portfolio and how they will judge it. Learners are unlikely to worry much about transfer and generalizability; and cost, because it is not a burden on them per se. As the hypothetical learner questions just presented indicate, however, learners are likely to worry about efficiency in terms of how they are affected by a heavier requirement of doing more writing or rewriting, preparing materials, producing supporting documentation, and so forth.

But there is little empirical research into learners' attitudes to portfolio-based assessment, either in its own right or by comparison with other kinds of writing assessment: All our statements here are qualified ones because, although we believe these things about learners' perceptions, we are aware that we do not know them. N. Baker (1993) conducted a study comparing portfolio and nonportfolio classes, but the end of semester assessment was still a timed essay, and so her data are not very useful in understanding learners' attitudes to portfolio-based teaching coupled with portfolio-based assessment. At the University of Michigan, students reported that they trust the portfolio more than they trusted the timed essay—that they felt the portfolio was fairer, because it allowed them more directly to demonstrate what they could do in writing. However, these were impressionistic results, and not the outcome of a careful study.

Clearly, learners have the right to have their questions about portfolio-based writing assessment answered (as they do about any assessment). Research that evaluates the extent to which portfolio-based writing assessment programs are providing students with answers to their questions about this assessment is needed. In effect, students need to know how portfolios constitute a better mousetrap from the students' point of view.

Classroom Teachers

Teachers' first questions are likely to concern the consequences of portfolio-based assessment for their learners; their next questions will concern consequences for themselves. Questions that teachers will want answered about the learner's perspective on portfolio-based assessment include the following:

- Does having a portfolio as an end-of-course assessment lead students to put more work into their writing class?
- Do students prefer portfolio assessment to standard grading methods or timed essay test assessment (in a range of contexts)?
- Do students believe more in the results of an assessment if it is done using a portfolio base than in other, traditional forms of assessment?

From the teacher's perspective these questions elicit key evidence for or against a shift to portfolios. If learners like portfolios and if portfolios lead learners to work harder at their learning, then teachers will be willing to entertain a shift to the method. Evidence so far is positive, but anecdotal, so teachers have an open field for research into the affective dimensions of portfolios.

Besides investigations into portfolios from the learner's point of view, teachers will be interested in questions that probe the portfolio as an agent for improved pedagogy, fairness, and other classroom implications. They will want answers to questions like those that follow:

- Does a portfolio-based assessment support the kinds of teaching I believe in more than do standard grading methods, essay tests, or multiple choice tests?
- Do portfolios give fairer results than other measures?
- What do the scores given to portfolios mean?
- Does a portfolio-based assessment place students into appropriate classes more effectively than do other measures?
- How much more work do portfolios involve for me?

Teachers want to be sure their students will not get lower scores or poorer results than in other forms of assessment the portfolio is replacing. They would like to think the portfolio will not cause more work for themselves (the efficiency issue) but most teachers are willing to put in some more work if they believe that the portfolio-based assessment will have beneficial consequences for their students and for their teaching. Teachers expect to understand what the scores reported for portfolio-based assessment actually mean in terms of real writing performance, whereas they have no such expectation of transparency (Frederickson & Collins, 1989) for indirect forms of assessment. Although not unaware of the financial pressures on colleges, teachers do not generally have cost as a significant issue on their agendas as they consider portfolios as assessments, although required, lengthy sessions reading portfolios will be a major factor in influencing teachers to feel negative toward the whole concept.

A frequent complaint about traditional measures of writing ability is that they undermine regular classroom instruction. An underlying premise of this book, which has frequently surfaced overtly, is that portfolios reflect the kinds of instruction valued in composition and that portfolios are therefore an inherently more meaningful form of assessment. Among the beneficial consequences of portfolio-based assessment claimed to make it a more meaningful assessment are the following:

- Promotion of richer concepts about good writing by using the portfolio as a repository and record of good writing and the processes and drafts by which it has been reached.
- The opportunity for students to apply higher order thinking skills, including metacognitive skills.
- The possibility of building good reflective practices up to and including the assessment.
- Greater ease for noticing growth in each student's writing, and the range of capabilities the writer has shown through the range of texts as well as the self-reflection) both for the teacher and for the assessor.
- Richer possibilities for feedback to the learner both during the course and in evaluative response to the portfolio.
- The more concrete benefits of delayed evaluation such as enabling writers to have time to correct their errors either themselves or by going for help to a writing center.

These and other benefits ascribed to portfolios fall under the cognitive complexity criterion and the content coverage criterion. Because of these visible benefits teachers generally feel that portfolio-based assessment supports the kinds of teaching they believe in more than more traditional methods for assessing and grading writing do: Yet here too studies are needed, and these questions provide a very rich site for classroom research.

Teachers' desire to know whether portfolio-based assessment is fairer to students usually focuses on wanting to know that portfolio-based assessments are not giving students lower scores, grades, placements,and so on, than students have earned under the older forms of assessment. The evidence on this question is limited, and, to the extent that it exists, conflicting. Such answers as we have are at present based on the superficial view that fairness means higher or lower test scores on one form of test than on another. The other definition of fairness that concerns teachers, and that has been discussed at several points in this book, is whether the assessment is free from racial or ethnic and gender bias. Hamp-Lyons' (1995) observations of portfolio groups reading and discussing the portfolios of native and nonnative writers, coupled with her examination of grading patterns for native and nonnative writers' portfolios, suggests that although some nonnative writers are actually advantaged by the process of reading and scoring portfolios, others are equally disadvantaged. Her results suggest that there is nothing automatic or inherent about the claimed fairness of portfolios: as we have continually stressed throughout this book, portfolios are only "a better mousetrap" for any constituency if the seven Cs, and especially "care" are continually exercised. The questions about fairness, then, remain to be researched.

The question, "How much more work do portfolios involve for me?" is perhaps the only one of the teacher's questions that can currently be answered clearly and in specific detail. Many of the early studies about portfolios, particularly those in the Belanoff and Dickson (1991) collection, describe in detail the functions of portfolio-based assessments and the implications for teachers' workloads.

Among the many other questions for which teachers would like the answer are whether having a portfolio as an end-of-course assessment leads students to put more work into their writing class; and whether a portfolio-based assessment places students into appropriate classes more effectively than other measures. There are, then, a number of very important questions that classroom teachers need to pursue. Most of this research can and should be done by teachers themselves in their own classrooms. McLaughlin (1991) pointed out the following:

> Almost four decades of experience with planned efforts to reform education have taught us that (1) teachers are not inclined to take responsibility for carrying out goals and objectives about which they have had no say and (2) teachers have important knowledge and expertise to contribute to the enterprise. (p. 250)

Teachers or researchers who focus on the needs of their "external" audiences are most likely to provide information describing the changes in teaching and learning that result from introducing a portfolio-based writing assessment.

Writing Program Administrators

The WPA occupies a niche between the classroom and the administration. WPAs are both teachers and administrators, and the kinds of questions they want answered address both those roles. Concerns of WPAs, like those of the teachers, begin with the students in the writing program. How does portfolio assessment affect learning? WPAs also have teachers in their charge, ranging from very experienced specialists in rhetoric and composition, to inexperienced master's students in literary studies. Thus, another set of questions addresses the needs of teachers and the ways the portfolio assessment may or may not support those needs. Finally, the WPA has to establish the program's accountability. What does the program accomplish? What kinds of evidence can the portfolio provide to establish the program's effectiveness? Here, focused as well as possible at this point in time, is a list of the research questions that address the needs of the WPA as an audience for portfolio research:

- What features of writing does the portfolio test for? Which does it not test for?
- What are the intended consequences of portfolio assessment?
  —Can we achieve those consequences?
  —How will we know?
  —How will we demonstrate that achievement?
- What are the unintended consequences of portfolio assessment?
  —Are those consequences positive or negative? Singly? Taken together?
  —How can we make the most of positive consequences?
  —How can we eliminate (or, if need be, justify) negative consequences?
- Does portfolio assessment enable a writing program to be more accountable to students, teachers, and the institution? How? How can we increase accountability?
- What are the mechanisms that integrate assessment with instruction?
- How do we know that those mechanisms continue to operate?
- Does portfolio assessment promote consistency in teaching and learning across sections of a single course? How? How do we know?
- What role, if any, does portfolio assessment play in faculty development? Does portfolio assessment promote effective teaching? How? How can we know? How can we assure that this role continues? That it expands?
- Does portfolio assessment help teachers and learners spend their time productively thinking about and pursuing course and program goals?
- Will teachers "teach to the test" (i.e., the portfolio)? If so, what are the effects of teaching to the portfolio? Does teaching to the portfolio increase or decrease the effectiveness of instruction?
- How will the writing program provide enough background training to allow teachers to help students produce valid portfolios? How

will the program train teachers to promote learning without yielding to the temptation to dominate or over coach the student writer?

- How will the writing program or the portfolio assessment provide enough background training to enable portfolio readers to understand fully either the processes or the implications of assessing writing with portfolios?

This list of questions reveals that all the dimensions of portfolios are significant to the WPA audience—as they are to the testing and measurement audience. At present, we believe that none of the other audiences attends to all eight dimensions. As teacher, the WPA shares similar concerns over consequences and fairness, and WPAs also share the more formal assessment-oriented concern for fairness—that the test not discriminate on the basis of race, ethnicity, gender, and so on. In addition, as the figurehead for the writing program, the WPA is aware, more than any other person, of the participants' reactions to the test and the impact of the testing program on participants (Messick, 1989).

As the person in charge of the program's curriculum, the WPA deals centrally with cognitive complexity, with the ability of the course to address and the assessment process to test for the degree to which students have mastered complex cognitive tasks (Linn et al., 1991). In addition, the WPA has to be concerned that whatever measure teachers use to assess students' progress be capable of content coverage, and that the measuring tool incorporate as much of the course's content as possible (content quality).

These concerns enable the WPA to assert that the program is accountable to the needs of its constituents, from learners all the way to the public at large because addressing these dimensions establishes the degree to which the course fulfills its role within the university (which, in turn, has its role to fulfill in society at large). Transfer and generalizability and meaningfulness are also important to accountability, as is the final dimension, cost and efficiency. As the person in charge of the program's budget, the WPA has to assure that those in other contexts can perceive the program's benefits (Linn et al., 1991; Moss et al., 1992) and that what students learn is stable enough for them and their future teachers and employers to rely on it (M. Miller & Legg, 1993). If the WPA can ensure that much, then justifying the cost or supporting the efficiency of the program or the assessment is simply done.

To date, not much of this territory has been explored, and most of what we know comes from the literature on essay testing and educational measurement, generally. These studies provide a clear context for research into portfolio assessment, but, except metaphorically, they provide little substance to arguments for or against portfolio assessment. In terms of curriculum, McLaughlin (1991) pointed out that what is tested matters: "because today's tests don't measure . . . higher-order skills, they discourage classroom practices that are directed toward teaching them" (p. 249). This comment—which, again, does not speak to portfolio assessment—links traditional testing and teaching in a relation that is viewed as damaging to teaching. This is a common view among teachers, yet there is relatively little evidence for it, of which the largest and most well-known study is that by M. Smith (1991). (And M. Smith's study, too, addresses large-scale standardized testing, not portfolio assessment.) The basic problem is that too many people confuse standards with the fact that tests are standardized (McLaughlin, 1991). A kind of false accountablility arises from this confusion, an accountability that focuses on the test, rather than on the classroom:

> ironically, accountability schemes that rely on existing testing technology trust the system (the rules, regulations and standardized procedures) more than they trust teachers to make appropriate, educationally sound choices . . . and they protect that system . . . more than they protect the students served by the system. (McLaughlin, 1991, p. 250)

Program administrators, whether WPAs, school principals, or department heads, will want to know whether such claims are true, and whether portfolio-based assessment permits a less damaging relation between testing and teaching.

In addressing programmatic concerns, WPAs and other program administrators should take heed of Linn et al.'s (1991) cautionary words: "High priority needs to be given to the collection of evidence about the intended and unintended consequences of assessments on the ways teachers and students spend their time and think about the goals of education" (p. 17). One consequence of portfolios that teachers and WPAs must address is the drift toward teaching to the portfolio, replacing old habits of teaching to the test. In the sense that the "test" in this case encourages the learner to revise further, to pay more attention to, and to heap more time on his or her writing, teaching to the test may be a positive consequence. To the extent that delayed evaluation encourages particularly the inexperienced teacher to provide too much help, to the point that the portfolio may no longer represent the student's level of ability, clearly teaching to the test is a negative consequence. We do not know, at this point, which, if either, of these scenarios is more frequent. Nor do we know, beyond the general or the anecdotal, what other positive and negative consequences accompany portfolio assessment. We need to know.

Finally, WPAs have to be concerned about whether their programs can actually sustain a portfolio-based assessment. How great a level of expertise is needed in the teacher corps? Who will supply the knowledge of assessment that will enable the program to respond to inevitable challenges? Who will provide the theory—and later the research—that justifies the labor and expense of mounting such an effort? Professional preparation for composition teachers rarely includes any form of training in testing, and any survey of assessment bibliography in rhetoric and composition or in educational measurement quickly reveals that these two communities simply do not read each other's work.[1] WPAs, school principals, or department heads will want to know whether their portfolio program is providing sufficient background training for teachers or portfolio readers to enable them to understand either the processes or the implications of assessing writing with portfolios.

Educational Measurement Experts

The current direction in the measurement community, as represented by, for example, Linn et al., is to concern themselves with all of the dimensions in the matrix.

Consequences

This new dimension of concern in educational measurement can be said to focus on test use and the impact of test use on teaching and access to or events in wider contexts, first labeled as *backwash* by Wiseman (1956) and currently usually known as *washback* (Alderson & Wall, 1993). It leads to questions like those that follow:

- Does the assessment lead teachers to spend more time on concepts and material covered by the portfolio assessment, and on activities supportive of improved performance on the assessment?
- If so, does that lead to improved or diminished classroom experiences for students?
- Is the "portfolio" being defined in such a way that it enhances teaching and learning?

---

[1] The CCCC Committee on Assessment's Bibliography on postsecondary writing assessment (1992) does not contain publications by Messick, Moss, Cronbach, Eisner, Kettle, Baker, and several others—all of whom write extensively about performance assessment, and all of whom would be central reading for anyone in the testing and measurement community. Similarly, a cursory examination of the bibliographies of articles in journals such as *Educational Researcher, Educational Measurement: Issues and Practice*, or *The Journal of Educational Measurement* will fail to turn up the key figures in portfolio assessment in college: Elbow, Belanoff, Haswell, Yancey, Sommers, and so forth. In effect, this phenomenon sets up another research need, for both these communities. We have to read—and heed—each other's work.

- Is it being defined in such a way that it enhances the possibilities of interpretable information about student learning emerging?
- How are portfolio results used by other client groups, such as college admissions officers and employers?

Fairness

Fairness concerns access to and equitable treatment in testing contexts for all learners and potential test-takers. The question of whether portfolio-based assessment is fairer to students (in the sense of not giving them lower scores, grades, placements, etc., than older forms of assessment) is a complex one, more complex than many teachers and WPAs are equipped to realize because of their underpreparation in assessment theory. The answer cannot simply be obtained by looking to see whether students from identified minority groups have or have not received higher scores on a portfolio-based assessment than on an essay test; as discussed elsewhere in this book, many factors affect access to education and therefore to assessment; and many factors affect the ways students from different groups perform on tests. The main tools the educational measurement community has are statistical, of course, and of these the differential item functioning (DIF) procedure is the main one, but as Linn et al. (1991) noted, because these procedures rely on data that has all students doing a large number of items it will be difficult to apply them to portfolio assessments, where the portfolio is one "item," or may at most be given multiple trait scores on four or five categories, thus generating four or five "items." Two major questions represent the complexity of these issues and the research that will provide answers:

- Is access to the assessment equally available to all students?
- Are there consistent differences in performances across racial, ethnic and gender groups that are not attributable to actual differences in ability or performance by the individuals assessed?

Meaningfulness

Described by Linn et al. (1991) as "like motherhood and apple pie" (p. 20) questions about whether an assessment is meaningful to students are important but often ignored.

- Do students find the portfolio assessment more meaningful and worthwhile than they do other forms of assessment?
- Do students get to perform important tasks?
- Can students demonstrate measurably improved performance on skills when being assessed by portfolio before and after a teaching

sequence (e.g., between a college entry portfolio and an exit portfolio from first-year composition)?

Transfer and Generalizability

Portfolios are highly context-dependent and task-specific, both of which have been argued to mitigate against traditional reliability (Koretz et al., 1994) because individuals' performances will differ not only according to their own abilities but according to task differences, teacher expectations, and, presumably, teaching quality. But if results from a portfolio-based assessment do not make sense beyond the single classroom they are unlikely to be valued by the groups in the outer circles of our heuristic. The educational measurement community has a more powerful consciousness of the demands of those groups than we in the universities and colleges do because they are employed by and answerable to them much more directly and immediately than we are. They will ask questions like those that follow:

- How are we to report scores on performances on portfolios?
- Are scores or grades on the portfolio assessment meaningful to people outside the classroom or other immediate context in which they were generated? (e.g., do scores from multiple sections within a Writing Program have the same meaning?)
- Does the portfolio instrument reflect transferable abilities, that is, would the students perform about the same if they had to write on other assignments "at the same level"?
- Would these same portfolios receive similar scores if scored by equally well-trained portfolio judges from different contexts?
- Are portfolios reliable, in the traditional sense?

Cognitive Complexity

Although the measurement community does not inherently care whether an assessment is cognitively complex, it must concern itself with these issues as far as the demand for such a characteristic in a test is prompting the test design, and as far as the existence of cognitive complexity makes the test design and validation process more problematic. Questions they will ask about cognitive complexity, then, are likely to be ones such as:

- Is this behavior or performance one that it is critical to assess?
- What are the ways available within our expertise to assess it?

- Can we break it down into smaller components of contributive behavior in order to assess them more simply?
- How might we report information on performance?

Content Quality

Ensuring that content of tests is relevant and a good representation of the behavior to be assessed has long been a major concern of test developers and others in the educational measurement community, and is a key reason for the current shift of attitude toward the acceptance of performance assessment among them. To ensure content quality they will ask such questions as:

- Are the tasks included in the assessment reflecting the domains of knowledge and ability that need to be tested?
- Are they tasks inherently worth doing?
- Are scores based on characteristics of performance that are truly worthwhile?
- Do scores encompass performance on the full content range?

Content Coverage

Because this is at once a strong argument in favor of portfolios and a significant complicating factor in their use as assessments, educational measurement people look to see the truth of claims that portfolios do in fact provide more content coverage than former kinds of assessment. They are likely to focus on such questions as the following:

- Do portfolio-based assessments sample a larger range of content than essay tests?
- Do they sample a larger range of content than a 50-item, multiple-choice test?
- Is the content sampled by portfolios more representative of what learners can do, and are required to do, than the other kinds of tests?

A very new kind of question on this group's agenda might be:

- Will testing writing ability with a portfolio lead to better instructional practice than testing writing ability with other test types?

Cost and Efficiency

These issues have been perhaps of less concern to educational measurement than they have needed to be: The temptation has been to spend as much money as funding agencies could be convinced to provide. Questions, then, tend to be limited to the following:

- Will the client for whom we are planning an assessment instrument be willing to pay for this assessment?
- How can we design an efficient data-collection system for a portfolio-based assessment?
- How can we efficiently score portfolios?
- How do we report scores on portfolios efficiently?

School Administrators

College administrators—deans, provosts, presidents, and so on—represent the first "external" audience in the widening circles of Figure 5.2. Typically, these officials are several steps up (as they see it) the institutional hierarchy from the classroom, and they are less interested in what works there than in how to represent what happens there as positive, effective, responsible, efficient, and educational. This audience often finds itself caught between the conflicting desires to pursue innovation and to stay within the boundaries of established practice. In addition, this audience has to justify budgets—and balance them—so those who promote portfolio assessments must also provide data that satisfy cost-benefit analyses, as well as risk-benefit analyses. Finally, this audience seeks evidence that can be used to justify actions to their external audiences—to the legislature, to the media, to contributors and funding agencies. This evidence must address, at minimum, the following questions:

- What evidence is available that establishes the effectiveness of portfolio assessment?
  —What kinds of "hard" data support that effectiveness?
  —How does the evidence justify the expense of portfolio assessment, both in dollars and in human resources?
  —Can the assessment be a showpiece? Can it generate funds, either in the form of grants or donations?
- Will a portfolio assessment generate positive attention for the institution?
- How will a change to portfolio assessment affect students? Will they be attracted by it? Will it motivate them to enroll somewhere else?

- How will a change to portfolio assessment affect funding from the legislature? Can portfolios help the institution build the perception that it is meeting its obligations to the public?
- What data or other evidence establishes reliably what the portfolio assessment will cost?
- What data or other evidence establishes reliably that the portfolio assessment will be worth what it costs?

Administrators will be concerned with some dimensions that focus inward, so to speak, on the educational effectiveness of a new measure or a new program, but for the most part, the administrator's focus turns the dimensions outward, toward audiences above the administrator in the chain of command (e.g., dean ⟶ provost) or audiences outside the institution itself (contributors, legislators, accreditors, etc.).

Looking inward, administrators want to see evidence that the assessment will produce beneficial consequences for all its participants—that it helps students learn, that it supports sound educational practice, that it helps faculty achieve the levels of teaching excellence, publication, and service that lead to tenure and promotion, and so forth.

Looking outward, administrators are concerned with how evidence centering on several dimensions will allow them to portray themselves and the institution in public forums. For example, the fairness of an assessment measure is important to the extent that it can help the institution portray itself as unbiased, as seeking ways to address the needs of minority populations within the student body and the faculty. Similarly, cognitive complexity and content coverage matter to the extent that they can provide substantial evidence for the rigor of the institution's curriculum and its teaching practices. Probably the dimension of greatest import for the administrative audience is transfer and generalizability, for that dimension allows administrators to use the outcomes of the assessment to portray what the institution is doing in terms that other audiences can understand and accept. All these dimensions together, then, help administrators address questions of cost and efficiency to their satisfaction.

So far, the kinds of evidence that satisfy the administrative audience have come from the testing and measurement community. Administrators are more likely to rely on quantitative studies than on qualitative evidence, and the measurement community is the source of most quantitative studies on assessment. As we in the teaching community construct our own studies, we will do well to accommodate our research to the needs of these external audiences. In doing so, we will find a more and more willing partner in the community of researchers who focus on educational measurement.

Government and Politicos

There is a serious disjunction in the attitude toward education in this country. Teachers are entrusted with teaching, that is, with making sure that students learn, and learn appropriate material; despite continually encroaching attempts at control from larger administrative structure, it is still generally accepted that appropriate education for students as individuals can safely be entrusted to teachers. However, teachers are not entrusted with assessing student learning, except in low stakes contexts, such as within their own classrooms. This attitude is well publicized at the public school level, but less attention has been paid to the fact that it exists at the college level, too. The accepted attitude by the outer circles seems to be that assessment must be trusted to systems because teachers cannot be trusted with it. Teachers, then, are trusted with the life-shaping role of educator, but not with the job of reporting to others what they know about the individuals they have educated.

The reasons for this seem to be based on the need for public accountability. There is a culture of credibility that has built up in the United States around quantitative data: It rarely occurs to people to disbelieve quantitative data they are given, and there is a tendency to be suspicious of claims that are not backed up by such data—by numbers. What this audience seems to want, then, is data about large groups of people that can be shown to be statistically inviolable (i.e., reliable in the classical sense). It is not interested, it seems, in what those numbers are based on, or whether they realistically represent the performance of the individuals within the groups. It is worth keeping in mind that this audience rarely includes anyone who has any expertise either as an educator or as a psychometrician. Its questions are based on lack of knowledge of the issues that concern students, teachers, WPAs, and even the measurement community; it responds to information from administrators at top levels, and to the push and pull of "public opinion" as fed to it by pollsters and the media. A major stumbling block for the acceptance, even for the awareness, of portfolio-based assessment by this audience is the relatively small amount of work that has been done so far toward increasing their transfer and generalizability, so that there is little information about what portfolios do in general that can be fed to the politicos for regurgitation in the forums where they are asked to account for the state of education in the country.

Government seems to pick up on the lowest common denominator of the patterns of public opinion about education; witness the unquestioning acceptance of the claim, repeated every decade, that standards are declining. President Bush's determination to be considered "the education president" led him to develop the Education 2000 initiative, the chief mechanism for which was—tests. Tests were to be used and valued for their consequences, for their assumed ability to solve problems that are little if at all understood. Through tests we would assure that every citizen was literate by the year 2000, among other things. Yet, tests constitute a limited lever of reform, and to achieve any reform at all they require funding; but the teaching they are supposed to measure and mystically improve has even greater requirements for funding. Education 2000 provided no new money for literacy initiatives: The big stick of testing was supposed to do it. The problem of portfolios may be that they don't look like a big enough stick. We would like to think that these groups care about such features of portfolio-based assessment as cognitive complexity, content quality, and content coverage, but we regret to say that we have not seen the signs of that yet. We would like to hear them asking questions about fairness, but we have not.

What are the questions that this group asks? They seem to be restricted to cost-efficiency, and consequences (for the politicians themselves):

- Does the public want us to support portfolios?
- How much is portfolio assessment costing?
- Are portfolio assessments telling us things we want to know and couldn't find satisfactory information on before?
- Is there any evidence that having these portfolios is improving students' literacy skills?
- What's wrong with the way we've been testing all along?

The Public/The Media

We have linked these two groups together because it is not clear to us how far the public, seen as an undifferentiated mass, has information or opinions about educational issues in general other than as provided or shaped by the media. The public is, in addition, a constantly shifting set of special interests: Any one of us as a member of the public may be at one moment a parent and at the next a taxpayer, and perhaps that explains why we, as a group, seem to be completely fickle in our support of any sound reform initiatives, educational or other.

In terms of public perception, there is a special problem for portfolio-based assessment. In traditional assessments, objective testing, and even essay testing, test developers hold control over test tasks and the scoring procedure. Although such control is often deplored, one of the ways the test developers and testing agencies use that control is to provide information publicly about task types to be expected on the test, the criteria and standards by which test responses are to be judged, and typical standards of performance and success rates (see, e.g., the *Test of*

Written English Guide by ETS). This public availability of information and "data" acts as an important component of accountability by the test agency because their practices are open to scrutiny by the public. Although it allows the media to find grounds to attack any test, it also provides them with grounds to applaud it, depending on the way the political wind is blowing. But the variability of tasks, assignments and procedures within any single portfolio assessment make it extremely difficult to provide exact or generally applicable information to the public about what students must do to succeed on any particular portfolio assessment, or to state any fixed criteria or scoring standards by which portfolio assessments generally can be interpreted. These limitations on the openness of a portfolio assessment, caused by its environmental sensitivity, act as counters to the effectiveness of portfolio assessments, making it hard for to publicize them or to "sell" them to the media and the public. In the future, test development efforts will need to confront these issues if portfolios are to be taken seriously by the public and by groups concerned about the accountability of educators for the effectiveness of educational efforts, and if they are not to be questioned by the media as a gratuitous waste of public funds.

The media has so far given relatively little attention to the portfolio assessment movement; like most good educational ideas, it seems to be hidden from the public gaze. Indeed, it is hard to imagine how the media would take up portfolios and run a one-page article in the local daily, or a John Leo column in *Newsweek.* How (and why?) might Barbara Walters present a *20/20* slot on portfolios and college writing assessment? Simply considering the size of one portfolio and the amount of text to be processed, we must confess that the portfolio, by its nature, does not lend itself well to a 30-second sound-bite, or even to a 5-minute exposé. We celebrate this about portfolios: They are not a sop to anybody's quick and dirty interests; but the price of that is that they do not serve the baser of our own interests well either.

The kinds of questions the public and the media may ask are first and foremost about cost, and secondly about consequences and meaningfulness as defined from their own point of view:

- How much does this cost me?
- How do I know if I am getting value for money?
- How much is this costing our state (federal government)?
- How does the public know if it is getting value for money?
- Is the literacy of college students getting any better as a result of these portfolios?
- Will my child do better in college because the college uses a portfolio-based writing assessment?

- What are these portfolios and why are those people making such a big deal about them?

CONCLUSION: A CAUTIONARY TALE

All multiple-choice tests should be eliminated. The current approach to assessment of students achievement which relies on multiple-choice student response to a narrow scope of desired student outcomes must be abandoned because of its deleterious effect on the educational process. An assessment system which measures students achievement on performance-based measures is essential for driving the needed reform to a thinking curriculum in which students are actively engaged and are successful in meeting expectations for transition to various goals beyond high school. (*Meeting the Challenge*, the final report of the California Education Summit, December 1989)

The California Assessment Program (CAP; 1989) provides an illustrative note on which to conclude this chapter, in which we have set out a paradigm for designing research along established dimensions and according to the needs of different audiences with interests in portfolio assessment, vested or not. CAP began and developed hopefully. It involved instruction and assessment in just the ways we have advocated as desirable within the rhetoric and composition community, and it attended to the consequences of assessment in all its contexts, following the direction recently set by the educational measurement community (Messick, 1989; Moss et al., 1992). As Murphy and Smith (1992) described the project, CAP provided samples of students' work that demonstrated learning of many kinds and at many levels. Portfolio-based and performance-assessed, CAP portfolios exhibited all the characteristics that we described in chapter 2, and they provided fertile samples for investigating students' achievement, their strengths and needs, the richness or thinness of their schools' curricula, and so forth. And yet this project, which began so well, could not survive the budget axe that fell on the California education system in the early 1990s. Why?

We would answer that, by the time the legislative committees turned their eye to the project, it had not generated the kinds of evidence that audience needed in order to justify the project's expense. Murphy and Smith talked about "the potential of portfolio assessment." Noting that portfolios are still evolving, they talked about what portfolio assessment "can be," about what we "might do" with it, about what it "gives us a chance" to do (p. 58). This kind of talk is suited to the "inner circles" in our diagram of audiences (see Figure 5.2). It is effective in addressing teachers and learners, writing program directors, even members of the measurement community, who would at least see the constant reference to "potential" as framing interesting questions for research. Beyond that circle, however, believing must become knowing, and it must become knowing of a definite type.

When portfolios were in their infancy, Decker, Robinson, and Condon could get permission to run a pilot entry portfolio project and, ultimately, to shift to portfolios as an entry requirement, on the basis of the definite negatives now associated with essay tests (Brown, 1986; Camp, 1993; Huot, 1990). Or Haswell, Wyche-Smith, and Johnson-Schull (1994) could gain approval to develop a rising junior portfolio assessment based on the promise of integrating assessment with instruction, a promise they have made good. As portfolios become more widely known and used, the questions will become more focused, and the audiences will demand more solid proof of effectiveness, rather than being content to rely on potential, on what portfolios might do, or could provide. That is the rock on which CAP foundered, and if we wish to avoid the same obstacle, then we had better busy ourselves with our research agendas.

REFERENCES

Alderson, J. C., & Wall, D. (1993). Does washback exist? *Applied Linguistics, 14*(2), 116-129.

Anson, C., & Brown R. L. (1991). Large-scale portfolio assessment: Ideological sensitivity and institutional change. In P. Belanoff & M. Dickson (Eds.), *Portfolios: Process and product* (pp. 248-269). Portsmouth, NH: Boynton/Cook.

Aschbacher, P. R. (1991). Performance assessment: State activity, interest, and concerns. *Applied Measurement in Education, 4*, 275-288.

August, B., Jones, J., Markstein, L., Parry, K., & Smith, J. (1994, March). *Experiments in portfolios: The City University of New York*. Colloquium presented at the 28th annual convention of Teachers of English to Speakers of Other Languages, Baltimore, MD.

Bachman, L. F., & Palmer, A. S. (1996). *Language testing in practice*. New York: Oxford University Press.

Baker, E., Freeman, M., & Clayton, S. (1990). *Cognitive assessment of subject matter: Understanding the marriage of psychological theory and educational policy in achievement testing* (CSE Tech. Rep. No. 317). Los Angeles: UCLA/CRESST.

Baker, N. W. (1993). The effect of portfolio-based instruction on composition students' final examination scores, course grades, and attitudes. *Research in the Teaching of English, 27*(2), 155-174.

Bartholomae, D. (1985). Inventing the university. In M. Rose (Ed.), *When a writer can't write: Studies in writer's block and other composing process problems* (pp. 134-165). New York: Guilford Press.

Batzle, J. (1992). *Portfolio assessment and evaluation: Developing and using portfolios in the classroom.* Cypress, CA: Creative Teaching Press.

Belanoff, P., & Dickson, M. (Eds.). (1991). *Portfolios: Process and product.* Portsmouth, NH: Heinemann/Boynton Cook.

Belanoff, P., & Elbow, P. (1986). Using portfolios to increase collaboration and community in a writing program. *Writing Program Administration, 9*(3), 27-40.

Berlin, J. A. (1982). Contemporary composition: The major pedagogical theories. *College English, 44,* 765-777.

Berlin, J. A. (1984). *Writing instruction in nineteenth-century American colleges.* Carbondale: Southern Illinois University Press.

Berlin, J. A. (1987). *Rhetoric and reality: Writing instruction in American colleges, 1900-1987.* Carbondale: Southern Illinois University Press.

Bizzell, P. (1986). Foundationalism and antifoundationalism in composition studies. *PRE/TEXT, 7,* 37-56.

Black, L., Daiker, D. A., Sommers, J., & Stygall G. (n.d.). *Handbook of writing portfolio assessment: A program for college placement.* Miami: Miami University of Ohio/FIPSE.

Britton, J. (1982). Writing to learn and learning to write. In G. Pradl (Ed.), *Prospect and retrospect: Selected essays of James Britton.* Montclair, NJ: Boynton/Cook.

Brown, R. C. (1986). Testing black student writers. In K. L. Greenberg, H. S. Wiener, & R. A. Donovan (Eds.), *Writing assessment: Issues and strategies* (pp. 98-108). New York: Longman.

Bruffee, K. A. (1973). Collaborative learning: Some practical models. *College English, 34,* 634-643.

Burns, H. (1984). The challenge for computer-assisted rhetoric. *Computers and the Humanities, 3-4.*

California Assessment Program. (1989). *Writing portfolio project.* Berkeley: University of California.

Camp, R. (1985). The writing folder in post-secondary assessment. In P. J. Evans (Ed.), *Directions and misdirections in English evaluation* (pp. 91-99). Ottawa: The Canadian Council of Teachers of English.

Camp, R. (1989). *Portfolios evolving: Backgrounds and variations.* Paper presented at the seventh annual conference of the National Testing Network in Writing, New York.

Camp, R. (1993). Changing the model for the direct assessment of writing. In M. Williamson & B. Huot (Eds.), *Validating holistic scoring for writing assessment: Theoretical and empirical foundations* (pp. 45-78). Cresskill, NJ: Hampton Press.

CCCC Committee on Assessment. (1992). A selected bibliography on postsecondary writing assessment, 1979-1991. *College Composition and Communication, 43*(2), 244-255.

Chaplin, M. T. (1988). *A comparative analysis of writing features used by selected black and white students in the national assessment of educational progress and the New Jersey high school proficiency test* (Research Rep. No. 88-42). Princeton, NJ: Educational Testing Service.

Chiste, K., & O'Shea, J. (1988). Patterns of question selection and writing performance of ESL students. *TESOL Quarterly, 22,* 681-684.

Collins, J. (1993). The troubled text: History and language in American university basic writing programs. In P. Freebody & A. Welch (Eds.), *Knowledge, culture and power: International perspectives on literacy as policy and practice* (pp. 163-186). London: The Falmer Press.

Condon, W.C., & Hamp-Lyons, L. (1991). Developing a portfolio-based writing assessment program: Progress through problems. In P. Belanoff & M. Dickson (Eds.), *Portfolios: Process and product* (pp. 231-247). Montclair, NJ: Boynton/Cook.

Condon, W.C., & Hamp-Lyons, L. (1994). Maintaining a portfolio-based writing assessment: Research that informs program development. In L. Black, D. A. Daiker, J. Sommers, & G. Stygall (Eds.), *New directions in portfolio assessment: Reflective practice, critical theory, and large-scale scoring* (pp. 277-285). Portsmouth, NH: Heinemann.

Connor, U., & Johns, A. M. (1989). *Argumentation in academic discourse communities: There are differences.* Paper presented at the 23rd annual convention of Teachers of English to Speakers of Other Languages (TESOL), San Antonio, TX.

Corbett, E. P. J. (1971). *Classical rhetoric for the modern student* (2nd ed.). New York: Oxford University Press.

Daiker, D. A., Sommers, J., Stygall, G., & Black, L. (1990). *The best of Miami's portfolios.* Oxford, OH: Miami University.

Decker, E. (1995, Fall). The new portfolio requirement: Why change? *LSA Magazine,* pp. 4-7.

Decker, E., Cooper, G., & Harrington, S. (1992). Crossing institutional boundaries: Developing an entrance portfolio assessment to improve writing instruction. *Journal of Teaching Writing, 12,* 1.

DeFina, A. A. (1992). *Portfolio assessment: Getting started.* New York: Scholastic.

Dietel, R. (1993, Spring). What works in performance assessment? The proceedings of the 1992 CRESST conference. *Evaluation Comment,* 1-15.

Elbow, P. (1973). *Writing without teachers.* New York: Oxford University Press.

Elbow, P. (1991a). Foreword. In P. Belanoff & M. Dickson (Eds.), *Portfolios: Process and product* (pp. ix-xvi). Portsmouth, NH: Boynton/Cook.

Elbow, P. (1991b). Reflections on academic discourse. *College English, 53*(2), 135-155.

Elbow, P. (1994). Writing assessment in the 21st century: A utopian view. In L. Bloom, D. Daiker, & E. White (Eds.), *Composition in the twenty-first century: Crisis and change* (pp. 83-100). Carbondale: Southern Illinois University Press.

Elbow, P., & Belanoff P. (1991). SUNY: Portfolio-based evaluation program. In P. Connally & T. Vilardi (Eds.), *New methods in college writing programs* (pp. 95-105). New York: Modern Language Association.

Emig, J. (1971). *The composing processes of twelfth graders* (Research Rep. No. 13). Urbana-Champaign, IL: NCTE.

Erickson, F. (1986). Qualitative methods in research on teaching. In M. C. Wittrock (Ed.), *Handbook of research on teaching*. New York: Macmillan.

Fader, D. (1986). Writing samples and virtues. In K. L. Greenberg, H. S. Weiner, & R. A. Donovan (Eds.), *Writing assessment: Issues and strategies* (pp. 79-92). White Plains, NY: Longman.

Farr, M. (1993). Essayist literacy and other verbal performances. *Written Communication, 10*(3), 4-38.

Flanagan, A. (1993). New standards takes close look at portfolios. *The Council Chronicle, 3*(2), 1-3.

Flower, L. S. (1979). Writer-based prose: A cognitive basis for problems in writing. *College English, 41*, 19-37.

Flower, L., & Hayes, J. (1981). A cognitive process theory of writing. *College Composition and Communication, 32*, 365-387.

Fox, T. (1990). Basic writing as cultural conflict. *Journal of Education, 172*(1), 65-83.

Frechtling, J. A. (1991). Performance assessment: Moonstruck or the real thing? *Educational Measurements: Issues and Practice, 10*, 23-25.

Frederickson, J. R., & Collins, A. (1989). A systems approach to educational testing. *Educational Researcher, 18*(9), 27-32.

Fulkerson, R. (1979). Four philosophies of composition. *College Composition and Communication, 30*, 343-348.

Gere, A. R. (1981). A cultural perspective on talking and writing. In B. M. Kroll & R. J. Vann (Eds.), *Exploring speaking-writing relationships: Connections and contrasts*. Urbana, IL: National Council of Teachers of English.

Gere, A. R. (1987). *Writing groups: History, theory, and implication.* Carbondale: Southern Illinois University Press.

Graff, H. (1988). *The labyrinths of literacy.* London: The Falmer Press.

Guba, E., & Lincoln, Y. (1989). *Fourth generation evaluation.* Newbury Park, CA: Sage.

Guion, R.M. (1995). Commentary on values and standards in performance assessment. *Educational Measurement: Issues and Practice, 14*(4), 25-27.

Hairston, M. (1982). Winds of change: Thomas Kuhn and the revolution in the teaching of writing. *College Composition and Communication, 33,* 76-88.

Hale, C., Mallon, T., & Wyche-Smith, S. (1988). *Student writing groups: Demonstrating the process.* Tacoma, WA: Wordshop Productions.

Hale, C., Mallon, T., & Wyche-Smith, S. (1991). *Beginning with writing groups.* Tacoma, WA: Wordshop Productions.

Hamp-Lyons, L. (1988). *Moving to portfolios.* Paper presented at the Michigan Educational Research Association, Lansing.

Hamp-Lyons, L. (1990). Second language writing: Assessment issues. In B. Kroll (Ed.), *Second language writing: Research insights for the classroom* (pp. 69-87). New York: Cambridge University Press.

Hamp-Lyons, L. (1991). Scoring procedures for ESL contexts. In L. Hamp-Lyons (Ed.), *Assessing second language writing in academic contexts* (pp. 241-278). Norwood, NJ: Ablex.

Hamp-Lyons, L. (1991a-1992). *Holistic assessment of LEP student writing.* Paper presented to the OBEMLA Invitational Conference on Assessment of Limited English Proficiency Students under Education 2000, hosted by the Office of Bilingual Education and Minority Student Affairs, Washington, DC.

Hamp-Lyons, L. (1993, April). *Components of portfolio evaluation: ESL data.* Paper presented at the annual meeting of the American Association of Applied Linguistics, Atlanta, GA.

Hamp-Lyons, L. (1995, March). *Portfolios with ESL writers: What the research shows.* Paper presented at the annual convention of Teachers of English as a Second Language, Long Beach, CA.

Hamp-Lyons, L. (1996). Applying ethical standards to portfolio assessment of writing in English as a Second Language. In M. Milanovich & N. Saville (Eds.), *Performance testing, cognition and assessment* (Studies in Language Testing 3, pp. 151-164). Cambridge: Cambridge University Press.

Hamp-Lyons, L. (1997). Washback, impact, and validity. *Language Testing, 14,* 295-303.

Hamp-Lyons, L., & Condon, W.C. (1993). Questioning assumptions about portfolios. *College Composition and Communication, 44,* 176-190.

Hamp-Lyons, L., & Reed, R. (1988) *Development of the new Michigan Writing Assessment Instrument.* Report to The College of Literature, Science, & the Arts, Ann Arbor, University of Michigan.

Harrington, S., & Condon, W. (1998). Don't lower the river, raise the bridge: Preserving standards by improving students' performances. In J. Galin & J. Latchaw (Eds.), *The dialogic classroom: Teachers integrating computer technology, pedagogy, and research.* Urbana, IL: NCTE Press.

Harrison, S. (1995). Portfolios across the curriculum. *Journal of the Council of Writing Program Administrators, 19,* 38-49.

Haswell, R., & Wyche-Smith, S. (1994). Adventuring into writing assessment. *College Composition and Communication, 45,* 220-236.

Haswell, R. H., Wyche-Smith, S., & Johnson-Shull, L. (1994). Shooting Niagara: Making assessment serve instruction at a State university. *WPA: Writing Program Administration 18*(1/2), 44-53.

Hoey, M. (1979). *Signalling in discourse.* Discourse Analysis Monograph, English Language Research, University of Birmingham.

Holt, D., & Baker N. W. (1991). Portfolios as a follow-up option in a proficiency-testing program. In P. Belanoff & M. Dickson (Eds.), *Portfolios: Process and product* (pp. 37-45). Portsmouth, NH: Boynton/Cook.

Hult, C. (1994). *Using portfolios for assessment across the curriculum.* Paper presented at Portfolios for Learning and Beyond: Portfolios, WAC, and Program Assessment, Scottsdale, AZ.

Huot, B. (1990). Reliability, validity, and holistic scoring: What we know and what we need to know. *College Composition and Communication, 41,* 201-213.

Instructional "good pratice" indicators in undergraduate education. (1994). Washington, DC: OERI.

Jaeger, R.M. (1995). Setting standards for complex performances: An iterative, judgment capturing strategy. *Educational Measurement: Issues and Practice, 14*(4), 16-20.

Kemp, F. (1990). Review. *College Composition and Communication, 41,* 339-342.

Kilian, L. J. (1992). A school district perspective on appropriate test-preparation practices: A reaction to Popham's proposals. *Educational Measurement: Issues and Practice, 11*(4), 13-15, 26.

Kinneavy, J. (1971). *A theory of discourse.* New York: Norton.

Koretz, D., Stecher, B., Klein, S., & McCaffrey, D. (1994). The Vermont portfolio assessment program: Findings and Implications. *Educational Measurement: Issues and Practice, 13*(3), 5-16.

Larson, R. L. (1991). Using portfolios in the assessment of writing in the academic disciplines. In P. Belanoff & M. Dickson (Eds.), *Portfolios: Process and product* (pp.137-150). Portsmouth, NH: Boynton/Cook.

LeMahieu, P. G., Gitomer, D. H., & Eresh, J. T. (1995). *Portfolios beyond the classroom: Data quality and qualities.* Princeton, NJ: Educational Testing Service.

Lincoln, Y., & Guba, E. (1985). *Naturalistic inquiry.* Beverley Hills, CA: Sage.

Linn, R.L., Baker, E.L., & Dunbar, S.B. (1991). Complex, performance-based assessment: Expectations and validation criteria. *Educational Research, 20*(8), 15-21.

Lovett, C.R., & Young, A.. (1994). Portfolios in the disciplines: Sharing knowledge in the contact zone. In L. Black, D.A. Daiker, J. Sommers, & G. Stygall (Eds.), *New directions in portfolio assessment* (pp. 334-346). Portsmouth, NH: Heinemann.

Lunsford, A. (1986). The past—and future—of writing assessment. In K.L. Greenberg, H.S. Weiner, & R.A. Donovan (Eds.), *Writing assessment: Issues and strategies* (pp. 1-12). White Plains, NY: Longman.

Lunsford, A., & Ede, L. (1984). Audience addressed/audience invoked: The role of audience in composition theory and pedagogy. *College Composition and Communication, 35,* 155-171.

Macrorie, K. (1970). *Uptaught.* Rochelle Park, NJ: Hayden.

McLaughlin, M. (1991). Test-based accountability as a reform strategy. *Phi Delta Kappan, 73,* 248.

Medina, N., & Neill, D. (1990). *Fallout from the testing explosion: How 100 million standardized exams undermine equity and excellence in American public schools.* Cambridge, MA: FairTest.

Mehrens, W.A. (1992). Using performance assessment for accountability purposes. *Educational Measurement: Issues and Practice, 11*(1), 3-9.

Mehrens, W.A., & Kaminski, J. (1989). Methods for improving standardized test scores: Fruitful, fruitless or fraudulent? *Educational Measurement: Issues and Practice, 8*(1), 14-22.

Messick, S. (1988). The once and future issues of validity: Assessing the meaning and consequences of measurement. In H. Wainer & H. I. Braun (Eds.), *Test validity* (pp. 33-45). Hillsdale, NJ: Erlbaum.

Messick, S. (1989). Validity. In R. L. Linn (Ed.), *Educational measurement* (3rd ed., pp. 13-103). New York: American Council on Education, Macmillan.

Messick, S. (1994). The interplay of evidence and consequences in the validation of performance assessments. *Educational Researcher, 23*(2), 13-23.

Messick, S. (1996). Test validity: A matter of consequence. *Social Indicators Research, 45,* 35-44.

Miller, G. F. (1926). *Objective tests in high school subjects.* Norman: University of Oklahoma Press.

Miller, M.D., & Legg, S. M. (1993). Alternative assessment in a high-stakes environment. *Educational Measurement: Issues and Practice, 12*(2), 9-15.

Mislevy, R. J. (1995). *On inferential issues arising in the California learning assessment system.* Princeton, NJ: Educational Testing Service.

Moss, P.A. (1994). Validity in high stakes writing assessment. *Assessing Writing, 1*(1), 109-128.

Moss, P.A. (1996). Enlarging the dialogue in educational measurement. Voices from interpretive research traditions. *Educational Researcher, 25*(1), 20-28.

Moss, P.A., Beck, J.S., Ebbs, C., Matson, B., Muchmore, J., Steele, D., Taylor, C., & Herter, R. (1992). Portfolios, accountability, and an interpretive approach to validity. *Educational Measurement: Issues and Practice, 11*(3), 12-21.

Murphy, S., & Grant, B. (1996). Portfolio assessment: Breakthrough or more of the same? In E. White, W. Lutz, & S. Kamusikiri (Eds.), *Assessment of writing: Politics, policies, practices* (pp. 284-300). New York: Modern Language Association.

Murphy, S., & Ruth, L. (1993). The field testing of writing prompts reconsidered. In M. Williamson & B. Huot (Eds.), *Validating holistic scoring for writing assessment: Theoretical and empirical foundations* (pp. 266-302). Cresskill, NJ: Hampton Press.

Murphy, S., & Smith, M. A. (1992). Looking into portfolios. In K. B. Yancey (Ed.), *Portfolios in the writing classroom: An introduction* (pp. 49-61). Urbana, IL: NCTE.

Murray, D. (1980). The feel of writing—and teaching writing. In A. Freedman & I. Pringle (Eds.), *Reinventing the rhetorical tradition* (pp. 67-74). Conway, AR: L&S Books for the Canadian Council of Teachers of English.

Myford, C., & Mislevy, R. J. (1995). *Monitoring and improving a portfolio assessment system.* Princeton, NJ: Educational Testing Service.

National assessment of college student learning: Getting started. (1993). Washington, DC: OERI, National Center for Education Statistics.

National assessment of college student learning: Identification of the skill to be taught, learned and assessed. (1994). Washington, DC: OERI, National Center for Education Statistics.

National assessment of college student learning: Identifying college graduates' essential skills in writing, speech and listening, and critical thinking. (1995). Washington, DC: OERI, National Center for Education Statistics.

Nickerson, R. (1989). New directions in educational assessment. *Educational Researcher, 18*(1), 3-7.

Perl, S. (1980). Understanding composing. *College Composition and Communication, 31,* 363-369.

Poole, D., & Patthey-Chavez, G.G. (1994). Locating assisted performance: A study of instructional activity settings and their effects on the discourse of teaching. *Issues in Applied Linguistics, 5*(1), 3-36.

Popham, W. J. (1991). Appropriateness of teachers' test-preparation practices. *Educational Measurement: Issues and Practice, 10*(4), 12-15.

Pratt, M. (1991). Arts of the contact zone. *Profession 91* (pp. 33-40). New York: Modern Language Association.

Raimes, A. (1985). What unskilled writers do as they write: A classroom study. *TESOL Quarterly, 19,* 229-258.

Resnick, L. B., & Resnick, D. P. (1991). Assessing the thinking curriculum: New tools for educational reform. In B. R. Gifford & M. C. O'Conner (Eds.), *Changing assessments: Alternative views of aptitude, achievement and instruction* (pp. 37-76). Boston: Kluwer.

Ritchie, J. (1989). Beginning writers: Diverse voices and individual identity. *College Composition and Communication, 40,* 152-174.

Roemer, M., Schultz, L. M., & Durst, R. K. (1991). Portfolios and the process of change. *College Composition and Communication, 42,* 455-469.

Rorty, R. (1982). Hermeneutics, general studies and teaching. *Synergos: Selected Papers From the Synergos Seminars* (Vol. 2). Fairfax, VA: George Mason University Press.

Rose, M. (1989). *Lives on the boundary.* New York: Penguin.

Sheingold, K., & Fredericksen, J. (1995). *Linking assessment with reform: Technologies that support conversations about student work.* Princeton, NJ: Educational Testing Service.

Sheingold, K., Heller, J. I., & Paulukonis S. T. (1995). *Actively seeking evidence: Teacher change through assessment development.* Princeton, NJ: Educational Testing Service.

Smith, M. L. (1991). Put to the test: The effects of external testing on teachers. *Educational Researcher, 20,* 8-11.

Smith, M. L., & Rottenberg C. (1991). Unintended consequences of external testing in elementary schools. *Educational Measurement: Issues and Practice, 10,* 7-11.

Smith, W. (1994). Assessing the reliability and adequacy of using holistic scoring of essays as a college composition placement technique. In M. Williamson & B. Huot (Eds.), *Validating holistic scoring for writing assessment* (pp. 142-205). Cresskill, NJ: Hampton Press.

Stephens, W. R., & van Til, W. (1972). *Education in American life.* Boston: Houghton-Mifflin.

Stiggins, R. (1991). Facing the challenges of a new era of educational assessment. *Applied Measurement in Education, 4,* 263-274.

Swales, J. (1984). Research into the structure of introductions to journal articles and its application to teaching academic writing. In R. Williams, J. Swales, & J. Kirkman (Eds.), *Common ground: Shared interests in ESL and communication studies* (pp. 77-86). Oxford: Pergamon Press.

Swales, J. (1990). *Genre analysis: English in academic and research settings.* Cambridge: Cambridge University Press.

Sweedler-Brown, C.O. (1993a). The effects of ESL errors on holistic scores assigned by English composition faculty. *College ESL, 3*(1), 53-69.

Sweedler-Brown, C.O. (1993b). ESL essay evaluation: The influence of sentence-level and rhetorical features. *Journal of Second Language Writing, 2*(1), 3-18.

Tedick, D. (1993). *A multidimensional exploration of raters' judgments of ESL writing.* Paper presented at the annual convention of Teachers of English as a Second Language, Atlanta.

Valencia , S. W., & Calfee, R. (1991). The development and use of literacy portfolios for students, classes, and teachers. *Applied Measurement in Education, 4,* 333-346.

Walvoord, B., & McCarthy L. (1990). *Thinking and writing in college: A naturalistic study of students in four disciplines.* Urbana, IL: National Council of Teachers of English.

Weiser, I. (1992). Portfolio practice and assessment for collegiate basic writers. In K. B. Yancey (Ed.), *Portfolios in the writing classroom* (pp. 89-101). Urbana, IL: NCTE.

White, E. M. (1991). *The practices and politics of holistic essay scoring: The past as a guide to the future.* Paper presented at the annual Conference on College Composition and Communication, Boston.

White, E. M. (1994). *Teaching and assessing writing: Recent advances in understanding, evaluating, and improving student performance* (2nd ed.). San Franciso: Jossey-Bass.

White, E. M., & Thomas, L. (1981). Racial minorities and writing skills assessment in the California State University and Colleges. *College English, 42,* 165-188.

Williamson, M. (1994). The worship of efficiency: Untangling theoretical and practical considerations in writing assessment. *Assessing Writing, 1*(2), 147-173.

Williamson, M., & Huot, B. (Eds.). (1993). *Validating holistic scoring for writing assessment: Theoretical and empirical foundations.* Cresskill, NJ: Hampton Press.

Willis, M.S. (1993). *Deep revision.* New York: Teachers and Writers Collaborative.

Wiseman, S. (1956). Symposium: The use of essays on selection at 11+. *British Journal of Educational Psychology, 26*(3), 172-179.

Witte, S., Trachsel, M., & Walters, K. (1986) Literacy and the direct assessment of writing: A diachronic perspective. In K.L. Greenberg, H. S. Weiner, & R. A. Donovan (Eds.), *Writing assessment: Issues and strategies* (pp. 13-34). White Plains, NY: Longman.

Young, R. (1987). Recent developments in rhetorical invention. In G. Tate (Ed.), *Teaching composition: 12 bibliographical essays* (pp. 1-38). Fort Worth: Texas Christian University Press.

Zamel, V. (1982). The process of discovering meaning. *TESOL Quarterly, 16,* 195-209.

AUTHOR INDEX

A

Alderson, J. C., 185, *197*
Anson, C., 26, 56, *197*
Aschbacher, P. R., 25, *197*
August, B., 135, *197*

B

Bachman, L. F., 9*n*, *197*
Baker, E. L., 21, 175, 183, 184, 202
Baker, N. W., 25, 27, 178, 186, 194, *197, 202*
Bartholomae, D., 46, 111, *197*
Batzle, J., 15, *198*
Beck, J. S., 21, 133, 171, 175, 183, *203*
Belanoff, P., xii, 15, 27, 34, 52, 73, 188, 181, *198, 200*
Berlin, J. A., 38, 48, *198*
Bizzell, P., 46, *198*
Black, L., 26, 86, 92, *199*
Britton, J., 40, *198*
Brown, R. C., 14, 195, *198*
Brown, R. L., 26, 56, *197*
Bruffee, K. A., 44, 46, *198*
Burns, H., 48, *198*

C

Calfee, R., 22, 28, *205*
California Assessment Program, 194, *198*
Camp, R., 28, 195, *198*
CCC Commitee on Assessment, 185*n*, *198*
Chaplin, M. T., 14, *199*
Chiste, K., 14, *199*
Clayton, S., 25, *197*
Collins, A., 179, *200*
Collins, J., 13, *199*
Condon, W. C., 6, 26, 27, 28, 33, 52, 73, 74, 79, 80, 91, 118, 126, 134, *199, 201*
Connor, U., 46, *199*
Cooper, G., 133, *199*
Corbett, E. P. J., 39, *199*

D

Daiker, D. A., 26, 86, 92, *198, 199*
Decker, E., 26, 133, *199*
DeFina, A. A., 15, *199*
Dickson, M., 27, 73, 181, *198*
Dietel, R., 22, *199*

SUBJECT INDEX

A

Accountability, 18-20, 23, 24, 26, 29, 110, 133, 135, 136, 140, 182-184, 191, 193

assessment

  alternative, 4, 15-18, 20, 116

  authentic, 11, 18, 23, 126, 171, 172

  bias, 14, 20, 110, 181

  conditions, 3, 4, 7, 12

  context(s), 3, 4, 6, 7, 9, 11, 14, 15, 27, 28, 31-33, 36, 51, 55, 58, 59, 61, 124, 139, 186

  criteria, 36, 37, 39, 45, 52, 54, 55, 74, 80, 81, 91, 97-99, 104-108, 111, 112, 121, 128-130, 133, 136, 137, 141-143, 145, 146, 162, 162, 192

  diagnostic, 27

  direct, 2, 5, 7, 11, 12, 14, 118, 119, 135, 163, 171

  educational, 16,17, 19, 20

  entry, 3, 14, 15, 59, 63, 76, 86, 88-92, 103-105, 134, 145, 159, 195

  essay test(s), 4, 11, 14, 15, 60, 61, 77, 83, 91, 92, 99, 110-112, 126, 134, 142, 171, 179, 186, 188, 195

  exit, 3, 6, 7, 13, 15, 28, 56, 61, 63, 76-83, 86, 87, 102-108, 120, 134, 135, 142, 145, 154, 155

  history, 9, 13, 166, 169

  holistic, 6, 11, 12, 33, 91, 127, 133-135, 139, 144

  indirect, 7, 9-12, 14, 33, 171, 172, 179

  instrument(s, 3, 4, 6, 7, 12, 23, 26, 27, 77, 90, 110, 112, 126, 127, 137, 141, 142, 189

  large-scale, 14, 64, 91, 105, 146, 184

  multiple-choice, 9, 10, 14, 60, 90, 145, 176, 179, 188, 194

  multiple-trait, 11, 139, 142, 186

  national, 14, 24

  objective, 7, 9, 10, 14, 146, 192